unlock your
CREATIVE GENIUS

Also by Bernard Golden

Healthy Anger

New Hope for People with Bipolar Disorder
(Coauthored with Jan Fawcett and Nancy Rosenfeld)

unlock your
CREATIVE GENIUS

BERNARD GOLDEN, PhD

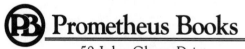 Prometheus Books

59 John Glenn Drive
Amherst, New York 14228-2197

Published 2007 by Prometheus Books

Inquiries should be addressed to
Prometheus Books
59 John Glenn Drive
Amherst, New York 14228–2197
VOICE: 716–691–0133, ext. 207
FAX: 716–564–2711
WWW.PROMETHEUSBOOKS.COM

11 10 09 08 07   5 4 3 2 1

Library of Congress Cataloging-in-Publication Data

Golden, Bernard.
  Unlock your creative genius / Bernard Golden.
      p. cm.
  Includes bibliographical references and index.
  ISBN-13: 978–1–59102–456–9 (pbk. : alk. paper)
  ISBN-10: 1–59102–456–0 (pbk. : alk. paper)
  1. Creative ability. I. Title.

BF408.G565 2006
153.3'5—dc22

                                                              2006022922

Printed in the United States of America on acid-free paper

To my parents—
who nourished and supported
my child's curiosity

CONTENTS

ACKNOWLEDGMENTS

This book marks the completion of another portion of my creative journey. Like any such venture, it has been supported by the efforts of a team.

Once again, I want to express my deepest gratitude to Nancy Rosenfeld, my friend, agent, coauthor (with Jan Fawcett) of my first book, and truly an "encourager extraordinaire." She has continued to provide support, feedback, inspiration, and a gentle nudge whenever I needed one.

I am extremely grateful for the continued support and feedback of Dr. Patricia Robin. Also, I wish to thank Dr. Bonnie Holstein, who patiently read the entire manuscript and provided ideas that helped me to further expand on and clarify my thoughts. Additionally, I wish to express my appreciation to Mindy Gold and Matthew Williams for their support and meaningful dialogue.

A special thanks to my friend Robert McElroy, with whom I spent many hours in thought-provoking conversation regarding aspects of creativity.

I also want to thank Steven Mitchell, editor-in-chief at Prometheus, for his probing questions from the very beginning of our first contact. He helped me to find direction and clarity in what I wanted to express.

I am extremely indebted to Brian McMahon for his masterful editing. He inspired my trust and confidence beginning with his initial feedback and helped me invaluably in supporting my creative expression.

I want to again thank my mother for her love, support, and ongoing good wishes regarding this project.

Thanks, too, to the many clients with whom I have worked and whose creative journeys I have been privileged to share. They have been tremendously courageous and have informed much of my thinking.

Finally, I want to thank the many individuals who have taken time to further explore and identify the many facets of the creative process. These creative individuals, by having the courage to share their ideas, inspire and move us to trust our own.

INTRODUCTION

*U*nlock *Your Creative Genius* is an outgrowth of a partially completed manuscript that never matured to become a full-grown book. To be honest, this present volume was triggered, in part, by the rejections I received from publishers in response to that earlier manuscript. The seeds for creativity can often be found in very surprising places! "Too vague," "too broad in its scope," "good ideas, solid writing, but it does not address a targeted issue. It would be hard to promote," and "somewhat dry" were just a few of the publishers' comments forwarded to me in an e-mail from my agent.

Even I was surprised by my reaction! Initially disappointed, upon reviewing the feedback, I was very quick to acknowledge a sense of relief. I had not looked at that manuscript for about six months prior to its submission. However, I had felt that it was lacking even at that time. The publishers' comments only confirmed what I had already suspected. In fact, while I attributed prior rejections to other manuscripts (that did become books) as based simply on the personal preference of editors, I could not honestly accept that rationale in this instance.

Although it was late in the evening when I read that e-mail, I stayed awake, spending the next hour in thought. In that brief duration I came to identify a new direction to take that would capture the essence of my manuscript in a better-defined way. I had similarly identified a stylistic approach that would help it become more alive and much more interesting for you, the reader. Emotionally excited and charged by the time I went to bed, I had some difficulty falling asleep.

Two hours later I woke to thoughts that seemed to tumble like coins from a winning slot machine. Each idea built upon another until I realized that I had once again felt intense passion for my writing, a passion that would define the direction of my creative energies for the next few years. Consequently, I chose to stay awake for a couple of hours to capture my thoughts so that they would not disappear by morning.

Clearly, I was having a creative moment, one in which inspiration flourished and was welcomed by my receptive mind. The process that unfolded involved a sequence of distinct moments in time, during which I could be nonjudgmental, open, and fluid in my thinking. During those moments, I experienced joy, hope, satisfaction, and thoughts that further supported and encouraged me to continue my efforts. Simultaneously, I became energized by a slight but welcome physical tension, marked by an openness and alertness that further fostered my engagement with the task at hand.

In sum, these reactions helped to nurture and enhance my creative passion. I yearn for such moments whenever I write. And yet, through experience, I realize that the intensity of both my creativity and my passion often ebb and flow like the ocean tides, though lacking their consistency and predictability.

I have always been pulled toward such moments. Even in elementary school I much preferred writing a paper for a class than having to take a short-answer test. Perhaps it was the sense of empowerment I experienced playing with ideas, words, sentences, and paragraphs—choosing and organizing them in such a way that they succeeded in capturing concepts and ideas that resonated with me. While as a child I had passion for other toys and games, overall, words became my Legos. With words, I could build edifices of ideas, express and generate emotions to reveal, to hide, to inform, and to persuade.

Whether I wrote a social studies paper on the government of Canada or a revealing composition about my eighth summer vacation, I was able to access a deep passion in the adventure of writing. I was enamored with the entire process. I could get lost in the brainstorming of ideas, in sorting through words, and in shuffling phrases. It has always been exceedingly gratifying to put my ideas into concrete words in such a way as to clearly reflect my internal experience, whether in regard to my attitudes, perceptions, or emotions.

During childhood, while my most consistent creative efforts increasingly focused on writing, in hindsight, I seemed to be attracted to the creative realm in other areas as well. Though I had a few favorite toys, clay was always my first choice. No, that medium never grew to become the target of my adult passion, but I marveled at the many things I could make with clay, from forts filled with soldiers to a zoo filled with animals. I even used clay to make a model of the internal anatomy, which I entered in my seventh-grade science fair.

In addition, I liked building things and taking them apart. I still recall my childish impatience as I waited for electronic appliances to fail so that I could explore their inner workings. I was fascinated by the construction of radios, clocks, toasters, and watches.

While I had attempted a few autobiographical short stories when I was in my early twenties, most of my writing focused on satisfying academic requirements. Even my doctoral dissertation pushed me to the limits of my creativity. I conducted research on the effectiveness of a self-help book I had written for teenagers to work with individually or in group formats.

Although I had longed to devote more time to writing, upon graduation I let life interfere with this ambition while I focused my attention on developing my skills as a clinician. Then, in the mid-1980s, I began working on a book about managing anger. I went so far as to submit a proposal to several publishers and, although their feedback was supportive, the manuscript was not accepted for publication. As before, life interfered with my desire to write. It was not until the late 1990s that I once again pursued my passion more seriously.

I was most fortunate when Nancy Rosenfeld, now my friend and agent, asked if I would be interested in being a coauthor of *New Hope for People with Bipolar Disorder*, with her and Dr. Jan Fawcett. The invitation came at a perfect time. I was finally receptive to more actively embracing my creativity, and I have continued to do so for the past eight years. I embraced this passion so completely that I decided to leave my half-time position as an associate professor to further immerse myself in writing (and expand my practice).

This book is about helping you foster that same capacity for creative passion. It is about helping you access and experience your creative genius. It is about empowering you to reclaim and embrace the natural openness, curiosity, and excitement you had as a child when you first explored your new world and began to realize that you could impact it with your ideas and actions. Although I focus much of my attention on writing, this book is not really just about writing. It is about enhancing courage, freedom, openness, acceptance, self-trust, and commitment, the essential ingredients to fully embrace your creative genius in any endeavor. It is intended to help you address feeling "creativity challenged" as well as to further increase your engagement and connection with your creative passion. *Unlock Your Creative Genius* is also for those who have become blocked in their ability to identify a deeply felt passion for being creative. In sum, it is intended to help you find greater joy and meaning in your life by reconnecting with and unlocking your creative genius.

This book will help you embrace your creative passion whether your interest is in the arts, in science, in starting a new business venture, in creating a new career, in deciding how to live your retirement, or in any activity in which you desire to reflect and elaborate on what is most deeply meaningful for you.

My premise is that the capacity to unlock our creative genius is based on our ability to overcome the tension we feel when we dare to create. Only then can we develop free and open access to explore our internal realities— our emotions, thoughts, images, and sensations. This ability depends on our resourcefulness in overcoming inhibitions such as fear, guilt, and shame, which may block access to and the expression of our creativity.

The freedom to access creative genius is nurtured during distinct moments when we have an overriding, comprehensive, mind-body experience that is life affirming and involves positive emotions, supportive and nurturing thoughts, and energizing physical states. Joy, satisfaction, contentment, excitement, anticipation, and surprise are just a few of the emotional states that encourage creative freedom—the capacity for self-acceptance, openness, and an ability to act.

Creative freedom is further enhanced by supportive "self-talk," thoughts that consciously and unconsciously communicate, "You can do it," "Trust yourself," "You deserve to pursue your passion," and "You can handle the tension of creating." Such freedom is further fostered during most of the creative process by thoughts that are compassionate and nonjudgmental.

Similarly, increased freedom and enhanced creative passion are associated with a physical state that involves a positive but heightened excitement that pushes us toward thoughts and action in contrast to disturbing physical tension that stifles or inhibits forward movement.

Creativity and the creative passion that fuels it depend on the interplay of these forces to foster free access to and the expression of our selves. All levels of creativity require these basic ingredients, but it is when they come together in strength that we can most firmly embrace our creative passion. Whether painting, creating photographs, composing music, writing, generating ideas for the company conference, or simply organizing a party for a group of one's best friends, this positive mind-body interaction is essential in order to nurture and embrace creative passion.

In contrast, difficulties in accessing and embracing our creative genius are associated with experiencing discrete moments and series of such moments when our mind-body interplay thwarts acceptance, openness, and action. Specifically, negative emotions such as fear, shame, anxiety, and guilt, and constrictive and devaluing thoughts and negative physical tension interact to foster decreased creative passion and promote withdrawal from creative engagement. To the degree that we can learn ways to identify and effectively manage and overcome such tension, we increase our freedom to connect with ourselves, to be self-accepting, and to more fully engage our creative passions.

Throughout my years as a clinician I have worked with clients to overcome the paralyzing impact that anger, depression, and anxiety can have on their lives. In doing so I have helped them to develop a wide variety of strategies to reduce and manage the negative emotions that are associated with these symptoms, including fear, guilt, shame, and the hurt that results from rejection, abuse, and loss. These strategies derive from my focus not just on helping clients reduce their symptoms, but on positive psychology, helping clients to foster strengths such as the courage, resilience, persistence, and commitment to cope with life's challenges and to achieve their goals. In essence, both require the same skills I offer the reader throughout this book. In both situations, whether dealing with a symptom or pursuing a creative passion, we face the challenge to be authentic and to find real meaning in life. And, while it is a challenge we all face, we especially confront it as we attempt to be creative.

I begin by discussing creative genius, the creative process, and the essential strengths that support it. In chapter 2, I offer a detailed analysis of one individual's "moments of challenge," those distinct moments that can potentially impede, inhibit, and block creative engagement. These are discrete points in time when, rather than embrace the creative process in the forefront of our awareness, we fixate on and become distracted by fears and anxiety, crippling and inhibiting thoughts, or physical discomfort. Throughout the book, I offer numerous examples from my own experiences, as well as those of clients and others, that demonstrate the vacillation between engagement and disengagement that so often occurs when attempting to embrace creative passion.

This book offers understanding, specific strategies, and exercises that you can use to once again access and embrace your creative genius and to overcome the paralyzing potential of your moments of challenge. Through reading, practicing the skills described, and completing the exercises, you will be able to increase your capacity to generate positive emotions, supportive and nurturing thoughts, and positive physical tension essential for creativity. Through these same activities, you will be helped in strengthening your self-compassion, an attitude of positive self-regard that feeds your ability to flourish.

Each chapter concludes with suggestions for further exploration and exercises, questions, or discussion that will help you to further advance your understanding of the chapter and increase your self-awareness. I recommend writing your answers so as to maintain a log of your reflections. Additionally, I present quotations regarding the chapter content that I find to be inspiring.

Creativity is a hallmark of the human spirit that echoes who we are and who we are becoming. In every act of creativity we feel connection with ourselves and with others. And, when engaged in such moments, we once again view ourselves and our world through the eyes of an innocent child engrossed in play; filled with joy, imagination, and empowerment; and without self-deception or the tyranny of fear. I wish you increased openness and commitment to experience such moments and great joy and gratification as you embrace your creative genius throughout your life journey.

I

THE CHALLENGE TO UNLOCKING CREATIVE GENIUS

Chapter 1

THE NATURE
OF THE CHALLENGE

"It arouses in me a range of intense emotions, some of which I fight to avoid. And yet they are all a part of the acute gratification I experience when I write. It is part desire and part compulsion, something I feel I have to do. It is in my genes to be a writer."

"The joy of my music is in those moments when, although I gently guide them, I feel like the notes, chords, and harmony just seem to flow from some deeply hidden, vast musical reservoir within me."

"At times I feel like my painting is my mistress. Each day I awake with visions of her. I long to spend time with her. There are times when all else feels like a distraction. How fortunate I am that my wife feels the same about her writing!"

"I add colors, heat them, blow into it and rotate it at various angles. Sure I have some idea of how I would like it to be, but the true excitement comes from seeing where it goes and recognizing that one precise moment when I know it is time to retract the glass from the fire."

CREATIVE PASSION AND CREATIVE GENIUS

Creative passion is an all-powerful and compelling desire to engage in a creative endeavor. Whether involved in writing, composing music, painting, glass blowing, pottery, photography, or any similar adventure, creative passion is the driving force that propels us to immerse ourselves in the journey of sustained creativity. While grounded in emotion, such passion reflects an all-encompassing embrace of the creative venture by our mind, body, and spirit as well.

Such passion is rooted in the child's natural curiosity and openness in exploring his surroundings and himself. At its core, creative passion is the same uninterrupted joy experienced by the healthy, bright-eyed, and beaming child as he regards with awe everything around him, from his mother's face and the colors of his toys to the sounds of the human voice and the taste and texture of food entering his mouth.

It equally originates from the sense of mystery, excitement, and empowerment we feel as children when we discover our ability to have an impact on our surroundings. Whether launching his milk bottle into flight, causing a mobile to move, tapping a spoon against a bowl, or making a parent smile, a child becomes engrossed in his observations, making sense of them and recognizing the impact he can have on his environment. Such excitement only intensifies when he is encouraged to draw, paint, move blocks around, or roleplay super heroes. Deeply rooted in creative passion is a drive to imagine and to express that imagination. In doing so we demonstrate our distinctly human capacity, through sheer will, to temporarily transcend time and place.

This book is about helping you develop skills to reconnect with, nurture, and enhance your creative passion, whether you are a full-time artist or seek to become more engaged in a hobby, whether you already feel intense passion or are seeking ways to strengthen your drive to be creative. It is more about fostering openness and freedom to create than it is about identifying specific games, techniques, or skills to become creative. Specifically, the focus of this book is on helping free you emotionally, physically, and mentally to access, trust, and express your creative genius. While it is intended to help you to more consistently engage in sustained creativity, it can also provide you increased openness to engage in being creative in all aspects of daily living.

Creative passion is very much like a loving relationship. After all, creative passion is a form of love. At its best, it leads to joy, excitement, inspiration, gratification, and companionship. Sculpting a bronze figure, transforming a canvas into a captivating sunset, writing a novel or a poem, or striving to perfect a pirouette can impact us emotionally as deeply as many moments of a relationship. From conception, through production, to the moment when we expose our creation to others, embracing creativity can bring us to peaks of ecstasy and long-term gratification. At the same time, sustained creativity forces us to confront challenges that, like those in a romantic relationship, are sometimes difficult and unsettling—the challenge to be true to yourself and to be authentic.

And like a loving relationship, sustained creativity demands an overriding commitment, a promise to maintain the bond in spite of challenges to and fluctuations in the intensity of that passion. We make that commitment with the determination, hope, and optimism that we can manage any challenges that threaten our pursuit.

At the same time, as in a loving relationship, sustained creativity can also lead to a variety of tensions that may include hurt, fear, anxiety, frustration, anger, and even guilt and shame. These are moments of tension that challenge our commitment and can lead our creative passion to diminish in intensity. Some of this tension is associated with various forms of performance anxiety.

Although driven to follow our creative passion, doing so leads us to concerns about our performance and fears that we are incompetent. We may be anxious when we move the brush across the canvas and conclude that our efforts do not exactly reflect the vision we hold in our mind's eye. When writing fiction we may feel fear or guilt about revealing our most sacred personal secrets through the words and actions of our characters. We may approach a blank page and experience unyielding anxiety regarding how we should begin a story.

"What will others think?" and "Is this really good?" are a duet of paralyzing concerns that to some degree are a very natural part of every creative endeavor. This is in part because any act of creativity reveals to others and to ourselves certain facets of who we are. Words, music, photography, dance, and pottery are just a few of the many languages that communicate aspects of one's unique identity. Sustained creativity often leads to a finished work that is as revealing and as personally unique as a fingerprint. It should not be surprising that, just as many of us experience tremendous anxiety about public speaking, we would also experience anxiety related to expressing and revealing ourselves in a manner other than the spoken word.

Many of the most successful actors, entertainers, artists, and writers indicate that they experience fear and anxiety during the pursuit of their craft.

Those who are most successful report that they have learned a variety of strategies to manage it so that it does not become overwhelming. At the same time, many also acknowledge the beneficial aspect of such anxiety and actually experience uneasiness in its absence.

CREATIVE ENGAGEMENT

Anxiety can be a powerful resource that heightens your attention to your surroundings and to yourself. It prompts you to become hypervigilant and alert to the details of your perceptions, thoughts, experiences, and sensations. This sharpened focus is essential when exploring both the world around you and your internal landscape. Through this focus, you become more deeply engaged and present with the creative process, attending to and sorting through the observations that will become and already are a part of your memory bank. Similarly, heightened attention helps you attend to the details of imagination, the generation of new ideas, images, and perceptions. Anxiety, aside from increasing the attention required to find what you seek, also enhances your openness to the surprises you may discover along the way.

I embrace this form of anxiety as an essential component of my creative passion. It accompanies the most rewarding and productive moments of my writing. At such times, I feel alive, challenged, and empowered. I am in a state of what Mihalyi Csikszentmihalyhi has described as flow.[1] It is a state of mind and body during which I feel totally absorbed by the task at hand, a loss of self-consciousness, and loss of a sense of time. It is a unique form of flow, one characterized by excitement and a genuine sense of fluid movement, even though I am sitting still in front of my computer. It is creative passion taking center stage in my focused attention.

While my conscious thoughts revolve around the content of my writing, interspersed among them are positive, supportive, and encouraging bits of self-commentary such as "I really *can* do this," "This is fun," "Wow! I really like the ideas I am addressing," "I deserve to have fun," "I like where this is going," "I know I can trust myself," and "I have no idea where that thought came from, but it certainly fits in!" These are just a few of the thoughts that consciously and unconsciously buoy my passion and enable me to embrace the momentum and content of my flow. At such moments, I feel joy, satisfaction, contentment, hope, and empowerment.

During moments of creative flow, you also react on a physical level. You feel energized, and may even experience the subtle changes in breathing that often accompany such tension. At times you may notice a leg shake, a finger tapping, or your tongue periodically darting against your teeth. These physical responses are symptoms of a nervous energy, a tension that is predominantly one of excited exploration against a backdrop of low-level, threatening anxiety.

Although perhaps less intense, I find it comparable to my experiences when scuba diving or flying in a glider plane; it is the feeling of soaring associated with the miracle of defying gravity. As with these activities, self-consciousness periodically interrupts my experience of flow. Sure, there is some apprehension, a distant thought or fleeting image of my vulnerability, but these are soon placed where they should be, in the distant recesses of my awareness.

During such moments, I step back to observe myself and marvel at the experience. These moments of reflection further escalate my enthusiasm and a full embrace of the moment. There is a sense of freedom in such moments of creative passion, very much like the soaring that is a part of those sports. My experience of flow is also accompanied by a heightened attention to detail and a desire to further explore all that I feel and observe.

I wish that I could easily access this intensity of passion each and every time I write, but the reality of the creative journey does not always follow my preferred route. While I may embark on a creative venture with some sense of direction, embracing creativity also demands that at times I let the momentum of the process be my guide. Likewise, remaining somewhat passive to the medium with which you create will further fuel your passion. Whether you are dealing with words, ideas, music, paint, dance, clay, or crafts, creativity requires that you freely step back and let the medium lead you.

Another factor that contributes to the vacillating intensity of creative passion is the nature of the aforementioned creative process. At its best, true creativity is characterized by collaboration between your conscious and unconscious mind. You can consciously work at being creative, but you are also dependent on your unconscious mind, that part of your psyche over which you have no direct control, to provide inspiration. And yet, such dependence does not imply that you should sit idly and wait for your unconscious to give inspiration as a gift.

By consciously valuing and embracing those attitudes favorable to creativity, including self-compassion, you become more fully alert and receptive to what the deepest part of your psyche has to offer. And by consciously maintaining this mind-set, your unconscious is reassured that it is appreciated and welcome to work its miracle and share its riches—what we then call "inspiration." Inspiration may arrive as a phrase, a concept, an image, a framework of a short story, several lines of a poem, a melody, or, as Mozart describes, a complete symphony.

Once that inspiration arrives, you resume your chosen creative journey with increased intensity and momentum, only to once again stimulate your deeper mind to further action. In essence, this is what this book is about, helping you to increase access to and collaboration with that part of your mind that, though hidden, is essential for the rewards of sustained creative engagement.

MOMENTS OF CHALLENGE

But being creative, freely exploring yourself, and allowing the process to occur can be extremely threatening. While it can bring elation, it is also marked by discrete moments of intense anxiety that distract, inhibit, or even block you from moving forward in your creative quest. At such moments, your willingness and capacity to fully engage in sustained creativity is strongly challenged. Judgment appears much too early and impedes the freedom of thought and action that is essential for creativity to flourish. Self-critical and pessimistic thoughts may form the overriding content of the assessments you make about your ability as well as the products you create. These thoughts may give rise to experiences of fear, anxiety, and even guilt or shame that may, in turn, cause physical tension. This all-encompassing impact, experienced both consciously and unconsciously, threatens your passion. Consequently, you are at risk of losing focus and concentration. Ultimately, you may experience less connection and presence with yourself and with the medium with which you are working.

At times, negative emotions intensify and foster reduced production and flexibility in your thoughts.[2] Discomfort, as well as the fear of experiencing discomfort, dominates your efforts to move on. Like deer mesmerized by the glow of headlights, you may experience a form of tunnel vision and become fixated on the paralyzing impact of the negative tension. Creative passion often fails to compete with such powerful forces, resulting in an urge to with-draw from further engagement in the creative process. In response, you may refrain from thinking and taking actions that further your creative quest. Not only do you experience pressure to disengage from the creative moment; simultaneously, concerns that previously held a low ranking in your interest suddenly seem to necessitate your focused attention.

CREATIVITY AND THE CHALLENGE TO BE AUTHENTIC

At such moments, the challenge to be creative reflects the lifelong task that each of us faces. As we progress from childhood through adolescence and into adulthood, our needs to feel secure, connected, adequate, and loved often compete with our needs to be ourselves. When they do, we may overly value the concerns and expectations of others (as well as unrealistic expec-tations for ourselves), failing to recognize, trust, and accept our own emo-tions and thoughts and the imperative to embrace a forever changing and evolving self-identity.

Pressured by these needs and our culture's socializing influence, we are often held hostage by our fears, anxieties, and feelings of shame and guilt regarding who we are and who we wish to become. Even when we're able to identify our feelings and thoughts, we become paralyzed in expressing them. In the extreme, many of us lose touch with our feelings and beliefs, including those that define our experiences as being truly meaningful in our lives. For some of us, anxiety, depression, and anger develop as reactions to feeling alienated both from others and from ourselves.

It is this very concept that resonates so strongly with a statement made by one of my graduate school psychology professors.[3] He suggested that "all techniques in psychotherapy, regardless from what school of thought they originated, were ways to help individuals give themselves permission to be themselves." After over thirty years of clinical practice, I still have not come across another statement that is as succinct or accurate with regard to the purpose of psychotherapy. Stemming from a combination of life experiences and biological factors, many of our emotional problems result from barriers we have unwittingly created to avoid acknowledging who we really are, what we believe in, what we feel, and who we want to become.

Much of my passion in clinical work derives from helping individuals gain the freedom to reconnect with themselves in ways that allow them to increase access to their internal realities, emotions, beliefs, and values. In the process my clients learn to distinguish between those thoughts and feelings they can trust and those that are driven by the need to conceal their true selves, thereby developing the ability to overcome obstacles to living an authentic life journey. They become more fully engaged in choosing a more satisfactory career path, pursuing a passion, or improving their relationships with themselves and others.

This challenge to remain authentic to oneself and firmly connected with one's internal reality is a universal challenge, whether or not one seeks psychotherapy. When I help an individual cope with deep-seated anxiety, depression, or self-esteem issues; when I work with clients to specifically enhance their creative passion; and when I struggle with my own barriers to creativity, it is a response to this same fundamental challenge. Each of these examples requires a capacity to recognize, understand, and manage a certain level of tension in order to hasten an embrace of authenticity. Compared with other human activities, the process of unlocking creative passion forces us to more directly confront this challenge.

THE COURAGE, TRUST, AND OPENNESS TO CREATE

I contend (and it is the premise of this book) that sustained creativity demands that you work at maintaining your creative passion at a level sufficient to move you beyond those distinct moments of challenge. Additionally, such passion very much rests on your capacity to sufficiently manage these moments of unrest, experienced in your mind and body. However, just as you need certain attitudes and skills to maintain romantic passion in a relationship, you also need more than passion to remain creative; both require courage, trust, openness, resilience, and willingness to work.[4]

Courage is perhaps the most important building stone for sustaining creative passion. Courage eases the way for creative momentum to take hold. To assertively express yourself requires boldness and a daring attitude. As the eminent psychoanalyst Rollo May states,

In human beings, courage is necessary to make being and becoming possible. An assertion of the self, a commitment, is essential if the self is to have any reality. This is the distinction between human beings and the rest of nature.[5]

Courage allows you to venture forth through your inner reality to explore your thoughts, perceptions, images, emotions, and values. Courage supports your journey even though you may be forced to recognize uncomfortable or frightening parts of yourself that challenge your core beliefs about who you are. Courage is also essential to the willingness to take the risk of expressing yourself in ways that may potentially lead to rejection or even ridicule. Courage helps you move forward even though doing so may force you to visit your deepest fears, anxieties, and shame. Whether writing fiction, painting a picture, or composing music or a photograph, every creative journey demands the courage to face stiff challenges.

Coupled with courage, the creative journey also demands trust in yourself and overriding optimism that you can handle the challenges of this exploration and that all will ultimately go well. It is the same element of optimism that allows one to invest the family fortune in the opening of a restaurant despite the fact that only one in five survive beyond the five-year mark. It is similarly comparable to the optimism one draws upon when taking a marriage vow despite the fact that half of marriages in this country end in divorce.

The need for openness and optimism is poignantly reflected in the introduction to *Applied Imagination*, Alex Osborn's classic book on creativity. Osborn describes a vaudevillian who when asked, "Do you play the violin?" replies: "I don't know. I've never tried!"[6]

This type of optimism is not based on realistic statistical probability. Rather, it is derived from faith and hope. For some, this optimism has been encouraged by a rich history of past experiences that have had positive outcomes. Others may be supported by family relationships, by observations of others, by faith in God, or by some other sense of spirituality. For some, courage involves a true leap of faith against a history that offers not a single reason to embrace it.

Trust supports your courage to be open in the creative process. Openness in the creative process involves both trusting yourself and being receptive to the possibility of seeing things in a different perspective. Openness helps develop your capacity to observe not just the details of your exploration but also the uniqueness of how you observe them. It helps you to postpone premature judgment or criticism and, in doing so, fosters the free flow of creative thoughts and actions. Just as a river depends on many streams to feed it, a creative current depends on an open flow of thoughts to gain real momentum and generate new ideas. The following examples provide different scenarios regarding courage, trust, openness, and the ability to create.

A college senior, Stacey sought treatment regarding academic underachievement. She had been an excellent student up until the end of her junior year. During that time she gradually lost motivation to do well in school. Although she had majored in education with the intent to become a teacher, she had harbored a desire to become a writer. Stacey's fears of disappointing her father and competing with her mother (an author of children's books) were identifiable as major stumbling blocks for truly embracing her creative passion. As she finally began to pursue her path by taking a creative writing class, she struggled immensely and had to overcome critical thoughts, fear and anxiety, and a low-level physical discomfort. Throughout this process, she worked hard at promoting her courage, trust, and commitment.

Sean was a thirty-year-old man who sought help dealing with anxiety regarding public speaking. He worked in an advertising agency and his increasing success brought with it increased demands to make presentations. In the process, he shared his procrastination about resuming one of his favorite leisure activities, oil painting. Through shared discussion and exercises, he became increasingly aware of his internalized need for perfection. He soon realized that he had maintained a notion that he should be able to create an image on canvas without making mistakes. In addition, he identified an intense need to justify his desire for painting, a need that only further interfered with trusting himself to do so.

Brent did not pride himself at all on being creative. He found himself especially challenged by a desire to creatively express how deeply he cared for his girlfriend, Rachel, who was going abroad for two weeks. At first, he thought of just getting her a gift or taking her to dinner. After much thought, he arrived at an idea that he later described as being very much out of character for him. Though hesitant in following through with his plan, he really wanted to make a statement. Brent hoped to surprise her in a way that reflected how zany he could sometimes be. Anxious at first that he would seem silly, he roused his courage to take action. The evening before she was to leave she came home to find that her fichus tree had two hundred one-dollar bills, three disposable cameras, and a bon voyage card hanging from its branches!

These are just several examples of individuals who were challenged to trust themselves and to muster their courage in the face of powerful inhibiting forces.

I learned a great deal about my fears and the courage needed to overcome them during my collaboration with Nancy Rosenfeld and Jan Fawcett on *New Hope for People with Bipolar Disorder*.[7] Nancy had already authored two impeccably crisp and articulate books, and Dr. Fawcett was the chairman of the psychiatry department of Rush–Presbyterian St. Luke's Hospital in Chicago and an acclaimed authority on depression and bipolar disorder. He had traveled to distant parts of the world to offer education and consultation regarding his specialty.

While I had been in clinical practice for many years and had started writing a book about anger several years prior to our meeting, I was suddenly forced to face my own apprehension regarding my ability to meet the challenge. "What am I doing with these two people?" became the underlying impetus for a degree of anxiety that preoccupied me for the next few months. Over and over again my doubting internal voice intruded on my conscious thoughts, asking, "What if I just can't do it?" "What will my colleagues think?" and, most important, "What will I think of myself—knowing that writing a book has been a lifelong ambition for me?"

Excitement and pure joy vacillated with tension that at times felt unrelenting and insurmountable. Fortunately, such moments of discomfort subsided in intensity and frequency. How that happened is explained by the strategies that I discuss throughout this book.

I learned a great deal about myself throughout that experience. I learned to nurture my courage, trust, and openness regarding my writing. I learned to give myself the freedom to revise, revise, and revise, and to never feel so overly attached to one version of a sentence, paragraph, or page that I would not consider an alternative way of expressing it. I have learned to have the flexibility to rearrange the order of chapters; to eliminate certain portions; to discard entire chapters; and even to cut, paste, and reassign them as parts of other chapters.

THE COURAGE TO CREATE AND SELF-SOOTHING

While creative passion rests on courage, trust, and openness, it is your capacity to be resilient that sustains you when confronted by the most difficult challenges of being creative. Resilience involves the capacity to navigate the waves of discomfort that are an inherent part of pursuing one's passion. It involves the ability to sit with, experience, and ultimately to soothe the anxiety, fear, disappointment, frustration, guilt, or shame that accompanies most creative pursuits.

Being resilient involves managing disappointment when the printed phrase, the stroke of the paintbrush, or the finished photograph does not adequately reflect your expectations. It involves coping with the challenges inherent in submitting your work for review, whether to a friend or to a curator or publisher. It provides you strength to continue in spite of critical feedback or outright rejection.

A key aspect of resilience is the capacity to effectively endure extended periods of time during which you may feel inadequate to the creative task you have set for yourself. It is only as you continue to engage in the creative challenge that you develop the new skills necessary for a true sense of competence. Regardless of how talented you may be, pursuing your passion will inevitably involve a sizable dose of self-doubt. As a writer, I often question my ability to clearly and eloquently express my ideas, yet that has not stopped me from completing entire manuscripts. Each book I have written has brought new opportunities and challenges as well as the familiar anxieties of self-doubt.

Resilience also helps you to cope with the inevitable feelings of deprivation that periodically arise as the demands of the creative pursuit compete with other deeply felt longings. And, if it is truly a passion, creativity often requires a great commitment of time and energy. Similarly, it is resilience that is necessary to cope with the extended periods of solitude that are so often required in the pursuit of creativity.

The capacity to be patient is another source of resilience, and is essential during every phase of the creative endeavor. While some creativity is the product of spontaneous thoughts and actions, sustained creativity is a prolonged process involving decisions and actions that build upon each other to achieve their overall impact.

While Van Gogh is said to have completed some of his paintings in just several hours, he committed many brush strokes over many years to develop that degree of aptitude. Similarly, while forming an elegant glass vase may not take too much time in the hands of an expert glassblower, time is essential to develop the skills and craft that are required to make the creation of such high-quality art look easy.

In both situations, these artists demonstrate commitment and persever-ance, essential strengths that underlie resilience. Creativity requires that we persevere in spite of discouragement, opposition, and other setbacks. As will be emphasized throughout subsequent chapters, the capacity to embrace cre-ative passion may be challenged by limits to your ability to persevere. From the moment you first listen to the inner voice that guides your creative flow, through every aspect of creativity, it is perseverance that supports the progress that leads to a true reflection of your inner experience.

For many years I worked with children and adolescents in addition to seeing adults. Unfortunately, the experience described by fourteen-year-old Jeff was quite common. During one of our sessions he excitedly reported to me that he had purchased a guitar and was going to take lessons to become accomplished in his new endeavor. I inquired about his progress shortly after. Jeff indicated he was progressing and that he enjoyed the challenge. Several weeks later he gave me an entirely different response. He had prac-ticed for four weeks and had then decided to give up his pursuit. When I questioned him, he said, "I had no idea your fingers had to become cal-loused! Also, after practicing for a half hour every day, I could not play any songs that I like to listen to!"

Jeff lacked the resilience needed to sit with the frustration of not pro-gressing at his expected pace. In part, his frustration also seemed related to his feelings of inadequacy in attempting to master the instrument. Most important, Jeff lacked one of the final strengths for pursuing a creative pas-sion. He had difficulty making a commitment to work at developing his skills, a commitment to training and practice that demands time and effort, requires some form of deprivation, and only slowly yields tangible rewards. Generating ideas, whether for the major focus of a book, the composition of a painting, the script for a play, or the lyrics for a song depends on commit-ment. In any creative pursuit, some of the activities that support your cre-ative progress are more rewarding than others; some require greater demand of your resources, and some activities may at times be unproductive. How-ever, it is dedication to work at your craft that leads to increased mastery.

Each of us varies in the degree to which we have developed these strengths and capabilities. However, the good news is that there are very spe-cific strategies that you can practice to attain or strengthen them. And when you do, you will more effectively manage the distinct moments of challenge that arise throughout the creative process. You will also gain increased access to your creative genius and an enhanced ability to sustain your creative passion.

Chapter 2 explores in detail the vacillating nature of the mind-body tension that we experience when we dare to embrace our creative passion.

*** FOR YOUR EXPLORATION ***

1. Recall how your creative passion was experienced as a child. Are you currently pursuing similar areas of interest? If so, what has helped you nurture them? If not, what experiences are you aware of that may have inhibited you from further pursuing them?
2. What are the physical reactions you experience during the creative process?
3. What are your strengths and weaknesses in regard to your creative passion? Courage, trust in yourself, commitment, resilience, willingness to work?
4. What have you done in the past to improve on your weaknesses?
5. What are the most effective strategies you currently use to nurture and enhance your creative passion? Are they effective?
6. On the continuum of creative engagement, during what phases of creativity do you experience your greatest challenges?
    a. identifying passion
    b. thinking about expressing it
    c. taking initial actions
    d. following through in middle stages
    e. completing projects or achieving creative goals
7. Briefly describe your specific challenges.

REFLECTIONS

Do not forget the most important fact that neither heredity nor environment is a determining factor. Both are giving only the frame and the influences which are answered by the individual in regard to his styled creative power.—Alfred Adler

It is the function of art to renew our perception. What we are familiar with we cease to see. The writer shakes up the familiar scene, and as if by magic, we see a new meaning in it.—Anais Nin

Genius is nothing but continued attention.—Claude A. Helvetius

Creativity belongs to the artist in each of us. To create means to relate. The root meaning of the word art is "to fit together" and we all do this every day. Not all of us are painters but we are all artists. Each time we fit things together we are creating.—Corita Kent

NOTES

1. Mihalyi Csikszentmihalyi, *Flow* (New York: Harper and Row, 1990).
2. Martin E. P. Seligman, *Authentic Happiness* (New York: Free Press, 2002).
3. Erwin Singer, personal communication in City College of New York graduate psychology class, 1967.
4. Robert J. Sternberg, *Handbook of Creativity* (New York: Cambridge University Press, 1999).
5. Rollo May, *The Courage to Create* (New York: W. W. Norton, 1994), p. 4
6. Alex Osborn, *Applied Imagination* (New York: Charles Scribner's Sons, 1963), p. xiii.
7. Jan Fawcett, Bernard Golden, and Nancy Rosenfeld, *New Hope for People with Bipolar Disorder* (New York: Three Rivers/Random House, 2000).

Chapter 2

MOMENTS
OF CHALLENGE

Regardless of the form it takes, embracing creative passion offers you the opportunity to live authentically as you increasingly accept your uniquely evolving individual identity. It offers you the opportunity to connect with yourself by truly identifying what you feel and believe about the world and your role in it. At the same time, pursuing your creative passion is almost always accompanied by challenge, the confrontation of forces within you that resist and undermine authentic being.

Whether you write, paint, dance, compose music, work with ceramics, or are choosing a new career, your capacity to proceed rests on your ability to effectively manage those moments of great opportunity that are usually accompanied by moments of great challenge. In short, exploiting these opportunities depends on your ability to manage the mind-body tension aroused during the challenging moments that may strain, diminish, or entirely erode your creative passion. How you resolve the tension of such moments largely determines whether you live authentically or betray who you are.

A FORM OF SELF-BETRAYAL

Take a moment to observe a healthy young child and you will be immediately struck by his energy, drive, and determination to explore and take in every part of his new world. From out of darkness he has arrived to observe

35

dazzling colors, rich textures, and a vast variety of fragrances, sounds, shapes, and lines. Like a plant craving sunlight, he reaches out to taste, smell, touch, see, and hear what this world is about. To a great extent it is this exuberance that draws us to children. We see hope, potential, a sense of novelty and complete abandon, and unrestrained engagement with the process of taking the first steps of life's journey. We need no further proof to know that a child is innately fearless, open, curious, and awestruck as he explores himself and his new environment.

At the same time, accompanying this life force, we observe frailty and a deep sense of helplessness, even weakness, as we recognize and perhaps even recall from our own experiences how completely dependent he is on others for his psychological and physical well-being. These two driving forces, the assertive embrace of the great adventure of his unfolding life and the intense need for security and stability, will impact him now and for his entire adult life. How he manages them and how others respond to them will determine the degree to which he will be able to live authentically and embrace his creative genius.

Through such interactions, some people learn very early to ignore, minimize, or even deny yearnings to be creative (or even to be imaginative). Prompted by fear, anxiety, guilt, shame, and other reactions, these individuals become almost phobic about engaging in even the initial steps essential to embracing and fostering creative passion. With and without full awareness, based on the need for approval and acceptance from both others and themselves, they draw back from valuing their uniqueness and the wider creative process. By denying, ignoring, or suppressing their innate curiosity and openness to both self and world, they soon lose touch with their interests, needs, and passions.

More specifically, these individuals develop what I describe as a negative "mind-body set," which works against and can ultimately stifle their capacities to access, accept, and express creative genius. This negative mind-body set entails distinct moments in time when fears and other negative emotions, critical and constrictive thinking, and uncomfortable physical states hold them hostage and lead them to betray their own potentials. An individual caught in a negative mind-body set risks becoming an adult cut off from his own creative passion. A more severe outcome is the development of a sense of alienation from what he believes to be truly meaningful.

When you retreat from yourself, you also betray others by robbing them of the contributions your creativity may have on their lives. While your individual life is certainly enriched by your creativity, it is also accurate to say that civilization depends on creativity to meet the challenges of its evolving identity. When you exert restraints on your individual creativity, you may deny others a style of painting that inspires them, words that increase their depth of self-understanding, music that resonates with their moods, the one idea that will offer someone an impetus to start a new career or find a cure for a disease, or a plan that will bring accord among nations.

This same inhibition can impact the most intimate of relationships. Many of us passively wait for our partners to create excitement, surprise, structure, and novelty. Yet, maximizing the joy and bond in a relationship very much depends on what *each* partner does to keep the passion of love vibrant and alive. It is not an exaggeration to say that the quality and even the survival of a relationship very much depends on how much creativity you bring to it.

In contrast, many of us recognize a particular passion but rarely, if ever, pursue it. It often seems that the realities of life can interfere with actively following through with your deeply cherished dreams. However, the failure to nurture your passion is often due in large part to overvaluing the things that appear to be more "practical" and immediately rewarding. These perceptions may motivate you to flee from the tension of the creative moment.

Subsequently, you may put off writing until retirement or postpone painting until you find the perfect workspace or subject matter. You may wait for just the right mood to hit you, or until you once again feel your passion intensely enough to embrace it more fully. It may take anger or depression to move you to create, as if these emotional states were the only sources for your creativity. You may be the type to indefinitely postpone acting on your creative passion, choosing instead to obsessively read books and attend seminars to understand theories or techniques that you might never apply.

Others partake in the creative process in such a way that can best be described as "intermittent sustained creativity," durations of engagement alternating with periods of avoidance. One client described working on a painting for four years. Another purchased a piano and described intense daily practice for several weeks at a time, only to then skip weeks or even months of practice. I began working on my book *Healthy Anger: How to Help Children and Teens Manage Their Anger* nearly fifteen years before it was published![1]

Some of us experience the proverbial "block," a more consistent and intense inhibition of our creative efforts. If you are blocked, you may fail to engage in the creative process for extended periods of time that may range from a few days to a few years.

Finally, you might be able to successfully cope through almost all phases of the creative journey only to become overwhelmed and paralyzed in your efforts to complete the final steps of your venture. You put your manuscript in a drawer and never submit it to a publisher for review, or you complete nine recordings of a song but fail to perform the final cut. Similarly, you may view a painting as being "not quite finished" and yet put off defining what you need to do to make it complete.

WHAT IT FEELS LIKE

As stated previously, barriers to creativity involve the arousal of tension in a mind-body set. Specifically, they are negative emotions such as fear, anxiety, guilt, or shame, combined with critical thoughts and physical tension that dilute your focus and encourage you to reject and abandon your creative passion. Negative emotions compete with and leave little space for positive emotions.

Such discomfort evolves from a myriad of factors that may include fear of failure, fear of success, shame with regard to following your heart, and unrealistic expectations such as perfectionism, survivor's guilt, and uneasiness with the solitude that is so often a requirement for sustained creativity. (These and other related factors will be discussed in greater detail in part II).

Regardless of the unique issues that contribute to inhibit any individual's capacity to embrace creative passion, fear and anxiety are inherent in the creative process itself. Descending into the unknown, feeling vulnerable to the reaction of others, the tension you experience as you commit to temporarily suspend critical judgment; these factors interact in such a way as to threaten your progress and full engagement in the creative moment.

In part, this tension can arise even when you are not actually engaged in tangible acts of creativity. Even having a creative thought or daydreaming about engaging in such activities may lead you to revisit past fears and anxieties or anticipate having to experience new ones. This tension can impact you long before you more fully engage in specific actions that reflect your creative passion.

At such moments you may develop a type of "tunnel vision" in your awareness. It involves constriction and rigidity in your focus of attention that leaves little room for courage, trust, openness, and the positive tension essential to embracing creativity. Individuals who are severely depressed experience a constriction in awareness that is fixated on a constellation of thoughts reflecting pessimism, hopelessness, and helplessness. Those who suffer various forms of anxiety are similarly held captive by these types of thoughts. The tension that inhibits embracing creative passion is likewise dominated by a constellation of negative emotions, thoughts, and physical states. Their impact is more episodic and less pervasive, since they are directly triggered by creative engagement. This is reflected in the following case study.

KATIE'S CHALLENGE

The following scenario describes in detail a series of moments experienced by Katie over twenty-four hours as she struggled to pursue her passion for drawing. It identifies the various shifts in her mind-body set that foster her presence and engagement in the creative process at one moment, while sabotaging it at another.

Katie, age thirty-one and a mother of two, has worked as a computer analyst for the past seven years while harboring a strong desire to become an illustrator of children's' books. Although she has maintained this longing since completing college, she actually started drawing just six months ago. While she has made some progress, her efforts have been sporadic. Katie vows to sketch for one hour each day, but often skips several days or weeks before once again resuming her efforts. She describes her experience as follows.

In Her Own Words

> Several months ago I made a commitment to further develop my skills in illustration. I told myself that I would draw at least one hour each day even if I was not in the mood to do so. I reminded myself that whatever I drew would be fine and that I would try not to judge myself. I knew it would take time. I knew I had to be patient. I was sure that working just an hour a day would lead to my progress. I experience great fulfillment in illustrating and know that I will eventually succeed in this endeavor. I recall what I learned in my classes and I believe they helped me to develop some solid basic

skills in drawing. I know I can draw well even though I have not done so since then. Tomorrow morning I will again wake up at 6:00 AM, an hour earlier than usual, so that I can draw before the children awake and I have to get ready to go to work.

I have said this to myself for the last few months and yet something keeps me from consistently doing it. Oh, of course there have been many mornings when I actually followed through with my plan, but in total, I have only started several drawings in the last six months and they still need further revisions.

I do this for a few days and then skip a day or two, or even a week or so before I once again resume drawing. When I try to figure out what gets in my way, I often conclude that I am just trying to do too much. However, that was why I postponed pursuing my drawing until the children were older. And, while my job can be highly stressful at times, I have been taking work home less often during the past year. I know drawing is sometimes frustrating, but I really like doing it and want to complete a series of illustrations that I can be proud of.

The Dilemma

Katie is fairly self-aware and provides much detail regarding her experience. On one level it appears that Katie is motivated, confident, and knows exactly what she needs to do to reach her goal. She demonstrates strong determination and appears emotionally invested in her pursuit. Her desire to draw appears to emanate from her authentic self and resonates with an interest she has maintained for years.

Katie's description actually identifies a good degree of courage, resilience, trust in herself, and a commitment to work, all essential strengths for successfully embracing one's creative journey. For example, she demonstrates perseverance by her commitment to set aside time "even" if she is not in the mood to do so.

She also recognizes the need to suspend premature judgment of what she draws. This attitude reflects resilience, appropriate openness, and flexibility in her self-expectations. The fact that she has actually completed several drawings indicates that she experiences enough trust in herself to initiate the process. That she has completed several drawings also reflects her capacity to overcome challenges to her creative engagement.

Similarly, Katie's patience furthers the freedom she needs to move on with her creative endeavor. Her patience also strengthens her capacity to tolerate frustration and to be future-oriented, as opposed to needing immediate satisfaction.

Katie is practical in her commitment to her plan. She schedules a specific period of time to draw rather than passively waiting for it to become available. Similarly, she commits herself to an hour a day, in contrast to believing that she needs to schedule huge blocks of time to attain her goal. Her capacity for solid engagement is a strength that can counter the inhibiting tension associated with being creative.

However, despite the deep satisfaction she gains from drawing and her other identified strengths, she fails to consistently move forward in pursuing her craft. While she intermittently engages in the necessary steps of pursuing her dream, she is too often paralyzed by the challenges of tension and negative mind-body discomfort. We can best understand the pervasive impact of these forces by examining the delicate interplay of thoughts, emotions, and physical reactions that Katie experiences over a twenty-four-hour period during which she is able to make some gains in more fully embracing her creative venture but is simultaneously confronted by distinct moments of challenge, characterized by inhibiting mind-body tension. I begin with an exploration of the experiences she has the night before resuming her drawing.

Moment by Moment

The evening prior to resuming her drawing, Katie made a brief stop at a bookstore to once again review several children's books that included illustrations she greatly admired. These often inspired her. Even before entering the store, she acknowledged a low level of physical tension. In part, this reflected her excitement over her renewed commitment to resume drawing the next day. At the same time, she recognized a very familiar sense of discomfort.

She selected several books and retreated to a quiet corner to examine them. She thumbed through the first book, admiring the style as well as the facial features of the characters depicted in the drawings. Although they shared some similarity with her drawings, she favored a more impressionistic style in her work. For a moment she experienced a strong validation of her abilities. Being open, she also noted details of the drawing that inspired ideas regarding her style.

She then picked up a second book to review. With one glance at the cover of the book, Katie immediately experienced an initial knee-jerk reaction of uncomfortable tension. The illustration she noted was exceptional in color, style, characterization, composition, and combination of detail. Earlier in her development as an artist, Katie had aspired to draw like the illustrator of this book. Following this early fascination, she moved in a somewhat different direction. However, reviewing the illustrations of this book triggered an uncomfortable physical tension, a low-level emotional discomfort in the form of anxiety and some mild thoughts of self-doubt regarding her capacity to be "creative enough" to pursue her interest. Maybe I should take another class before I proceed," she thought. "My work does not compare to hers—am I fooling myself about my ability? Maybe I need to research more examples."

Fortunately, she reviewed several other books and was able to reconnect with her confidence, openness to experiment, and overall motivation to persevere. Clearly resilient in overcoming her tension, when Katie left the store she experienced once again the positive physical tension of excitement, a level of joy associated with buoyed confidence, and thoughts that were less judgmental and more nurturing and compassionate.

Just before going to sleep that night, Katie made preparations so that she could devote her full attention to drawing in the morning. Once in bed, she had some thoughts about the day and soon began to think about her drawing. She began to endure some moments of both positive and negative tension as she anticipated the resumption of her drawing. Though determined to get a good sleep, she initially found herself generating specific ideas for her illustrations. At this point, Katie formed a very positive appraisal of her ideas, her capacities, and the direction she was taking. She began to feel positive emotions of joy associated with hope and optimism that she would really be able to live her dream.

Her positive emotions helped foster increased openness and flexibility in her thinking. Essentially, her hope and optimism competed with and overshadowed her quickness to be judgmental. Consequently, she could be more present and engaged with picturing the details of her art. This further fueled both the development of ideas for her drawings and the satisfaction she anticipated as a result of making them. She then experienced positive physical tension from the interaction of her positive emotions and thoughts. This was reflected by a mild degree of restlessness that briefly interfered with her ability to fall asleep.

At that distinct moment, Katie's conscious experience was dominated by positive energy that influenced her openness to new ideas, increased her self-trust, and strengthened her desire to embrace her creative passion and genius. We can assume that any inhibiting tension that may have blocked her at other times was dormant and relatively weakened at that particular moment. She drifted into sleep shortly after she reminded herself to do so.

The alarm startled Katie the next morning, and while she was at first slightly irritated for having to wake up an hour earlier than usual, she very quickly remembered her reason for doing so. She splashed water on her face, prepared her morning coffee, and sat down to draw.

This was an important moment for Katie. While she had been more fully aware of positive tension the evening before, she was beginning to experience some very mild degree of negative tension. It was so mild and fleeting that she may not have consciously been aware of it. However, she would have become sensitive to it if she'd been directed to stop for a moment and specifically attend to her body. Even then, it may have been so slight that she would have experienced some difficulty discerning whether it reflected positive or negative tension. The fact that it was morning and one hour earlier than her usual time for waking may have further contributed to the decrease in her positive energy. In general, Katie sees herself as being more of a "night" person. She may not be able to function as well as she would have had she begun working on her drawing in the evening.

However, Katie did become engaged in her drawing. As she arranged her materials to begin work on a drawing she had already started, she was able to endure and move through the slight discomfort. Fifteen minutes passed before she began to review her progress. Her reactions following this quick review were crucial in that they influenced the tone of her mind-body set and, consequently, her capacity to continue the process at that moment. She judged her work favorably and was able to successfully begin making rough sketches.

Although influenced by positive tension, Katie first focused her attention on the task of sketching and not yet on selecting colors for her illustration. She continued to experience an overall positive mind-body set as she concentrated on this endeavor.

Although progressing, Katie was challenged in deciding how to create a character that best reflected the story she was attempting to illustrate. She began to experience mild frustration. The task of making this decision momentarily aroused inhibiting tension that fostered resistance to both trusting herself and remaining nonjudgmental. Negative tension related to fear, shame, or guilt regarding her success may have briefly impeded her advancement. Fortunately, she was able to manage her tension. She quickly settled on a particular style and was once again able to move on.

Overall, Katie's internal experiences during the first half hour of drawing were positive, only alternating briefly with moments of inhibiting tension aroused by a slight ebb and flow of fear, judgmental thoughts, and physical discomfort. At that point, she paused, sipped her coffee, checked the time, and briefly reflected on the day ahead of her. Katie's overall satisfaction with her progress led her to quickly resume drawing for a few more minutes before pausing to review the two sketches she had completed.

While Katie was pleased when working on the sketches, she now became more critical of their organization and style. As she reviewed her work, she became slightly negative in her evaluation. At that point, her critical thoughts regarding the quality of her achievement aroused already existing self-doubts regarding her overall drawing ability. At that instant, she felt the impact of escalating inhibiting tension.

This was another decisive moment. It was another point in time when either her positive tension would help her maintain momentum or the beginning rumblings of constricting tension would derail her focused efforts. At a deeper level, with or without awareness, she began to experience inhibiting forces. In part, these were based on her fears of failure. At the same time, while not fully aware of it, Katie was challenged by an inhibiting theme of guilt. Katie has always felt compelled to put the needs of others ahead of her own. So at this moment in time, she was also experiencing tension derived from the conflict between her desire to create and her sense of guilt that she was spending precious time on her drawing that she could have been devoting to her family.

As these reactions surfaced, her positive emotional reactions yielded to an increasing degree of disappointment, guilt, frustration, and even anger related to her negative self-assessment. While Katie initially had little sense of any physical discomfort, she progressively began to experience some visceral uneasiness. This was reflected by mild muscular tightness in her chest, characteristic of increased anxiety and apprehension. Had she been directed to observe her breathing, she might also have recognized that it had become somewhat shallow. During similar moments in the past Katie has experienced other physical reactions, including the sensation of an impending headache and strain across her shoulders. Her emotional, mental, and physical tension had escalated.

While she strongly desired to embrace her creative genius and knew what she needed to do in order to accomplish this, her negative mind-body states stifled her continued progress. At that moment, Katie was hostage to constricting tension that competed and conflicted with living authentically. The result was tension at both an unconscious and a conscious level of awareness that pressed her to move away from the task at hand.

She stood up, walked away from her desk, and went to the kitchen to refill her cup with coffee. She had a fleeting thought of stopping for the day. She glanced at a magazine on the kitchen counter, opened it to read a feature article, and then abruptly put it down to return to her project. Fortunately, Katie was once again able to regroup and endure the tension associated with working on her illustrations.

In reviewing her work for a second time, she was able to be less judgmental and instead focus on the positive aspects of her work. As a result, she was able to push on for a few more minutes and complete the hour of drawing with a sense of accomplishment. She put away her art supplies and began to face the rest of the day.

While experiencing an overall positive sense of accomplishment, Katie had experienced moments of tension in her thoughts and emotions and in her physical reactions. Similarly, while she had made progress, it had been challenging and had required much effort in order to maintain her commitment to the creative process.

The Outcome

Whether Katie stays on track the following morning will depend on a number of factors. She may focus predominantly on the positive emotions, thoughts, and physical reactions that she experienced while drawing the previous day. In doing so, she would embrace her authentic self and feel empowered to move forward. Alternatively, Katie may dwell on fears aroused by her frustration, self-critical thoughts, and physical tension. In doing so, she would be yielding to the influence of her inhibiting tension. Her ability to continue drawing will be based on the relative strength of these two competing forces and her ability to effectively manage them over the next twenty-four hours.

In addition, whether Katie persists may also be influenced by the degree to which other events in her day tap into and impact the ebb and flow of negative and positive tension regarding her ability to access, accept, and embrace her creative genius. These events, though they may or may not be directly related to her specific interest in drawing, may still influence her overall capacity to embrace this pursuit.

Feedback from colleagues and Katie's supervisor that she seems distracted from her work may briefly tug at her deeply felt concern that perhaps she is overextending herself by pursuing her passion for drawing. In contrast, events may occur that support the positive forces that promote her commitment to further developing her skills. Positive emotions, thoughts that foster them, and factors that contribute to physically energize her may strengthen her resolve to embrace her passion for illustration.

MEETING THE CHALLENGE

The sequential analysis of Katie's experience clearly highlights how underlying inhibiting mind-body tension can interfere even with our strongest desire to create change in our lives. It emphasizes not only the need for a positive mind-set but also the need for an overall positive mind-body set that promotes the openness to be present and engaged to the fullest in the creative moment. It also demonstrates how forces can compete with and diminish one's capacity to embrace creative passion and access one's creative genius. This description highlights the need to develop increased awareness of such forces and the specific themes they convey.

As I previously indicated, moments of challenge can occur when merely reflecting upon or evaluating your latest project, identifying new directions to follow, or considering the possible consequences of its completion. These are all potential moments that may either nurture and enhance or stifle your creative passion. How to more effectively take notice of such moments, understand them, and constructively manage the tension they produce is the focus of the rest of this book.

*** FOR FURTHER EXPLORATION ***

1. Recall a moment in your creative pursuit during which you experienced tremendous satisfaction. Describe in detail your positive reactions, listing your emotions, thoughts, and physical states.

2. Recall a moment of challenge that you experienced during your creative pursuit. Describe in detail your inhibiting reactions to that moment, listing your emotions, thoughts, and physical states.

3. What strategies are most effective in managing your moments of challenge? Do you use a variety of strategies? If so, what circumstances lead you to use one versus another? If you withdrew from pursuing your creative passion, what did you do instead?

4. Identify the objective and compassionate thoughts you use when trying to manage inhibiting or constrictive thoughts. Write them on flash cards or post them where you do your most creative work.

5. What, if anything, do you do to directly impact the physical reactions you experience during moments of creative challenge?

6. Have you used specific strategies to foster positive emotions as part of your preparation for creative engagement? If so, what strategies have been most effective for you?

7. Were you aware of any of your mind-body reactions while reading the description of my moments of challenge? If so, what were they?

REFLECTIONS

It's exhilarating to be alive in a time of awakening consciousness; it can also be confusing, disorienting, and painful.—Adrienne Rich

Every child is a genius, but is enslaved by the misconceptions of self-doubt of the adult world, and spends much of his or her time having to unlearn that perspective.—R. Buckminster Fuller

Artists don't get down to working until the pain of working is exceeded by the pain of not working.—Stephen DeStaebler

The cure for boredom is curiosity. There is no cure for curiosity.—Dorothy Parker

NOTE

1. Jan Fawcett, Bernard Golden, and Nancy Rosenfeld, *New Hope for People with Bipolar Disorder* (New York: Three Springs/Random House, 2000).

Chapter 3

PATHWAYS
TO INHIBITION

Most of those who study personality development maintain that openness, curiosity, and enthusiasm about life are a part of our innate heritage. It is in our nature to explore, discover, and observe what the world has to offer and ways we can have an impact on it. And yet, in spite of these predispositions embedded in our DNA, a number of factors contribute to inhibiting and, sometimes, completely stifling their expression.

Mihaly Csikszentmihalyi, a noted psychologist and researcher on creativity, suggests that

> each of us is born with two contradictory sets of instructions: a conservative tendency, made up of instincts for self-preservation, self-aggrandizement, and saving energy, and an expansive tendency made up of instincts for exploring, for enjoying novelty and risk—the curiosity that leads to creativity belongs to this set.[1]

He emphasizes that while the conservative tendency does not require support from others, our expansive tendencies can be impeded if there are too many barriers to risk and exploration and too few opportunities to experience the rewards of curiosity. Collectively, these obstacles play a general role in the formation of personality and can have a decisive role in the inhibition of our creative urges. Such obstacles derive from the combined impact of our interactions with others, neuropsychophysiological factors, and certain patterns of thinking.

INTERACTIONS AND PERSONALITY

From the first days of your interaction with others, your behavior is either encouraged and accepted or discouraged and punished. Through this interplay you internalize attitudes about others, the world in general, and yourself. In the process, you learn how you should feel, think, and act.

Many professionals in child development advise that it is appropriate to satisfy, as best as possible, the basic needs of a child during her first year of life. Doing so nurtures and validates her desires and needs and fosters a sense of security. By the end of the first year, it is usually appropriate to begin to increasingly set limits on a child's behavior. From this point on, the manner in which those limits are set greatly influences the child's sense of self in terms of what she learns about others, her environment, and how accepting she becomes of her own desires.

The task of limit setting is to socialize the child to the norms of the culture and behavior the parents define as being appropriate. To socialize a child without stifling her innate openness, curiosity, trust, and exploration is a difficult challenge that calls for a delicate balance of interactions.

During this phase, in addition to reward and praise, guilt and shame may also serve as valuable motivators that, to some degree, help children internalize both empathy and impulse control. (Guilt and shame will be discussed in greater detail in chapters 6 and 7, respectively.) For example, if it is discovered that a child has taken something from a sibling, she will feel bad when a parent or sibling expresses disappointment or hurt. The same is true when a parent reprimands a child in an appropriate way for hitting him or her. Following each of these situations, the child may feel guilt followed by remorse. This is appropriate and a well-learned lesson.

In contrast, some parents may communicate in a way that leads a child to experience shame rather than guilt. Their reprimands may be excessively harsh, communicating a type of rejection that focuses on the whole child rather than on the specific trespass. Shame can be especially debilitating, in contrast to guilt, as it leads to an overall sense of inadequacy about one's entire being and not just in regard to the specific error one has made.[2]

While these negative and uncomfortable emotions can be useful for socialization, when excessively experienced they serve as the initial foundation for the kind of emotional paralysis that leads to a lack of self-connection, a defeated will, or a view that one doesn't deserve to pursue one's inclinations. Such early childhood experiences may result in an adult who rejects her curiosity, striving, pleasure, assertion, and overall openness to living authentically.

While primary caretakers play a significant role in what their children internalize, siblings, extended family, peers, teachers, leaders in the community, the media, and an assortment of other cultural factors further contribute to the shaping of a child's attitudes and behavior patterns. These forces influence human development through both direct and indirect messages. Such messages either encourage or inhibit the child's capacity to live authentically and with an ability to access, accept, and act from her authentic self in embracing her creative genius. Some messages are learned through direct experience, as, for example, when one learns to be careful around a hot frying pan by touching it and getting burned. Messages are also direct when they are clearly articulated and convey expected standards concerning both how the child should feel, think, and behave and what she should expect of others and the world in general.

Indirect messages are those that are conveyed to children more subtly as they model the behaviors of adults around them. For example, a father indirectly communicates to his children how to express anger when he yells and becomes critical but never directly discusses his anger or the hurt behind it. Parents and others also communicate indirect messages to their children by how they relate to other people. Through their interactions, they model attitudes and guidelines for how to treat other people and what to expect from them.

IMPACT OF INTERACTIONS ON CREATIVE PASSION

Through these experiences you internalize attitudes that are either conducive to or inhibiting of your ability to be creative. Whether you had role models who actively valued creativity in any form may play a major role in the degree to which you embrace your creative genius. Throughout your development, these internalized messages regarding creativity form your attitudes and beliefs at both a conscious and an unconscious level, influencing your thoughts, emotions, and physical reactions when you engage in creative pursuits.

To the degree that parents nurture and support their children in living authentically, they help instill in them the capacity to access their creative genius. Through direct and indirect statements that encourage self-reflection, imagination, risk taking, exploration, and curiosity and openness, they help their children to pursue creative engagement. Such messages are further reinforced when others similarly communicate in words and behavior that creativity is exciting and that self-inquiry is life affirming. If you are truly fortunate, you have been encouraged to embrace creativity for the intrinsic joy it brings as well as for other rewards you may gain by doing so.

In contrast, creativity may be undermined by messages from parents and other adults that communicate a consistent lack of interest in a child's creative efforts. Parents who are dismissive or ignore a child's creative strivings inadvertently help to extinguish exuberance and, ultimately, creative desire. This may be the case when caretakers themselves have become inhibited in living authentically.

Additionally, one may learn to avoid novelty and change, developing the attitude that being curious, questioning, and exploring are dangerous. Simultaneously, one may learn to overvalue the opinions of others. In doing so, a desire to please, to conform, and to feel accepted may dominate and interfere with self-inquiry, acceptance, and actions related to living authentically and being creative.

Many of us may have received contradictory messages regarding creative passions during our formative years. For example, parents may have suggested we spend time writing, but through their behaviors really showed significantly greater excitement when a sibling successfully made the school basketball team. A child may be encouraged to pursue her artistic passion at the same time that her parents subtly communicate through their own behaviors that financial success should really be the most important goal in life. A teen may be directly told to focus on obtaining good grades but at the same time observe that his father's business success did not require a college degree and, in fact, depended more significantly on his being a creative entrepreneur. Similarly, a twelve-year-old girl may be encouraged to pursue her education and even a career while her mother repeatedly emphasizes how blessed she is that she pursued a more traditional female role of remaining home to raise her children.

Through the variety of your interactions you learn how to label, understand, and accept or reject your affinity for creativity. In essence, you internalize standards regarding how you should view your strivings, fantasies, and imagination, as well as your desire for recognition or success. Similarly, you learn attitudes regarding your emotions; when to trust or distrust them and when to share or hide them.

Such attitudes are communicated in the earliest of interactions. For example, an infant may become excited and laugh when a mother smiles at her or when she displays a colorful toy in front of her. The child is supported in her reaction when her mother communicates through her facial expression, tone of voice, and physical demeanor that she is accepting of her joy and exuberance regarding the toy as well as in being the center of attention. Her infant's excitement and enthusiasm are validated and further supported when she similarly echoes her reactions in a momentary volley of mirroring interactions.

In contrast, her mother may be so preoccupied with other concerns that she is not fully available to support her child's enthusiasm and joy. A mother's depression or anxiety associated with her parent's death, financial or marital conflict, or illness may further interfere with her capacity to echo her child's natural exuberance and curiosity. Or she may be very supportive during her child's first year but become less nurturing of her curiosity when her infant seeks greater independence during the "terrible twos." Similarly, her own negative attitudes about curiosity, excitement, and openness may lead her to be unavailable to provide her child a nurturing and supportive reaction to her initial steps at simply "being" herself. In the extreme, a parent may react by impulsively expressing disapproval in a harsh tone of voice, through the content of her communication, through her facial expression, or worse yet, through physical punishment. Most important, through these interactions, the child may learn to deny, minimize, or ignore her internal experiences. In doing so, she risks becoming disconnected from her emotions and beliefs.

Disconnection with oneself undermines the development of many of the qualities that are essential for fully engaging in creative pursuits. As you stifle your curiosity, openness, and predisposition to seek novelty, you step back from being true to yourself. Additionally, if you've been taught that you do not deserve to have your needs met, you unwittingly engage in behaviors that are distracting and self-defeating toward the attainment of your individual goals and the expression of your values. In addition, by persisting in the habit of stifling your predisposition to openness, curiosity, and novelty, you model such behaviors for others, unwittingly contributing to an increased likelihood that they will likewise stifle their own innate creativity. Through these interactions you also learn attitudes regarding how to cope with tension and frustration in general. How effective you become in soothing such tension greatly influences the degree to which you can fully embrace your creative desires.

THE CAPACITY TO BE SELF-SOOTHING

The major premise of this book is that openness to your creative genius depends to a great extent on your capacity to be self-soothing, your ability to "sit with," tolerate, and regulate the tension of negative emotions, thoughts, and physical states that accompany creative engagement. This ability to regulate and manage tension is just one of several significant areas of emotional development that noted psychologist Daniel Goleman describes as comprising "emotional intelligence."[3] Prominent among Goleman's areas of emotional intelligence are both the ability to identify and differentiate one's emotions and a capacity for empathy. Frustration, tolerance, and the ability to manage negative emotions together comprise the foundation for the resilience needed to cope with all of life's challenges, but particularly those moments of challenge triggered by creative engagement.

Although partially influenced by a biological predisposition, this capacity is also very much formed by early interactions with caretakers. Research suggests that mothers who communicate attunement to an infant through eye contact, tone of voice, hand gestures, and touch help a child develop an increased capacity to regulate uncomfortable affect. Attunement may best be described as being attentive to, sensitive to, and in synch with an infant's level of excitability while actively helping him to appropriately calm himself when his emotional excitement escalates.

Many years ago, while working in a clinical practice, I had the opportunity to observe parent-child interactions that reflected various degrees of such attunement.[4] As part of an assessment of parent-child bonding, mothers were asked to engage in the game of peekaboo with their young children. Even how this simple game was played revealed different degrees of parent-child attunement, so important to the development of children's capacity to be self-soothing.

Many parents played it engagingly, remaining hidden for an appropriate amount of time. Upon lowering their hands and "reappearing," they communicated reassurance through eye contact and tone of voice, showing their children that they were present and were not going away. They were attuned to the children's curiosity, capacity for some tension, and need to be comforted. They were likewise attuned to the playful intentions of the activity and to children's ability to cope with the escalating tension. They sensed when the infants needed reassurance in the form of quickly reappearing with calming smiles. Played in this manner, the children received lessons about their capacities to tolerate frustration in the future. They learned that they are able to cope with the anxiety of being alone, that others are dependable, and that some degree of tension can be effectively managed.

In contrast, with or without full awareness, some parents played the game in a teasing manner. Some evidenced this by hiding their faces too long, which consequently led their children to become overly excited. The children's excitement was reflected by rising tension in their faces that was accompanied by flurries of physical agitation. Some parents seemed more focused on the task and were not fully present to support the child's enjoyment. Some seemed to make it a challenge for the child to uncover their faces, even resisting their child's efforts to pull their hands away to reveal their faces. Their responses led the children to experience the game as tension provoking rather than as a joyful activity.

Certainly, the skills for self-soothing are taught over years and through a variety of interactions with those who are most important to the developing child. Through these interactions a child may or may not learn skills in self-soothing that are essential to manage the tension of positive excitement as well as negative emotions. However, in recent years, growing research has supported the idea that the quality of a mother's early interactions with her child actually influences the infant's maturing brain, particularly with regard to her capacity to be self-soothing. This component of resilience is highly relevant for understanding self-soothing and its impact on our capacity to remain engaged during the creative process. However, due to the limits of this present study, I will only briefly address the topic here.

NEUROSCIENCE RESEARCH AND SELF-SOOTHING

In recent years, advances in neuroscience research have provided increased understanding of how the interaction of nature and experience influence our behavior. Specifically, these findings emphasize that both genes and experience have a role in determining the structure of the brain through the modification of neuronal circuitry and the strength of firings at synapses, the connecting points between neurons along the information highways in our brains. Second, and especially relevant to our focus, it has been found that while early interactions play a significant role in the development of brain structure and neuronal circuitry, new learning can significantly alter earlier structures. This has important implications both for the management of emotions in general and, as will be addressed shortly, for how one can effectively manage the tension associated with creative engagement.[5]

Through the development of advances in imaging, research suggests that how a mother responds to her infant influences the infant's brain, including the arousal-regulating neurotransmitters and activity levels that relate to emotional arousal. The calmness of the mother is said to be transmitted to the child (and to his developing brain) through eye contact, voice, and touch. These interactions are said to evoke similar patterns of calming in the infant's brain, having a profound and lasting influence on the baby's neural development and, in particular, on the developing structures responsible for emotional regulation. These studies highlight "the fundamental principle that the baby's brain is not only affected by these transactions, but also that its growth literally requires brain-brain interaction and occurs in the context of a positive affective relationship between mother and infant."[6]

Essentially, these studies suggest that attuned interactions (like those described previously) promote the development of cerebral circuits that can predispose a child to be capable of self-soothing.[7] Such interactions are viewed as having an effect not only on the brain structure but also on the frequency, locations, intensity, and patterns of neural firings in various areas of the brain that impact emotional regulation. These include those areas associated with emotions and memory; among them are the prefrontal cortex, the amygdala, and the hippocampus. Increasingly, these studies emphasize that early interactions may be essential to activate certain genes related to affect-regulation.

Through favorable interactions the infant develops the capacity to manage both positive and negative affect. In a sense, when a child has developed the ability to transition from negative states of arousal to calmer states, it is because various collaborating parts of his brain have a predisposition for specific patterns of neuronal activation. In contrast, when a child is not able to effectively regulate his emotions, it suggests that the actual brain structure and patterns of neuronal firings are less prepared to do so. The implications of this are especially relevant to exploring both our capacities to manage the tensions aroused by creativity and the major roles that fear and other negative emotions may play in inhibiting our creative journeys.

THE FEAR FACTOR

How you respond to fear is embedded in your nervous system. Research in the last decade regarding fear emphasizes that much of your fear response derives from the activation of a part of the amygdala and other areas of the brain that play a major role in emotion.[8] This portion of your brain, considered the emotional brain, can make decisions and influence how you feel, think, and act even without having to coordinate with the more rational center of your brain. Some researchers suggest that this is nature's way of ensuring your survival. It is as if your body came with a heightened sensitivity to experience fear without having to check in with the administrative part of your brain that processes information and gives meaning.

As a consequence, however, you may be prone to experience fear even when there is no real threat to your physical welfare or your sense of self. It is the equivalent of reacting with a "false positive" assessment. This is a term used by researchers to refer to the indication of the presence or influence of some factor when in fact that factor is not present or has no influence. An example is a diagnosis that a dermal growth is cancerous when in fact it is benign. This type of response characterizes much of the fear you may have regarding life's challenges, including those aroused by your creative pursuits. You may react automatically with fear or anxiety to many aspects of the creative process when, in reality, they pose little or no actual threat to your safety. In a sense, your emotional brain holds you hostage when you desire to become creatively engaged.

Furthermore, research reveals that the more you have similar experiences, accompanied by thoughts, emotions, and physical states that arouse them, the more sensitive you become to react similarly in the future. In a sense, the circuitry and the patterns of responses become stabilized, leaving you predisposed to respond with fear.

It is the automatic response of this circuitry that may lead your body to demonstrate the physical responses associated with fear when you engage in creativity. With or without full awareness, when you seek to engage in the creative process, your attempts to violate certain internalized standards lead you to once again "revisit" uncomfortable states of being. At such moments, it is as if you are back in time, experiencing these unsettling states as a helpless, dependent, fearful child who lacks confidence, objective judgment, and a mature capacity for self-soothing in the face of such mind-body discomfort.

This occurs because at these distinct moments of creative challenge, you experience patterns of neuropsychophysiological reaction that have become embedded in your mind-body set over the course of your development. Whether the overriding inhibiting theme is fear of failure or success, being alone, being seen as inadequate, or being rejected, your reactions derive their energy from past learning. At such moments, your brain causes you to act "as if" you're in real danger.

As described earlier, the most exciting news of these findings is that new learning can alter and replace these habitual patterns of activation. The more you become aware of these "false positive" reactions, the more you can challenge them and replace these experiences with new ones. Essentially, by offering yourself new interpretations of potentially triggering events, you can raise the threshold for reactions. The more you practice new skills to calm yourself, the more you can literally change your brain structure and its patterns of activity. In effect, you can "rewire" such circuitry so as to alter your "knee-jerk" reactions. Every strategy described in this book offers you specific guidelines to achieve this goal.

INHIBITION AND "CHILD LOGIC"

One way of conceptualizing the negative impact you may experience when being creative is to understand such moments as being overly influenced by your "child logic." Child logic is self-centered and characterized by thought patterns that do not follow more mature cause and effect logic. It is more primitive logic, like that reflected in your nightly dreams. Such logic is dominated by emotions instead of reasoning. It is the underlying force of child logic that is triggered when you become blocked in your attempts to move forward in the creative process. As will be explored shortly, child logic leads to thinking that fosters fears, anxiety, guilt, and shame associated with creative pursuit. While I emphasize the term child logic as a form of thinking, much of such thought is also supported by children's immaturity in emotional intelligence.

Such logic is reflected when a child erroneously assumes that her behavior or thoughts have caused the illness of a sibling or his parent's divorce. It may also be involved for the adult who not only dreams about his first novel winning the Pulitzer Prize but who is compelled to believe that it is not worth writing if he is not assured that he will obtain that renowned symbol of recognition.

Child logic also has a positive side in that it allows us to think more creatively, not bound by the need for cause and effect relationships or reality in general. It is this type of logic that allows us to see different connections and novel patterns in ideas, images, and sounds, for example. But it is when child logic is coupled with powerful negative emotions and uncomfortable physical states that we become most inhibited in our capacity for creative pursuit.

CHILD LOGIC AND "SELF-TALK"

Whether you choose to direct your creative energies in the arts, the sciences, or in daily activities of living, the negative impact of child logic can undermine such desires. Suppose, for example, that you are thinking about enrolling in a woodworking class. As you contemplate doing so, a number of thoughts may surface. Some of these may be "loud enough" so that they are a part of your awareness. In contrast, others may be at a more "quiet" level, residing below the radar of your active attention. Some form a part of the unconscious while others remain closer to the "preconscious," that state of awareness on the threshold of complete awareness. Such thoughts and their related emotions very much influence your mind-body reactions at the moment you first contemplate pursuing a creative dream.

One may describe such thoughts as "self-talk." Everyone engages in this form of inner dialogue, whether at home, at work, in a car, in a store, when interacting with loved ones, or while observing others in a park. Each of us varies in the amount of self-talk we engage in. However, we may be so busy, focused on the challenges of the day, or preoccupied with what others are thinking, that we are not aware of our self-talk. In fact, we live in a time when we are increasingly bombarded by external stimulation that competes with our ability to really listen to our self-talk. Our society so strongly encourages us to be active and productive that we often lack awareness of such dialogue. In many ways, we are so strongly reinforced to instead be concerned with thoughts of others, with fitting in, or with achieving that we fail to take time to more fully explore our thoughts and what is truly meaningful to us. Most significantly, whether our past experiences have supported and encouraged self-reflection further determines our capacity to be sensitive to our ongoing internal dialogue.

So while some of the decisions you make every day are based on thoughtful consideration, others are based on self-talk that occurs without your full awareness. Recognizing such thoughts involves active attention, "tuning" into them, and "turning up" their volume. For example, as you were reading these last few paragraphs, you may have had thoughts regarding what you were reading. Take a moment to reflect on thoughts that may have been occurring at a deeper and quieter level. Did you find yourself experiencing critical thoughts about what you read? Were you inspired to form a connection with thoughts you have regarding your personal creative path? Did you tell yourself you would read several more pages before going to bed or walking the dog? Did you find yourself questioning how helpful this book will be? Did you experience thoughts that reflect impatience? It is only through such reflection that you can become more aware of how child logic influences your self-talk to either move you forward toward an embrace of creative passion or distract you from doing so.

Regarding your plan to enroll in a woodworking class, more mature logic would inform you that you have had this interest for some time. You may even recall a project you completed as a child or teenager. Mature cause and effect logic would help you recognize that you require time and persistence to develop your skills. Your past history regarding learning new skills may bolster your confidence regarding your capacity to acquire these skills and to effectively manage any frustration you encounter as you do so. Cause and effect logic suggests that you may make mistakes as you progress and such mistakes are a natural part of developing new skills. Having such thoughts reflects self-acceptance and self-compassion. Those thoughts may help you feel both hopeful and excited about the prospect of taking the class.

At the same time, you may be aroused by negative self-talk originating from your child logic that is accompanied by an arousal of negative emotions and uncomfortable physical states. Your inhibiting theme, fear of failure, for example, may impact your capacity to maintain your motivation. "I'm not really good with tools so those skills will be too difficult for me; besides, even if I build a bookcase, I know it will look really bad." This is merely one example of a potentially challenging and inhibiting dialogue you might experience, with and without your full awareness.

Accompanying your fear of failure, you may experience anxiety and self-criticism as you anticipate feeling disappointment, the criticism of others, and feelings of inadequacy. Similarly, you may feel physical tension that prevents you from taking any further action. Figure 3-1 depicts two possible scenarios of what can occur when we dare to be creative.

The arousal of creative longings sets into motion mind-body reactions that move you to either embrace or withdraw from becoming more fully present and engaged in your creative pursuit. To the degree that you can connect with your passion, in mind and body, and to the degree you can manage the discomfort of feeling threatened, you can move forward in a positive direction. To the degree that your positive states may compete with and remain dominant relative to the negative impact, you can remain actively engaged. Figure 3-1 emphasizes the fact that positive and negative reactions may be alternating or simultaneously occurring. Thus, you can be fully engaged at the same time that you experience a pull to withdraw from creative commitment. The forces of attraction and avoidance may vacillate in presence and dominance over time.

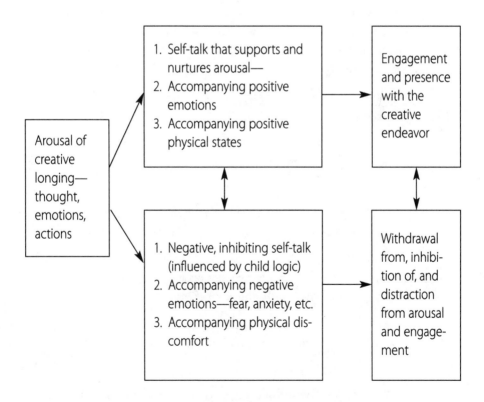

FIGURE 3-1: MOMENT OF CHALLENGE

CHILD LOGIC AND DISTORTED THINKING

In the last three decades, cognitive psychology has shown how our thoughts influence our emotions and behavior. This field of study has emphasized how the expectations and conclusions we form regarding the events in our lives very much contribute to how we react emotionally and the "meanings we make" out of events that occur. Specifically, by maintaining distorted thoughts we become more prone to experience negative emotions. I view child logic as being the basis of the type of distorted thinking described by the psychologist David Burns.[9] It is his premise that certain forms of thinking predispose us to feel depressed or anxious, which greatly interferes with our emotional well-being. Such thinking can similarly impact us at the moment of creative engagement. A description of several of these patterns follows.

Dichotomous (all or nothing) thinking: Thinking in extremes and labeling experiences in one of two extreme categories. Examples of such dichotomous either/or categories include flawless or defective and saint or sinner.

Example: "If I can't play the piano by now, I never will be able to do it."

Example: "If I don't devote eight hours daily to writing, I am not really a writer."

Overgeneralization: Drawing a general rule or conclusion based on one or more isolated incidents and applying that rule to related and unrelated situations.

Example: "Since my article was not accepted by that magazine, I am sure others will not be interested in it."

Example: "I had difficulty painting still life the first time I tried it, so I decided to focus on landscapes instead."

Discounting the positives: Focusing only on the negative aspect and discounting the positive aspects.

Example: "I really didn't like the way that one area of my montage came out. I don't think I'll try doing them again."

Example: "Sure I got great feedback about most of what I said, but nobody seemed to like one of the ideas I really felt strongly about. I don't know why I even bother sharing my thoughts with them!"

Clearly, these same patterns of distorted thinking play an active role in inhibiting creative engagement. As will be described in part II, each of the inhibiting themes is characterized by such categories of thought.

OPTIMISM AND PESSIMISM

The degree of optimism or pessimism you experience is another factor that can strongly influence the extent to which you are able to access, accept, and express your creative genius. Optimism is a strong expectation that, in general, things will turn out all right in your life. It is a positive attitude that you can successfully meet the challenges and frustrations that come your way. Martin Seligman, in his book *Learned Optimism*, emphasizes that optimists view a defeat as a temporary setback and its cause as being specific to the situation.[10] In addition, optimists believe that circumstances, bad luck, or other people cause the negative event to happen. Confronted by a bad situation, they perceive it as a challenge and try harder.

In contrast, pessimists tend to believe that bad events will be recurring, will undermine everything they do, and are their own fault.[11] Pessimism leads you to view yourself as having limited impact on your own life and fosters a sense of futility that discourages you from taking action.

Seligman believes that, like other aspects of personality, attitudes of optimism and pessimism are learned through our early interactions. Specifically, they are influenced by the explanations we have learned to use to account for our successes and failures.

If you consider yourself to be optimistic, some of this optimism may be based on your history of successfully mastering previous challenges. Some of your optimism may be a part of your learned capacity to be hopeful. To some extent, such optimism is based on faith, wherever you find it. It is the same optimism that helps a couple to feel determined that their new marriage will last forever in spite of the fact that, overall, marriages in our society fail 50 percent of the time. It is the same optimism that allows an entrepreneur to open a restaurant in spite of the fact that only one of six remains open for five or more years.

Optimism and pessimism may be viewed as thoughts overly influenced by our child logic, optimism a derivative from our open, expansive, curious, and hopeful child, while pessimism is a product of a more constrictive, cautious, and fearful part of our child.

A BUDDHIST PERSPECTIVE

Buddhist thinking has much to offer regarding the arousal of negative emotional states. Specifically, this perspective suggests that we are prone to have such reactions when we become overly attached to objects, whether ideas, possessions, or people.

Buddhist philosophy emphasizes the transience of all of life, the fact that we, and the world around us, are forever changing, and that nothing is permanent. According to this philosophy, all of our difficulties result from "cravings," our compulsive "attachments," or our "aversions" to people, things, or ideas. These cravings, attachments, and aversions are symptomatic of our effort to ignore or avoid the inevitable transience of life. Being neutral is a third reaction to our experiences.[12]

From this perspective, all of our inhibiting themes regarding creativity may be viewed as stemming from such attachments. Attachment implies a dependent and compulsive need to cling to objects as a way to experience one's sense of self as being stable, whole, and permanent; it is a result of compulsive perceptions we maintain without awareness. For example, our fear of failure stems from being obsessed with a need for approval and a drive to avoid the discomfort when others, or we ourselves, assess our efforts to have in fact "failed."

From this perspective, we may overly identify with our emotions. If I experience feelings of inadequacy, I may be quick to think of myself as being inadequate. If I have a fear of failure, I immediately react as if I am threatened. And, if I even have a positive experience of joy, I may come to expect that such emotion is part of my intrinsic makeup. I may compulsively strive to maintain it in an effort to avoid the recognition that even emotions are transient.

It is natural to have a concern about the reactions of others to our creative efforts. But to the degree that we are overly dependent on the approval of others we become prone to anxiety, fear, guilt, and shame. Similarly, becoming overly attached to our expectations for the quality of our creativity, the methods we use in its formulation, or the rate of progress we hope to achieve contributes to our being prone to negative mind-body states. In this light, perfectionism implies clinging to the ideal of perfection in order to experience one's self as worthy and stable. Such distraction helps us to ward off the full experience of our humanity; that we have strengths and weaknesses, that neither are permanent, and that neither solely defines who we are. Maintaining expectations about the orderliness of creativity or the way it "should" occur are further examples of such destructive attachment.

THE INHIBITING THEME AS A MORAL FOR LIFE

I have chosen to identify those guidelines that inform our child logic and that negatively impact our creativity as "inhibiting themes." In a sense, they can be described as reflecting predictable mind-body sets that interfere with your ability to embrace your creativity. Being able to recognize them and the hold they maintain over you is the first step in effectively managing their influence and unlocking your creative genius.

The inhibiting theme is like the concluding moral to a children's tale. Such morals are a summary statement that reflects the cumulative message of the story, sometimes actually stated, though more often left to the reader to infer. It offers a guideline for how you should live and what you should expect from yourself and others. Similarly, much of your child logic reflects a collection of morals, offering a summary guideline that you have internalized based on the cumulative experiences of your early years. In a sense, they reflect a summary predisposition of the brain circuitry that evolved throughout your development. They guide you in how you should live; how you should think, feel, and behave.

The chapters of the next section offer a detailed exploration of major inhibiting themes that can impact your capacity to embrace your creative genius. By reflecting on these you will become more sensitive and able to accurately identify those specific inhibiting themes that impact your creative journey. You may be influenced by more than one theme at any given moment and one or several may be dominant in inhibiting your ability to embrace your creative and evolving self. The major themes include the following:

Fear of failure
Fear of success
Variations of guilt
Eluding shame
Fantasies that get in the way of your dreams
Internal conflicts that challenge discipline
Discomfort with solitude
Fear of losing your identity

By accurately recognizing them, you will begin to reduce their impact by fostering the development of new patterns of thinking and new constellations of neuronal pathways that, cumulatively, endow you with a mind-body state more conducive to unlocking your creative genius.

*** FOR FURTHER EXPLORATION ***

1. How effective are you in managing negative emotions in general?
2. To what degree are you able to "sit with" and manage frustration?
3. What self-talk can you identify regarding
   a. being patient
   b. feeling inadequate when trying new activities
   c. expectations that things should come easy to you
4. To what degree do you experience the types of distorted thinking described in this chapter? Specifically, which forms of distortion do you most frequently experience?
5. To what degree are you optimistic or pessimistic? What if any situations tend to evoke a positive outlook versus a negative outlook?
6. To what degree are you overly attached to people or ideas with regard to your creative pursuits?

REFLECTIONS

Creative minds have always been known to survive any kind of bad training.—Anna Freud

No man has the right to dictate what other men should perceive, create, or produce but all should be encouraged to reveal themselves, their perceptions and emotions, and to build confidence in the creative spirit.—Ansel Adams

[The period from ages] seven to eleven is a huge chunk of life, full of dulling and forgetting. It is fabled that we slowly lose the gift of speech with animals, that birds no longer visit our windowsills to converse. As our eyes grow accustomed to sight they armour themselves against wonder.—Leonard Cohen

NOTES

1. Mihaly Csikszentmihalyi, *Creativity: Flow and the Psychology of Discovery and Invention* (New York: HarperCollins, 1996), p. 11.

2. Michael Lewis, *Shame: The Exposed Self* (New York: Free Press, 1995).

3. Daniel Goleman, *Emotional Intelligence* (New York: Bantam, 1997).

4. At the Theraplay Institute in Chicago. Described in Ann M. Jernberg and Phyllis B. Booth, *Theraplay: Helping Parents and Children Build Better Relationships through Attachment-Based Play* (San Francisco: Jossey-Bass, 1998).

5. Daniel Goleman, *Destructive Emotions: How Can We Overcome Them?: A Scientific Dialogue with the Dalai Lama* (New York: Bantam, 2003).

6. Allan N. Schore, *Affect Dysregulation* (New York: W. W. Norton, 2003), p. 42.

7. Ibid.

8. Norman E. Rosenthall, *The Emotional Revolution* (New York: Citadel, 2002).

9. David Burns, *Feeling Good: The New Mood Therapy* (New York: Avon, 1999).

10. Martin E. P. Seligman, *Learned Optimism* (New York: Pocket Books, 1998).

11. Ibid.

12. Kogen Mizuno, *Essentials of Buddhism* (Tokyo: Kosei Publishing, 1996).

II

INHIBITING THEMES

The chapters in this section identify and discuss the most common inhibiting themes that may interfere with your capacity to embrace your creative genius. These inhibiting themes reflect internalized standards that compete with and challenge your willingness to accept, trust, and act on your creative passion. By exploring these themes in detail, you will be helped to more accurately identify what specific factors interfere with your ability to access and sustain your creativity.

Each chapter offers specific statements that best reflect the key concerns associated with such themes as well as explorations of how the inhibiting themes may sabotage your efforts to live authentically when engaged in creative activities. The explorations help you to identify how these themes become internalized and how they impede your capacity for self-reflection, self-trust, courage, resilience, persistence, and tolerance for frustration, all of which are essential for the creative journey.

Being able to recognize and understand how these themes impact you is just a first step in overcoming their influence. In some cases, the simple step of identifying these factors helps you to exert more control over them. By being able to recognize and identify the specific emotions and physical states you experience at a deeper level, you take a major step toward more effectively managing their negative impact on your creative pursuit.

Chapter 4

FEAR OF FAILURE

Fear of failure is one of the most common obstacles to people's creative pursuits. Whether or not we are actually paralyzed by it, each of us has experienced it to some degree. Voiced out loud or declared as a low whisper by your internal critic, fear of failure robs you of your determination to be true to your creative spirit.

In an attempt to calm our feelings of apprehension, we often echo Franklin Delano Roosevelt's historic sentiment that "the only thing we have to fear is fear itself."[1] While this may offer some comfort, it provides little understanding about what it is we actually fear in any given situation. For when we attend only to fear, we fail to explore at a deeper level the real source of distress. To the degree that fear remains ill defined, it is experienced as vague but pervasive anxiety, a mind-body discomfort that has an increased potential to negatively impact our creative ventures. Only by identifying the many faces of our fear can we better understand and more effectively confront and manage it.

THE FACES OF FEAR OF FAILURE

Some of us have been besieged early in life by our fears of failure. Fear of failure gradually weakens your capacity to acknowledge and embrace your natural curiosity, diminishes your openness to exploration, and stifles your pleasure in creating. Such fear gradually begins to undermine and interfere with self-awareness and self-reflection, which forms the foundation of your creativity.

For some, just taking a small action toward being creative sets into motion a cluster of mind-body states that together reflect an intense fear of failure. This theme fuels a subjective experience that includes fear regarding the potential for failure, physical discomfort, and thoughts that are self-critical and constrictive in their impact on the capacity to create. Fear, in this case, is a warning signal to protect us from perceived threats to our safety and security. All too often, however, it is a false alarm that causes unnecessary retreat from encounters with who you are and who you can be.

Fear of failure masks your true fears and constricts your capacity to be connected with them. The following analogy offers some understanding of how this works and how fear of failure can intensify and become more pervasive when you fail to identify what it is you actually fear.

Over the years I have heard numerous clients discuss reactions to being involved in an automobile accident. The ways they managed their reactions reflect their individual ways of dealing with traumatic life events. These responses parallel how many of us deal with fear of failure.

Some clients reported making a vow to return to the scene of the accident as soon as they could physically do so. Their resolve reflected confidence and empowerment that they could conquer their fears by successfully driving through the area where the accident occurred. With determination and courage, these individuals formed corrective memories to help challenge and move them beyond the impact of their traumas. Others vowed never to drive past the intersections at which they had their accidents. Still others reported feeling paralyzed to drive anywhere near the vicinity of those locations. I met one woman from suburban Chicago who had not returned to the city for ten years following her misfortune. I have also had clients who promised never to drive a car made by the same manufacturer of the one they drove when they had their accidents.

All of these individuals handled their fear in the best way they could with the skills and resilience they had at the time. The variety of responses reflects their distinctly different capacities to manage such trauma. The range of their reactions also reflects a basic premise about fear. Their individual responses evidence the degree to which fear can paralyze and the degree to which fear becomes attached to other events, images, and experiences that may have nothing to do with the original source.

Those who immediately returned to the scene narrowed the impact of their fear. They were able to sit through and revisit the mind-body states they had experienced shortly before, during, and after their accidents. They more readily recognized and acknowledged confusion in their thoughts; feelings of helplessness, anger, guilt, and shame; and the range of other emotions that surfaced surrounding their accidents. Upon revisiting the sites where the accidents happened, some recalled having thoughts such as "I have no control over this car," "They're going through the light," or "If only I wasn't in such a rush." They similarly revisited images that occurred before, during, or immediately after impact. They identified physical sensations including tension, numbness, pain, and tunnel vision regarding their states of heightened attention to the various details of the accident scenes. Others subsequently became fearful of a location, a certain intersection, an area of the city, the entire city, or being in a car of a similar make or model. The scope of their fears had escalated and expanded so as to constrict the range of their travels as well as their capacities to experience the internal states associated with the accidents.

Your responses to the fear of failure are very similar to those evidenced by these drivers. Just as their fear served to protect them from the intense discomfort associated with their experiences of having been in car accidents, fear of failure helps you avoid the negative mind-body states that accompany "failure"; the hurt associated with anticipated rejection, feelings of inadequacy and shame, and self-critical thoughts and physical tension. While you may be in touch with your fear of failure, fully aware that it is a compelling force that competes with your attempts to be creative, it is your desire to avoid discrete moments of these other negative emotions that underlies your fear of failure. When you retreat from creative engagement, you are attempting to avoid these negative emotions as well as the thoughts and gnawing physical discomfort associated with them. Furthermore, your fear only intensifies the longer you avoid such experiences. The passage of time allows the fear to make deeper roots in your psyche as you continue to revisit it in your thoughts and emotions, and in your body.

Fear of failure is similarly a generalized fear of a variety of experiences you may anticipate having when you conclude that you have "failed" to reach a meaningful goal. Such fear then expands to include fear of experiencing emotions, thoughts, physical states, and images associated with that distinct moment you've identified as reflecting your failure.

Janice, a thirty-two-year-old mother of two, a seven-year-old boy and a five-year-old girl, had a strong interest in starting a home-based business. She had spent more than a year sporadically researching and thinking about her interests and had become enthusiastic about developing a line of gourmet candies. At times, Janice had worked on one recipe for several weeks only to abandon the goal.

> I really get excited when I even envision making them, deciding on and selecting the ingredients and actually forming them. It really varies. Most of the time I tremendously enjoy dreaming them up. And I really believe that a few of them taste great! At some point, though, I suddenly feel bored or disappointed. I'm not sure. I just stop working on them. I may not resume doing so for several months. I know, at times I feel like I am wasting my time. I then feel like I'm kidding myself. This happens especially when I think about actually going out to market them or even giving some samples to my friends.

Janice identified her fear of failure as interfering with more fully pursuing her venture. While she readily acknowledged a fear of being seen as a failure in the eyes of her friends, she was most preoccupied with fears about actually selling her product. Janice admitted ongoing thoughts and images of being told by the retailers that her candies did not measure up to expectations.

When encouraged to reflect on those specific encounters, she recognized that, coupled with rejection, she anticipated experiencing feelings of inadequacy. Further reflection led her to recognize that she had a predisposition to interpret being told her candies "did not measure up" as meaning that she herself did not measure up. While she had at times recognized this intellectually, she now felt it more deeply at an emotional level. Additionally, exploration of her distinct moment of challenge led her to recognize that she feared experiencing a sense of shame upon receiving a negative response.

Janice's fear of failure encompasses fears of rejection, inadequacy, and shame. But it is also a fear of experiencing the discomfort of critical thoughts as well as the physical tension that accompanies these emotions. While some disappointment would be natural, Janice's fear inhibits her creativity because of the intensity of the negative mind-body states she anticipates experiencing, even when merely visualizing her attempts to market her candies.

With Janice, as with anyone who is blocked by fear of failure, it is her child logic and associated emotions that, in spite of any real threat, make rejection appear to be potentially dangerous and threatening to her safety and security. Her child logic leads her to anticipate rejection with the same intensity of a dependent child who believes she needs acceptance and approval from caregivers in order to survive. Her sense of inadequacy parallels the same self-doubt of a child who lacks self-confidence. Similarly, it is her child logic that leads her to anticipate the rejection of her candies as an overall rejection of her entire being—the core experience of shame.

While she may be predominantly focused on her fear of failure, it is her inability and perceived inability to calm these reactions that causes her to vacillate in her creative venture between engagement and retreat.

LEARNING TO FEAR FAILURE

Fear of failure may be based on actual experiences of failure, observations of significant others failing, or learned attitudes based on messages about failure. Some of us who experience fear of failure may never have experienced serious failure. Instead, we may have witnessed how a parent, sibling, or peer responded to his or her failure to achieve a major goal. Observations of how others respond to failure can fuel such fear.

If while growing up you repeatedly heard a parent complain about a failure to achieve a career or personal goal, you may easily have internalized sufficient fear of failure to avoid even minimal pursuit of your own creative longings. You may have internalized the message that the world is not receptive to you when you live authentically, that there are punishments for being creative, or that there is little possibility to successfully pursue your creative desires. For a variety of reasons, some of us may instead reject such fear. You may, for example, foster enough determination, optimism, and perhaps even anger to ensure that you do not suffer the same fate. A variety of factors determine how you respond to such modeling.

Randy explained to me that witnessing his father's years of depression influenced his fear of failure. While Randy was growing up, he frequently heard his father express regret and self-criticism regarding his failure to become a professional basketball player. Although his father was financially successful as an owner of a fast-food franchise, he repeatedly complained about his job, focused on his past, and often described how good his life would have been if he had succeeded in professional sports. In addition, he consistently put himself down regarding his current line of work. For years he emphasized extreme hurt, disappointment, and anger about failing to achieve his goal. Such statements communicated feelings of inadequacy and shame as well as pervasive feelings of not being "good enough." Having witnessed his father's response to feelings of failure, Randy vowed never to give up trying to reach his goals. He treated his father's behavior as an example of how not to respond to failure.

THE POWERFUL NEED FOR ACCEPTANCE AND APPROVAL

While much of creativity is an individual endeavor, it is natural to question how others will perceive your work. When you write a poem, prepare a sketch, or compose music in solitude, you may only fleetingly consider the possible reactions of an imagined audience. Certainly, however, you become more concerned about the opinions of others when you are involved in a sustained creative endeavor that leads to the public display or performance of your work. This occurs regardless of whether you intend to share the fruits of your creative labor with a few friends or with the consumer public. When the negative impact of child logic overly influences your concern, fear and anxiety can build in intensity to thwart your creative efforts.

As children, we are dependent on our parents for all aspects of physical and emotional well-being. Because we cannot survive without them, we will do anything we can to win their acceptance. With sufficient love, security, encouragement, and support, we learn that we can make mistakes, disagree with our parents, and even live authentically while still feeling assured that our parents are dependable and can be counted on to be there for us. While we may at times experience rejection, feelings of inadequacy, and shame, we become sufficiently able to manage these reactions and move on.

In contrast, early experiences of rejection or of feeling devalued can make you more vulnerable to experiencing an absence of acceptance or approval as outright rejection. This is especially true when, over time, you have learned to experience the lack of approval of a particular behavior or creative product as all-encompassing rejection of who you are. It is rarely one incident that leads to such a conclusion. Rather, it is through repeated experiences of making this connection that you develop such vulnerability. It is this sensitivity to feeling rejected that leaves you prone to becoming an adult held hostage by fear of failure.

Facing new situations always arouses some of the feelings and thoughts associated with child logic, but it is the degree to which these feelings and thoughts inhibit you that determines your capacity to move on in your creative pursuit. This point was clearly evidenced in a self-publishing seminar I attended many years ago.

The instructor asked the twenty-five participants to raise their hands if they had written a book. Surprisingly, about two-thirds had completed a manuscript. She then asked how many had submitted the manuscript to a publisher. Only five in the audience raised their hands. Finally, the instructor inquired of those who had submitted their manuscripts, how many had continued to make submissions after getting several rejections. Only one person reported having the persistence to do so.

Those who had received rejections indicated that they had become paralyzed both with doubts about their abilities and with fears of again facing rejection. Those who had not yet submitted their manuscripts had even stronger self-doubts and fears. Each group was dealing with the same issue but at different phases in the creative process. Each reflected the same fear while evidencing varying capacities to manage it.

Trusting the ideas you generate, actually purchasing oils for painting, sharing with others your completed ceramic project, or designing a room can potentially arouse such intense reactions. Any forward movement and engagement in the creative process has the potential to awaken inhibiting child logic. At such moments, in mind and body, you may feel threatened, as if you actually risk abandonment or even annihilation. At such distinct moments, with or without awareness, you make an assessment from the mind-body set of a threatened child. Understandably, you may feel unprepared to manage such rejection. From this perspective, it makes sense to withdraw from experiencing such moments in order to maintain a sense of calm and inner security.

Your inhibiting fear of failure regarding trusting and accepting your creative spirit rests on reexperiencing those earlier moments in your life when you felt acutely threatened by criticism, rejection, or a sense of failure for not having measured up to your own expectations or those of others. The intensity of these negative mind-body states is influenced by your heightened need to be accepted, combined with a deficit of maturity with regard to effectively managing their impact.

PERFECTIONISM AND THE FEAR OF FAILURE

As emphasized through these examples, your fear of failure is a fear of experiencing those mind-body states associated with the hurt of rejection and related feelings of inadequacy and shame that they may trigger. However, the degree to which your fear of failure is incapacitating depends upon your capacity to be realistic, compassionate, and flexible in your assessment of your shortcomings. It depends on your ability to connect with that part of your child logic that is open, hopeful, and optimistic, as opposed to the constricting and inhibiting parts. These strengths offer you the resilience to intellectually and emotionally recognize that you can strive to be perfect, but that you can't expect to always attain perfection. When you maintain realistic expectations, you may still feel inadequate and disappointed, but the intensity of these reactions will not paralyze or significantly distract you from maintaining creative engagement. Falling short of your goals may arouse emotional pain, but you will be able to sit with the associated discomfort of disappointment, hurt, shame, or embarrassment and move forward.

In contrast, living with unrealistic expectations regarding your creative pursuit, including the need to be perfect, makes you overly sensitive to perceiving failure as overwhelming and pervasive. At such moments, your sense of self feels vastly diminished. This is the distinct moment in time that you have tried your best to avoid. But your fear of feeling inadequacy and shame only further fuels a need for perfectionism. Such perfectionism is based in the type of child logic that underlies self-talk, such as "I have to be perfect or I am a failure" or "If I fail, others will reject, abandon, or be angry with me, and I cannot live with that." Clearly, such logic leaves little room for self-acceptance.

As described in chapter 3, such thinking reflects "all or nothing" thought, a distortion of perspective in which you see things in black and white.[2] This thinking plays a part in skewing your self-evaluation, encouraging you to declare your entire self a failure when, in fact, your failure is limited to a shortfall in achieving a specific task.

A person who experiences fear of failure may also be prone to conflating his *feelings* with his *being*, habitually thinking, "I *am* my feeling." Reflective of this distortion in thinking, described by David Burns in *Feeling Good: The New Mood Therapy*, we view ourselves as failures when we have fallen short in maintaining the level of achievement we expect from ourselves.[3] Either conclusion mistakenly generalizes the sense that we have failed, resulting in the expansion of our fears of failure.

The desire to avoid experiencing shame is often a major contributing factor to the unrealistically high and rigid expectations that underlie perfectionism. As will be described more fully in chapter 7, shame arises from an overpowering negative evaluation that contributes to feelings of being inadequate and flawed. Rather than identifying your failure to achieve a goal as resulting from inattention to details, a lack of skill that can be corrected with more training or practice, or some other specific cause, you view your experience as an overall reflection of who you are and mistakenly evaluate yourself in globally devaluing terms.

Successfully embracing creative genius requires that you think in terms of "gray." It requires that you develop comfort with ambiguity. To do so, you need to master the skill of nurturing and soothing yourself following a failure to live up to your self-imposed standards. Most significantly, you need to be more compassionate in your expectations for yourself and in your self-appraisal. Such "self-compassion" will free you to be more flexible and realistic throughout every aspect of the creative process.

PROJECTED FEAR OF REJECTION

Fear of failure often derives its strength from the fact that you may already experience feelings of rejection based on your own assessment of your creativity. When you already feel inadequate about your abilities and accomplishments, you are likely to believe that others will react negatively to your work. It was this perspective that contributed to the reluctance of the authors attending the writing workshop I described earlier who, paralyzed by fear of rejection, were unable to submit their manuscripts to publishers. They had already evaluated their work as unacceptable. This reaction reflects the self-focused and self-centered nature of intensely emotional child logic. Intense emotions often lead you to assume that others feel as you do. If you are extremely angry, you may be quick to assume that others are similarly angry. If you are filled with joy, you may have difficulty imagining that others do not necessarily feel the same way. If you are convinced your work is not suitable, as measured against your own rigorous standards, you will be inclined to assume that others will likewise evaluate your work as unsuitable.

OPTIMISM, PESSIMISM, AND THE FEAR OF FAILURE

Fear of failure may be greatly influenced by the degree of optimism or pessimism you experience with regard to your capacity to be creative. In the extreme, severe pessimism is associated with depression that is characterized by a constriction in emotion, thought, and action. In addition to pervasive negative emotions and thoughts that are often unrealistically self-critical and devaluing, depression is also marked by fatigue and lethargy.[4]

When challenged by the possibility of failure, it is as if you fear a narrowly defined but nevertheless intense mind-body experience that parallels a state of depression. Emotionally, you experience a sense of inadequacy accompanied by a sense of hopelessness and helplessness regarding your creative abilities and persistence. You become self-critical, devaluing, and, in general terms, constrictive in the quality and depth of your thinking. Such constriction impairs your capacity to attend to details, to reflect, and to maintain flexibility in your thinking. It diminishes your freedom to imagine, organize, and even retrieve information. At such moments, you cease to attend to the details of both the world around and within you. All of your attention instead focuses on protecting yourself from imagined threats.

Optimism means looking beyond statistical probability. It is for this reason that some view optimism as unrealistic thinking. To a large extent, optimism rests on faith, however we come upon it. Optimism is likewise rooted in a commitment to succeed. It is an ongoing process of commitment, with and without full awareness, during which, though confronted by fear of failure, you choose to focus on the best possible outcome over and over again. The fact that it is a choice is reflected in figure 5-1.

Observe the cube in such a way that you view "Pessimism" on the top front face of the cube with "Optimism" displayed at the top of the inside rear face of the cube. Now shift your focus so that "Optimism" appears displayed across the top of the front face of the cube and "Pessimism" appears across the top of the inside rear face of the cube. Just as you are able to choose what to attend to when observing this cube, you have the capacity to repeatedly choose to focus on optimism rather than pessimism as you pursue your creative goals.

To a great extent, as the third section of this book emphasizes, any strategy that leads to this type of "realistic" optimism is a strategy that fosters your openness to creativity. This is what it means to manage the fear of failure even while you experience it.

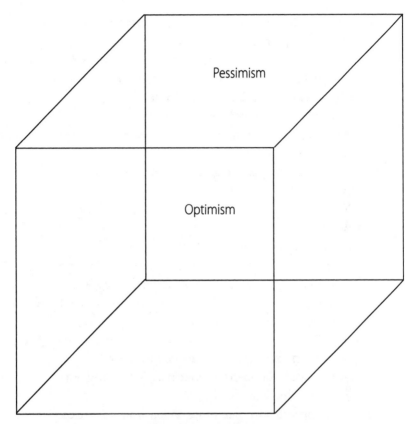

FIGURE 5-1: OPTIMISM/PESSIMISM CUBE

Though it is not necessary to eliminate your fear of failure, a major task in fostering creative engagement is to effectively manage it. Recognizing the actual fears that underly the fear of failure is a fundamental challenge you need to address if you are to more successfully tap into your creative genius.

*** FOR FURTHER EXPLORATION ***

1. Can you recall direct messages you were told about fear of failure? If so, who offered them and what did they say?
2. Do you recall messages regarding fear of failure that may have been communicated indirectly, either in words or through behavior? If so, who provided these messages and what attitudes did they convey?

3. Can you articulate in several statements the attitude you had regarding fear of failure as you were growing up?

4. To what degree do you believe perfectionism interferes with your creative pursuits? If it is a contributing factor, are you aware of anticipating feelings of rejection, inadequacy, or shame?

5. If and when you experience fear of failure, are you focused on your assessment, that of others, or both when imagining yourself failing in your creative endeavor?

6. To what degree does pessimism contribute to interfering in your creative pursuit?

7. What strategies do you currently employ to help effectively manage fear of failure?

8. Explore your experience of failure.
   a. Recall a time when you experienced a sense of failure.
   b. Describe the situation, including the responses of others who were witnesses. If other people were not present, did you anticipate how they would react?
   c. What were the physical states, emotions, and thoughts that accompanied your experience of failure?
   d. How did you manage your reactions? How effective were your management strategies?
   e. Compared to other times when you have experienced failure, how typical was your reaction in this instance?

REFLECTIONS

Fiction never exceeds the reach of the writer's courage.—Dorothy Allison

Creativity isn't about brilliance. It's about the exuberance, focus, and fearlessness.—David Bohm

Perfectionism is not a quest for the best. It is a pursuit of the worst in ourselves, the part that tells us that nothing we do will ever be good enough—that we should not try again.—Julia Cameron

Creativity—like human life itself—begins in darkness.—Julia Cameron

Mistakes are the portals of discovery.—James Joyce

NOTES

1. Franklin D. Roosevelt, Inaugural Address, March 4, 1933, as published in Samuel Rosenman, ed., *The Public Papers of Franklin D. Roosevelt,* vol. 2, *The Year of Crisis, 1933* (New York: Random House, 1938).

2. David Burns, *Feeling Good: The New Mood Therapy* (New York: William Morrow, 1980).

3. Ibid.

4. Martin E. P. Seligman, *Learned Optimism: How to Change Your Mind and Your Life* (New York: Knopf, 1991).

Chapter 5

FEAR OF SUCCESS

W hile many of us have experienced how fear of failure can inhibit our creative pursuits, the debilitating impact of fear of success is often more difficult to recognize and comprehend. Such fear may undermine the passion to engage in even the smallest of creative challenges. However, it is more likely to surface when we choose creative endeavors that have the potential to substantially alter our lives; for example, those that may lead to financial gain, improved social status, or psychological growth. Feeling threatened by these changes forms the core of this inhibiting theme.

The difficult challenges to success are reflected by the extensive media coverage of those who have achieved great creative success only to fall victim to the downside of their accomplishments. The ambivalence we sometimes feel toward success is similarly revealed by our quickness to emphasize flaws in those who have been most successful. For some of us, it is as if we are reassured in our shared opinion that "they're not that great" or that "success does not bring happiness after all." Unfortunately, these reactions may only echo our own fears, helping us to justify a hasty retreat from pursuing our own creative dreams.

Inhibiting themes associated with fear of success include the following.

1. My success may hurt others and even cause them to reject or abandon me.
2. Success will overwhelm me.
3. My success will expose me as an imposter.
4. Achieving creative success is selfish.

These themes can threaten your creative engagement during any phase of the creative process, but often become most challenging during periods of sustained creativity. Thus, a painter beginning his first work or starting to promote his art, a writer completing several chapters or seeking to publish a book, or an employee planning to start his own business or actually opening his shop to the public for the first time are all situations that may exacerbate fear of success.

MY SUCCESS MAY HURT OTHERS OR CAUSE THEM TO REJECT OR ABANDON ME

While fear of failure derives from anticipated rejection as a result of exposing our inadequacies, fear of success is rooted, in part, in the fear that others will feel hurt or reject and even abandon us because of our strengths. In reality, sustained creativity can put great demands on our relationships.

Your partner may feel threatened when you retreat to your studio to draw, paint, sculpt, or pursue your passion in any one of countless ways. Friends and family may feel unnerved as your striving forces them to face their own fears regarding creative passion. Your success may arouse in them a level of tension that stems from wanting to support you while also feeling threatened by your success. This may be especially pronounced when competitive strivings influence such reactions. This was the case with Ellen, a writer who had successfully published her first book.

After some hesitation, Ellen asked her best friend, Kathleen, if she would review one of the two chapters of a novel that she had completed after working on them for several months. Kathleen indicated she would do so but, in her tone of voice, reflected some hesitation. Two weeks passed and, although they had spoken several times, Kathleen made no mention of reading the chapters. Ellen finally inquired about them. Kathleen indicated that she had been very busy but would immediately get to them. Several days later, Kathleen returned them, offering feedback that was both brief and general.

Ellen was puzzled by her friend's response and directly inquired about Kathleen's reaction to her request. Through discussion, Kathleen admitted that she had felt somewhat neglected in the past months and that she was also envious of Ellen's ability to persevere with her writing. In that instant, Ellen's knee-jerk reaction was to experience guilt. This guilt was the price of her success, and it was a defining moment for Ellen. She felt bad, concluding that her creative success had led Kathleen to feel hurt and that she was somehow responsible for Kathleen's discomfort. As a result, Ellen experienced self-doubt and became reluctant to share her work. Ellen revisited her fears about being successful and calling attention to her accomplishments. Only upon further reflection was she able to acknowledge her disappointment, hurt, and anger regarding Kathleen's inability to consider her work in a more supportive and nurturing way.

This reaction reflects the moment of challenge that underlies the fear of success. It is a moment that encompasses fears of hurting someone or, even worse, being rejected or abandoned. Such emotions are accompanied by negative thoughts and uncomfortable physical reactions that together impede creative engagement. Deriving its strength from child logic, this inhibiting theme is characterized by the fear of experiencing the mind-body states associated with rejection, abandonment, and isolation, which may lead some to cease a creative venture just at the point when they are approaching a milestone in their creative success.

While creative success may lead some observers to withdraw or to become distant, the reality is that success also inspires others to pursue their dreams. When we dare to create, we serve as models for others. We inspire in them the courage to take risks and to listen to the inner voice that pushes them toward personal expression, in spite of their fears. As we confront moments of challenge inherent in the creative process, such relationships are mutually supportive and nurturing.

Anticipated isolation may also be a powerful motivator in the fear of success. With rejection comes a sense of abandonment and feeling alone. This is the reaction experienced by Kevin, a doctoral student in psychology, who visited his family during a holiday break. Shortly after his arrival home, his parents requested that he provide his older brother advice regarding a career choice. Kevin's parents had always cast him in the role of caretaker, but his suggestions were never well received by his older brother. In fact, his brother often resented Kevin's advice, finding it intrusive. Although he felt somewhat guilty, Kevin acted assertively, indicating that he came to visit his parents and would not offer his brother advice. His father responded in a sarcastic and irritated tone, "Oh, you're in a doctoral psychology program now! You don't want to help your family! You're too good to help us."

Kevin had struggled with his creative achievements and his fear of success in pursuing them. At that distinct moment, he revisited both his fear and the sense of rejection that he had anticipated. Kevin knew that although his father was in some ways proud of him for his success, he also seemed to feel threatened by it. In fact, his father had held himself back from pursuing his personal dreams as a musician. This was a theme that he experienced throughout his life, an ongoing regret for not having taken greater risks to pursue his passion.

SUCCESS WILL OVERWHELM ME

Some of your creative ventures are short-lived. You bravely respond with a quip in situations in which you would typically remain silent. You write a poem and add it to your cherished collection. You spend a weekend redesigning the décor of a bedroom or study or you enroll in a drawing class. Each of these activities can be termed a creative success. They are expressions of what moves you and helps you to enrich your life. Such creative outbursts may or may not be shared with others. And while they momentarily enhance your experience, taken individually, they may not significantly change your life.

In contrast, some of your creative pursuits are life altering. These may include starting a business or pursuing art, dance, photography, or any creative endeavor to the degree that it requires a major commitment of time, effort, and financial resources. Such creative paths require sustained creative passion and consequently are more apt to arouse fear of success. These pursuits more clearly define who you are and make a far deeper impact on your life.

Success in creativity brings with it new challenges as well as opportunities. Those who write and intend to publish their work need to negotiate with agents and publishers to promote their writing. Those who paint need to become involved in exhibiting their works if they are to transform their interest into a life career. Anyone who has ceased to be an employee in order to create their own business knows of the many challenges that need to be addressed when becoming an entrepreneur. These ventures simultaneously offer increased freedom and demand increased responsibility. This increased freedom is an essential ingredient for creativity. Managing the challenges of creativity involves recognizing and accepting the trade-off between responsibility and freedom.

Jesse, a highly motivated computer graphics illustrator, offers an example of how fear of being overwhelmed underlies fear of success. He had been employed for four years prior to undertaking freelance work. He thoroughly enjoyed the challenges these freelance projects brought, since they gave him the opportunity to expand his skills. For over two years Jesse thought about leaving the company to start his own business. He even went so far as to design a Web site, though he never activated it. Unfortunately, Jesse continually distracted himself in order to avoid making the final decision to go out on his own.

I recommended that he try several exercises in an effort to help him better understand those underlying issues that inhibited his ability to move on. I suggested that he begin by sitting at his computer and, while viewing his Web site, imagining that it was up and running. I then recommended that he spend several minutes thinking about actually being self-employed. I encouraged him to identify the details of his internal experience that were aroused while imagining this scenario, including his physical reactions, his emotions, and the nature of his internal dialogue.

His initial reactions were highly positive, including a sense of joy, excitement, and empowerment. He felt slight physical tension that he identified as being a part of that excitement and a sense of vitality flowing through his body. His self-dialogue included statements such as "Wow! I'm finally doing it," "This is really exciting," and "This should definitely get people's attention!"

I then encouraged him to visualize returning home the next day to find four inquiries e-mailed to his Web site. Again, he was asked to picture himself at the computer, imagining his reactions to them. Subsequently, I suggested he envision two more scenarios. On the following day he would find eight inquiries, and on the fourth day he would receive twelve.

Jesse took time to really engage in these exercises in an effort to fully experience and recognize his reactions. He indicated that his excitement and optimism were further fueled upon receiving four inquiries. He experienced increased confidence and a more solid sense of empowerment that comes with the experience of feeling competent in one's chosen area of creative pursuit. He encountered tremendous satisfaction and a sense that he could truly flourish as an artist while he earned a living from his work. At the same time, he also recognized that, while some of his physical tension was positive, there was a slight anxiety beginning to surface.

The eight inquiries further boosted his enthusiasm and he felt even more validated. The increased number of responses prompted a more intense physical reaction that he now described somewhere between excitement and trepidation, a combination of reactions very similar to that of the joy and fear of being on an amusement park ride.

Imagining the final scenario tilted the overall tone of his reaction and, in doing so, put him much more directly in touch with his fears regarding success. He described anticipating feeling overwhelmed regarding the number of requests for services. At that distinct moment, while imagining receiving twelve inquiries, he became more aware of his apprehension that he would be consumed by his work. At that distinct moment, the excitement of being creative, starting his own business, and gaining increased personal freedom were overshadowed by a fear that he would have no time for himself, that the joy of his work would be undermined by the pressure of deadlines, and that the business demands of such work would rob him of both his freedom to be creative and the balance he desired between work and leisure time. In part, this knee-jerk reaction was an outgrowth of a fear that commitment to work meant giving up much of what he valued in life, his leisure time with friends and family and the time and energy to indulge other creative pursuits.

Further reflection also helped Jesse to recognize that "all or nothing" thinking had influenced this assessment. At that distinct moment, he became more aware that his fear of success was based on his fear that he would be unable to exert limits on the demands of his work. Although he desired all of the advantages of being self-employed, he now sensed that it might require more deprivation than he was willing to tolerate. Further reflection helped Jesse identify the source of his fear. He realized that, for him, success implied being overwhelmed. He had seen how his father's life had been dominated by the demands of his custom picture framing shop for over twenty-five years. Yet, he soon realized that he did not necessarily have to follow that same path, that he really could have greater freedom to shape his life.

For others, achieving success is fearful when it is associated with the fear of having to denounce one's youth and youthful attitudes. In these situations, creative success is associated with having to be "grown-up," a very frightening challenge when one feels ill prepared for or resentful of doing so.

Success may carry with it fear of being overwhelmed when it is associated not only with a loss of time but also with a loss of youth. Depending on your experiences, you may have come to identify being successful as something that only adults do. Being successful in your creativity may be associated, in a negative way, with having to be too serious, being overly disciplined, lacking spontaneity, and maintaining other expectations that seem intensely inhibiting in your life. It may also be linked with the concern that making a commitment to be creative in one area may close the door on other choices. This fear rests on the view that discipline and commitment associated with creative success preclude the continued embrace of the spontaneity and exuberance associated with youth. For those in the grip of this fear, reconciling these opposing forces is the greatest challenge to their capacity to achieve their creative potentials. (This concern will be described in greater detail in chapter 9.)

THE IMPOSTER SYNDROME

Those who evidence an imposter syndrome have an underlying belief that they have fooled others into overestimating their abilities.[1] They view their success as resulting from luck, being evaluated by those who do not know better, being in the right place at the right time, or being of the "right" race, gender, or ethnicity; basically, any imaginable cause other than their genuine skills. The core concern of this syndrome is the fear that "I will make one mistake that will reveal me for the imposter that I really am." It is in this aspect that the fear of success is similar to the fear of failure. The predominating thought focuses on the fear that any decision or action will expose you and that others will finally recognize what you have believed all along—that your success has been based on deception. You fear that, as a result of this "unmasking," you will come face to face with rejection and feelings of inadequacy and shame, strikingly similar to the path of reactions associated with a sense of failure. The tension derived from this constellation of attitudes about yourself increases as you become more successful. At times it can become self-fulfilling, as when, without full awareness, you unwittingly sabotage your own progress.

Rachel was a successful lawyer whose performance in her company was outstanding. After many years of dedication and hard work she finally became a partner. Her specialty in corporate law had gained her extensive recognition and invitations to present at conferences.

While she had previously excelled in making presentations, Rachel developed severe anxiety about doing them once she became a partner in the firm. She experienced intense fear at the podium related to her fear of exposure. She soon realized that she could accept herself as a lawyer struggling to become a partner, but the change in her position led her to revisit the sense of having "fooled" her colleagues about her abilities. She had succeeded at a lower level, but the increased visibility, responsibility, and expectations likewise increased the potential that she might be exposed as a fraud. As a result, she experienced elevated fear of success.

This example also reveals the fact that this inhibiting theme is most often activated when you take on a new challenge or role. It is during this phase of creative challenge that you are most likely to experience increased self-doubt, feelings of inadequacy, and inhibiting tension. With further experience in the role, you most often develop increased confidence as you master the tasks that accompany it. The fear temporarily subsides with the passage of time until you are once again confronted with a new challenge.

ACHIEVING CREATIVE SUCCESS IS SELFISH

Another more subtle but often major barrier to seeking success, and one that underlies moments of challenge to sustained creativity, is the sense of guilt you may endure as a result of feeling or being successful. The young man who comes from a low socioeconomic background to achieve financial success may suffer the same internal conflicts as someone dealing with the challenge of acculturation. In both cases, individuals are challenged in dealing with being part of one minority while making a transition into (and seeking affiliation with those in) another group. The struggle involves an ongoing challenge to maintain one's identity while continually evolving new associations, values, interests, and pursuits.

Sid Caeser, the famed comedian, described struggling with this challenge in his biography.[2] He reported that one evening, as he exited the theater at which he had performed, he noticed an elderly woman across the street crouching under the awning of a storefront, protecting herself from a heavy downpour. He soon recognized the figure as his mother, quickly crossed the street, and inquired why she was there. His mother timidly described her desire to see the theater where her famous son performed. She had kept her distance out of her concern that she would appear too intrusive.

Caeser describes offering to drive her home, though she adamantly refused and indicated that she preferred to take the bus. It was a poignant moment for Caeser, and one that reflected some of his internal struggles with success.

Caeser's biography emphasizes that he came from very impoverished beginnings and had extreme difficulty in reconciling his success with the fact that his parents had not been as fortunate. He attributed his alcohol abuse to the pressure of his demanding schedule as well as to his internal conflict and underlying guilt about his success.

Individuals who are successful often have an intense desire to help parents, siblings, or friends share their success. This determination may stem from a genuine wish to share their happiness. At the same time, it can often derive from guilt regarding their accomplishments. Such guilt may arise from a genuine desire to pay back those who have supported one's success. However, it often rests on other factors, which I will more fully address in chapter 7. Extreme difficulty with success may even involve undoing the fruits of that success through overspending, the use of drugs or alcohol, or engaging in other risk-taking or potentially self-destructive behaviors. While consciously motivated to be successful, child logic may foster these behaviors as a distraction from the mind-body tension associated with it.

Pursuing success in creative endeavors can also arouse discomfort one has grown up associating success with being selfish. A child may directly or indirectly receive messages that success is selfish and should be punished. This may result from hearing a mother disparage her husband's success, a father devalue a sibling's accomplishments, or being the target of a parent's withdrawal or denigration for one's own achievement.

Alice Miller, noted psychoanalyst and author, writes extensively about those parents who see their children as an extension of themselves.[3] Such a parent exerts tremendous pressure on his child to succeed in certain endeavors because the child's success positively reflects on his own sense of achievement and recognition. At some point, however, he may be quick to feel threatened by such success. It is as if his child's attainments point the spotlight on his own sense of not measuring up. At such moments, he may feel slighted and react by threatening emotional withdrawal or even more serious abuse. Through words and actions, such parents communicate to their children that they are committing an act of betrayal by their creative pursuits. Children of such parents may become adults who face an extremely difficult challenge when attempting to sustain a creative pursuit for any period of time. As they move forward to express their individuality, they may intensely experience the guilty feeling that they are betraying their parents.

The overpowering fear of success is evidenced by the painter who never finishes his work, the writer who hides a completed manuscript in his closet, the musician who never performs a final take, and the psychologist who postpones sitting for the licensing exam. Certainly, there may be a combination of factors leading to one's inhibitions regarding creative pursuits, but fear of success is just one potential force that can derail your creative investment.

*** FOR FURTHER EXPLORATION ***

1. What direct messages were you given by caretakers regarding success? Were they positive and encouraging or did they undermine your ability to succeed?
2. What indirect messages do you believe you were given regarding success? How were these expressed?
3. What messages were provided by how your parents or siblings regarded creative success?
4. How did different members of your family respond when one member sought to draw attention to themselves for their creativity?
5. What are your attitudes toward the creative success of others? How might these attitudes impact what you believe others think of your success?

REFLECTIONS

Every creative person has a second date of birth, and one which is more important than the first; that on which he discovers what his true vocation is.—Brassai

Sadness usually results from one of the following causes—either when a man does not succeed, or is ashamed of his success.—Seneca

NOTES

1. Joan C. Harvey and Cynthia Katz, *If I'm So Successful, Why Do I Feel Like a Fake?* (New York: Random House, 1984).

2. Sid Caeser and Bill Davidson, *Where Have I Been: An Autobiography* (New York: Random House, 1982).

3. Alice Miller, *The Drama of the Gifted Child: The Search for the True Self* (New York: Basic Books, 1996).

Chapter 6

VARIATIONS OF GUILT

Guilt is an extremely powerful emotion that guides our behavior and influences how we view others and ourselves. It is considered to be a "self-conscious" and "moral" emotion, which develops from our most meaningful and earliest relationships with others.[1] Guilt is described as being self-conscious because it is in part the result of our reflecting upon and making judgments about ourselves. It is considered moral in that it plays a decisive role in promoting moral behavior. The painful experience of guilt arises from a self-evaluation of actions and an assessment that we have violated certain standards set for our behavior. Guilt carries with it an overriding experience of tension and remorse, and leads us to question what we could have done or should have done instead of what we did.

While guilt can be useful to prompt us to correct our behaviors, it can also be excessive and subsequently toxic as it interferes with living authentically and embracing creative passion. It becomes toxic when, in spite of attempts to make amends or to guard against future violations, we become obsessed with guilt. There are many variations of guilt, which can foster a mind-body set that competes with and inhibits our access to and trust of our creative genius. "Survivor's guilt" is one of the most powerfully debilitating forms of such guilt.

SURVIVOR'S GUILT

"Survivor's guilt" refers to the guilt experienced when one endures a shared tragedy and has escaped pain or even death while others have not.[2] Such guilt may arise from surviving natural or human-made catastrophes, including hurricanes, earthquakes, vehicle accidents, terrorist attacks, crimes, wars, suicides, or the death of loved ones. Survivor's guilt is guilt about living, which can include self-recrimination for surviving, striving, and especially for thriving. Such guilt sabotages your creative efforts, reflecting the core, inhibiting theme, "I do not deserve to live or to pursue my own needs."

Survivor's guilt forces you to play over and over again in your mind what you should or could have done to help a person close to you who became the victim of a tragedy. Like those who survived the Holocaust, those who escape an airplane crash, warfare, an automobile accident, or a natural disaster are often left scarred by recriminating guilt just for being alive. Even without full awareness, when such guilt is pervasive, channeling your energies toward individual growth and enrichment is experienced as betrayal and the epitome of self-centered arrogance. It is reflected in self-talk such as "How can I think about myself and enrich my life? I don't deserve to be alive, much less happy." Those who experience severe survivor's guilt may even believe they deserve to be punished. As a result, they may live with the constant fear that they will be punished if they let go of their guilt. Some may unconsciously or consciously experience intense pressure to do something to justify their survival. For example, they may devote their time to raising funds for a certain cause or even choose a profession that involves helping people.

Others with severe guilt may actually punish themselves, with or without full awareness that they are doing so. Some individuals sabotage their creativity by not taking sufficient time to do as well as they could on a project. Some may undermine their own work when trying to promote it, fail to do sufficient research, or even miss key deadlines when submitting their projects for consideration by reviewers. Others may unwittingly find themselves with ongoing financial difficulties so they forever lack the money to pursue their creative ambitions. Addictive and other self-destructive behaviors may also be influenced, in part, by the overriding tension of severe guilt. Fueled by toxic guilt, our unconscious minds can be quite relentless in undermining our attempts to live authentically and creatively.

Creativity is an assertive embrace of life. It involves placing high value on your life and nurturing and forging your unique identity. Any act of creativity forces you to confront survivor's guilt when it has become a prominent part of your repertoire of mind-body states.

When not effectively managed, such guilt is awakened even by initial attempts to identify, accept, or pursue your creative genius. Once awakened, such guilt results in distinct moments of mind-body tension that lead to withdrawal from engagement as well as the suppression or repression of your uniqueness and associated creative drives.

Sarah described frequent self-recrimination regarding her role as the driver in a car accident that claimed the life of her boyfriend. For almost two years she isolated, worked hard, and rarely socialized with others. Initially impacted by understandable grieving, she was depressed as well as paralyzed by guilt regarding her involvement in the tragedy. She repeatedly played over in her mind what she could have or should have done to avoid the accident. Gradually, her depression lifted. She volunteered to help injured patients in a rehabilitation facility. This was one way in which she dealt with her reactions.

For several years Sarah became excessively sensitive and was quick to feel rejected. Impacted by intense guilt, she could only assume that those around her viewed her with disdain for her role in the accident. While she was gradually able to let go of this attitude, she remained unable to resume her participation in a theater group that she and her boyfriend had helped promote. Her guilt regarding his death powerfully inhibited her ability to pursue her passion for theater without him. Only as she recognized that such participation led her to once again revisit her guilt was she able to begin to rekindle that passion.

Justin described a lifelong interest in photography. In fact, he came from a family where creativity was very much valued by his parents as well as by his siblings. His father was an art professor, extremely skilled in painting and sculpture. His mother, also an educator, was a freelance writer. Justin's brother Evan was two years younger, played in a band, and was full of passion for music. Tragically, Evan died in a boating accident, which Justin survived. He reported that for the next several years, while he moved on socially and in striving to achieve his academic goals, he only sporadically took pictures. Much of the last few months before Evan passed away, Justin had attended his brother's performances and had put together a photo album of his events. Since the accident, each time he had attempted to take pictures, his initial reaction was to once again revisit his guilt and grief. His guilt was accompanied by thoughts that he was being "frivolous" in pursuing his interest and that he should spend his time focused on something more meaningful.

Some individuals with survivor's guilt have taken up a cause as a way of managing their guilt. In this way, they deal with their guilt by being creative. For example, a survivor who killed someone due to drunk driving may make presentations to educate others and encourage them to refrain from drinking and driving. Many who survived the Holocaust wrote about their experiences in order to alert the world to the horrors of the past so that they would never happen again. Still others have channeled their feelings through artistic expression.

Clearly, survivor's guilt is a powerful deterrent to unlocking creative genius. While it is certainly understandable that it can interfere with creativity shortly after a tragedy, such guilt can endure and serve to undermine creative passion for many years.

We do not need to be survivors of tragedy to experience guilt that inhibits our creative engagement. Guilt and our attempts to avoid experiencing it can be more subtle in their development.

FOREVER THE CARETAKER

Some of us have learned that our entire lives should be devoted to the needs of others. Against this standard, we begin to feel guilt the moment we begin to attend to our own needs. Caring for others provides us connection and can deeply enrich our lives. However, there is a significant difference between an articulated clear choice to be a caretaker for others and the paralyzing and inhibiting compulsion to consistently value the needs of others above our own. In the extreme, such guilt can lead to anxiety and depression as we restrain from pursuing our passions or remain disconnected from our feelings and desires.

This type of guilt is especially compelling for those who have been rewarded for becoming a caretaker to parents and/or siblings. Similarly, as will be explored more fully in chapter 7, some of us may distract ourselves from the anxiety of living authentically by embracing the role of caretaker. With or without full awareness, a parent may come to emotionally depend on and seek support, guidance, and structure from his or her child. This may occur when a parent is physically ill, dealing with the loss of his or her own parents or siblings, experiencing marital conflict, or distracted with emotional difficulties such as depression or anxiety. Even the stress of work or parenting may lead parents to behave in ways that contribute to their children feeling responsible for their welfare.

Subsequently, a child may depend to an unhealthy degree on a type of self-esteem that is dependent on taking care of others. While women in general tend to prioritize their role as being responsible for maintaining relationships, those who are raised by parents in this style increasingly focus their attention on the needs and feelings of others to the neglect of their own. As a result, when they reach adolescence or early adulthood, they may experience tremendous discomfort in focusing on their own needs, interests, and opinions. Such guilt inhibits fully identifying and engaging in their creative passions. Experiencing the slightest joy associated with being creative may precipitate intense feelings of guilt when one has internalized the directives that "I am completely responsible for the happiness of others," "I should always put others' needs before my own," and "I do not deserve to pursue my life interests." Those who put others' needs before their own and are blocked in their creative urges may feel threatened and even engage in behaviors that, without their full awareness, undermine their capacities to sustain a creative enterprise for any extended period of time.

Barbara, aged thirty-five, described tremendous guilt in relation to her success in painting. She had worked with watercolors for several years and had consistently received positive feedback about her work from friends and family. In spite of such praise, she was unable to take the next step and share her work on a larger scale. She thought about submitting her work for exhibition in a neighborhood art fair, but could not bring herself to do so. Through exercises in self-reflection, like those described in part III of this book, Barbara soon recognized how guilt had played a part in her inhibition.

Her mother had always been supportive of her painting, and Barbara really believed she was sincere in her encouragement. However, upon reflection, Barbara recognized that she experienced tremendous guilt and shame in relation to her mother's thwarted desires for success as a painter. While growing up, Barbara recalled the many times her mother had talked about pursuing her own interest in painting. She never did pursue painting and periodically gave as her reasons that caring for the children and the financial burdens of raising a family following her divorce had prevented her from finding the time and energy to pursue her passion. It had been some time since Barbara had recalled her mother describing her wishes, and it was only at the moment when she thought about going public that her sense of guilt surfaced and competed with her capacity to enjoy the success of her creativity. Such guilt can also breed a sense of compliance that furthers the betrayal of self for the sake of others.

A SENSE OF BETRAYAL

Guilt that undermines the creative process may also be associated with achieving happiness and some forms of success while others may have been disadvantaged socially, psychologically, or economically. Such guilt may arise in relation to one's race, ethnicity, culture, disability, socioeconomic status, or family history. It is very much like the guilt experienced by many immigrants upon leaving their families behind in a quest for a better life.

Twenty-four-year-old Raphael described experiencing guilt as a child and adolescent when reading books in English. Both of his parents were born in Mexico and moved to the United States when he was eight years old. While they encouraged him to learn English, they demanded he speak Spanish at home. He experienced competing emotions regarding wanting to please and be loyal to his parents and heritage and his strong desire to succeed in his new culture. This guilt led him to postpone for several years a decision to go to college. While he acknowledged his doubts about doing well academically, he had a strong sense of betraying his parents by being the first member of his immediate and extended family to seek higher education.

Similar guilt is frequently a side effect of psychotherapy, a process that helps individuals achieve personal growth as they become increasingly connected with themselves; their thoughts, emotions, and attitudes; and what is meaningful for them. Through this journey of discovery, they often gain freedom and confidence to pursue their uniqueness while working on fostering meaningful connections with others. In essence, they are helped to feel empowered and confident in creating for themselves a life that is personally authentic and meaningful. However, as they continue to experience a sense of increased comfort with who they are, and as they begin to take new actions in spite of their fears, another form of guilt often surfaces. They want their loved ones to join them on the same journey, partly out of genuine love and, to some degree, because of the guilt they experience for being optimistic instead of pessimistic, hopeful instead of hopeless, and empowered instead of powerless. Sometimes such guilt arises out of the powerful compulsive drive to feel responsible for the happiness of others; sometimes it is part of the guilt and shame they experience regarding their strivings to identify, accept, and nurture their own needs. In either case, such guilt may be especially strong when parents or other loved ones have not had the same opportunities to better their lives.

Such guilt can be especially difficult for individuals who are perhaps for the first time in their lives focusing on recognizing and identifying their individual needs, thoughts, and feelings. Being able to creatively live their lives may set them apart from loved ones and friends. In spite of their desire to have others join them on the creative journey, others may not wish to join them or may not be able to do so.

Fully embracing and accepting one's creativity involves effectively managing this excessive and paralyzing guilt.

COMPLIANCE

Being overly compliant involves the excessive focus on the needs of others. In part, this attitude develops from guilt. However, it is also rooted in dependency and passivity. It involves deferring one's needs and desires with regard to both significant and less important decisions in one's life. As with other patterns of interactions that foster challenges to creativity, this inhibiting theme is developed early on and competes and interferes with maintaining genuine connection with oneself. It involves a hypervigilance to the needs of others and a powerful desire to conform to them.

Over time, such compliance and deferment causes one to lose touch with what is personally meaningful. It leads to a sense of self-alienation and an inability to identify one's personal emotions, interests, and desires. This manner of managing one's needs may impact simple decisions like the ability to voice an opinion when asked by friends to choose a restaurant for dinner. It may also have more serious negative impacts on creating and sustaining relationships. By being compliant we ignore our needs. Whether we do this consciously or unconsciously, this can lead to feelings of isolation, a lack of recognition, and a sense of being invisible.

Additionally, this pattern of avoiding self-expression can also lead to a heightened sensitivity to feeling controlled, as resentment increases about not having one's needs met. Similarly, it can strongly impact one's career, as when it leaves one unable to express or assert one's needs in the workplace. Most significantly, this is often the challenge faced by individuals who cannot identify a passion in their lives or are quick to disengage from meaningful progress during any stage of the creative process.

Chris, aged forty-two, had worked in his family-owned business for over fifteen years. While it had been challenging for him to work with his parents and one of two siblings, he had become quite successful in helping to run the restaurant. His confidence gave rise to an interest in opening his own restaurant. He endured tremendous guilt regarding his plan and could not voice it out loud to any members of the family for several years. During this time, as he increasingly suppressed his true desires, his resentment grew. He felt paralyzed and utterly incapable of making a change, especially in light of the success of the family business as well as the love and devotion he felt toward his family. And yet, he believed he needed a new challenge. He needed to break away from his family to pursue a business that more closely reflected his unique visions and aspirations.

As emphasized throughout this book, our capacity to make changes and pursue creativity may be challenged when others around us feel threatened by our pursuits. Fortunately, this story has a happy ending. After an initial period of strain and tremendous guilt, Chris finally opened his own restaurant. It took time for his family to adjust to their loss, but they grew to become extremely supportive of his endeavor.

Guilt of this form can arise even when your family is supportive and encouraging of your creativity. Gloria was part of a family of low socioeconomic status, living in the South Bronx. Her mother, who raised Gloria and her three siblings, was successful in instilling a love of learning. Although she herself had only attended one semester of a junior college, her three children completed graduate programs; one in education, another in nursing, and Gloria, in creative writing.

Gloria spent several years sporadically devoting time to her writing and rarely submitted her work. She achieved increasing acceptance, but experienced a great deal of guilt regarding both her mother and her friends and extended family who had not been as fortunate.

As a psychologist, I meet many people in their middle or late twenties who find themselves in their first jobs, several years after undergraduate or graduate school. They seek treatment because of a sense of boredom or a related sense that, having reached a goal they had worked hard to achieve, there is an emptiness and lack of enthusiasm in their lives. They even report having close friends and being involved in meaningful and rewarding relationships. No doubt this is a natural part of having reached a major goal and now being faced with identifying new goals. However, many report feeling lost in terms of experiencing meaning in life. As it turns out, many individuals who experience this loss are the same individuals who have been conditioned to be compliant. They have defined themselves by the expectations of others and how they believed they "should be," but have ignored or rarely reflected on what was really meaningful for them.

A lawyer explained to me that he had lived his entire life for the expectations of others. He was just finishing law school; had married a year previously; and his wife, parents, and in-laws all were pressuring him to have children. And yet, it wasn't until a year after graduating that he admitted to himself that he had little interest in law but had pursued that field because of career status and the expectations of family. He sought counseling to deal with the anxiety of these realizations. He had distracted himself with others' dreams to such an extent that he could not identify what would make his life more meaningful. For some, it takes this level of discomfort before they can begin to assertively create their own lives. This is not an early midlife crisis. Rather, it is the self-realization that one has neglected oneself in an effort to fit in or to manage the guilt of living authentically.

While the creative goals of the scientist may be to benefit humankind and the creative goals of the artist may be to entertain, inspire, or give a voice to others, the creative journey is one that involves individual exploration and evolution. It is an ongoing process of self-reflection characterized by the *need* to create and follow a personal path, sometimes in spite of the interests of others. It calls for self-knowledge as well as comfort in forging one's individual identity. All creativity, whether in the pursuit of art or scientific inquiry, requires an ability to put aside the needs or preferences of others so that you can be open and free to embrace your creative genius. It is a form of healthy selfishness in that it allows you to suspend judgment so that you can be more fully present and engaged with the creative process. Such pursuit can be a way of constructively managing guilt or, unfortunately, it can be persistently undermined by the impact of toxic guilt.

*** FOR FURTHER REFLECTION ***

1. To what degree have you assumed the role of the family caretaker, feeling responsible for the happiness and health of others?
2. To what degree has this drive expanded to your being the caretaker in relationships outside of your family?
3. To what degree does your assumed responsibility inhibit your capacity to have a more balanced perspective in considering and pursuing the satisfaction of your longings?
4. If you were to pursue your identified passion, in what ways do you believe you would be depriving others?
5. Have you had experiences that have left you with toxic guilt? If so, what, if anything, have you done to address it?
6. Are you aware of such guilt surfacing when you begin to pursue creative engagement, during your leisure time, at your workplace, or when defining your life goals? If so, to what degree has such guilt interfered with your capacity to accept and act upon your creative passion?
7. If you have survived a tragedy, are you aware of what you are telling yourself about embracing your creative passion? Write down what you believe those who did not survive the tragedy would tell you regarding your desire to be creative?

REFLECTIONS

True guilt is guilt at the obligation one owes to oneself to be oneself, to actualize oneself. False guilt is guilt felt at not being what other people feel one ought to be or assume that one is.—R. D. Laing

How unhappy is he who cannot forgive himself.—Publilius Syrus

It is only too easy to compel a sensitive human being to feel guilty about anything.—Morton Seiden

I can feel guilty about the past, apprehensive about the future, but only in the present can I act.—Abraham Maslow

NOTES

1. June P. Tangney and Ronda L. Dearing, *Shame and Guilt* (New York: Guilford, 2002).

2. Aphrodite Matsakis, *Survivor Guilt: A Self-Help Guide* (Oakland, CA: New Harbinger, 1999).

Chapter 7

STRIVING TO ELUDE SHAME

Shame can play a major role in inhibiting access to and expression of your creative genius. More specifically, much of the tension that leads you to withdraw or distract yourself from creative engagement is rooted in the motivation to elude the intense mind-body states that are associated with shame. Like guilt, shame is considered a "self-conscious" emotion.[1] It is a paralyzing negative emotion triggered by the awareness of not living up to your own or others' codes of standards, rules, or norms. In contrast to the self-reproach aroused by guilt, which focuses on behavior, shame arises when you judge yourself as being inadequate or flawed in the very essence of your being. Shame is global in perspective, an attack on every aspect of the self. In addition, while guilt is often focused on the fear of punishment, shame involves fear of isolation and abandonment.[2]

THE EXPERIENCE OF SHAME

Whether experienced with full awareness or when you are reacting to the tension arising from and influenced by the depths of your unconscious, shame can impact your thoughts, emotions, and physical states. The desire to hide is the dominant motivating force of this mind-body state and is a hallmark reaction to feeling shame. Thus, it is often the case that, prompted by growing tension, you flee from engaging in those activities that may give rise to it.

When actually confronted by shame, your thoughts are likely to become constricted with a focus on self-doubt. Objectivity in self-evaluation is lost, and confusion prevails regarding every aspect of your sense of self. When this occurs, you are likely to reflect on yourself and assess your shortcomings from an intensely negative and "all-encompassing" perspective; anxiety is pervasive and inhibits expression of the self through your thoughts, emotions, or actions.[3]

Intense pain and discomfort associated with shame may include hurt, sadness, disappointment, anger, and anxiety as well as feelings of inadequacy, isolation, and being unworthy. Low-level and vague anxiety, the fear of failure, and the fear of success often serve as the alarm to change your course so that you steer clear of facing this powerfully uncomfortable constellation of emotions. In effect, you may "substitute" somewhat more palatable emotions such as anxiety and fear for the less palatable experience of shame. You may even become more consciously aware of anger or depression in place of feeling the negative whirlpool of shame. Such substitutions may occur because your conscious mind can better tolerate the subjective experience of depression, anger, or anxiety than the intense pain of shame. In this manner, you protect yourself from discomfort through suppression, consciously choosing to ignore it, and by repression, unconsciously keeping it hidden from your awareness.

The overriding physical reaction associated with shame is pervasive tension that fosters a desire to hide or withdraw. Such tension can best be described as your body's revulsion with itself. Your shame may be expressed physically by averting your eyes, withdrawing, or even crouching, as if you can become smaller and less apparent.

SHAME AND ITS IMPACT ON CREATIVITY

Shame can be attached in a very narrow way to specific behaviors, thoughts, or emotions. For example, you may experience shame in association with certain sexual thoughts. Also, shame may become closely linked with a specific emotion such as anger. As such, the shame of experiencing anger may actually lead you to become even angrier. In each of these situations, shame may lead to a narrow impact on specific behaviors, thoughts, or emotions.

In sharp contrast, shame is most powerfully inhibiting of creativity when it is associated in a broad manner with your desires to live authentically. When this occurs, shame leads you to deny, minimize, or attack your individual strivings to express yourself in any manner.[4] Shamed strivings inhibit your creative engagement because they challenge your core sense of deserving to be who you are and become who we want to be. Such shame may cause you to suppress and repress your deepest desires and, subsequently, to lose touch with yourself—your passion and the innate curiosity you experienced as a child. Your natural tendencies toward increased autonomy, as well as the capacity to accept being different, are both undermined by shamed strivings. In this sense, shame may potentially inhibit your every step as you dare to acknowledge, attend to, and act upon your creative passion.

All of the elements essential for the creative process are paralyzed when you experience shame. Curiosity and openness, the main fuel sources for creativity, cannot exist in the presence of shame. Shame renders you unable to observe the details of your surroundings and the nature of your internal experience. It competes with the fluidity of your thought processes. When your thought processes stagnate, it becomes virtually impossible to act on and generate new patterns of thought, image, or movement. Instead, you are only able to support intensely critical judgments that interfere with your ability to ponder, discover, explore, and express yourself. Feelings of being unworthy overpower and replace the intrinsic pleasure that should normally accompany the creative act. Thus, powerful experiences of shame may undermine your capacity to access your creative genius.

Noted author and counselor John Bradshaw has highlighted the positive aspect that shame plays in relationship to creativity. He has suggested that the need to be right has a tendency to undermine one's curiosity. Feeling that one is right makes the process of seeking new information redundant. Accordingly, Bradshaw has suggested that

> our healthy shame, which is a feeling of our core boundary and limitedness, never allows us to believe we know it all. Our healthy shame is nourishing in that it moves us to seek new information and to learn new things.[5]

In addition, being shamed may not always lead to inhibition of creativity. In fact, much of creativity can be a way of managing the impact of shame. Painting, writing, dance, music, or any such creative pursuits are expressions of the authentic self or, at the very least, attempts to express the authentic self. As such, it is no surprise that many individuals who have had serious emotional difficulties have been attracted to these creative mediums. Such expressions are meaningful ways to manage the range of joy and hardships you have experienced on your journey through life.

LEARNING SHAME

Shame is rooted in the context of our relationships with parents, siblings, peers, extended family, teachers, religious leaders, and the wider culture. Through their combined influence, the experience of shame may become associated with specific standards for behavior, attitudes, and emotions. Most often, this occurs through direct and indirect messages that are shaming. Messages that are shaming maintain their powerful hold because of the intense longings we experience as children to feel accepted and loved by those who are important to us. Consequently, our fears of rejection or abandonment hold us hostage and compel us to conform and show our caretakers how "good" we really can be. It is in the way we are treated that we learn to treat ourselves.

Additionally, direct messages that induce shame include expressions of frequent and powerful criticism that are global rather than specific in focus. Being told you are stupid or ignorant for a belief you maintain, scolded for a feeling you experience, or intensely reprimanded regarding your behavior are all examples of messages that are shame inducing. For example, you may be reprimanded and viewed as being weak for experiencing certain emotions such as doubt, anxiety, anger, or even joy and pleasure. You may have been shamed even for caring, for expressing in words or actions the need to receive love and the desire to give it. Traditionally, for example, boys have been shamed for experiencing self-doubt, ambiguity, and anxiety while girls have been shamed for experiencing anger.

Shame may also be communicated nonverbally through facial expressions of disgust, by withdrawal, by dramatic sighs, and by other behaviors that communicate an evaluation that you, as a whole person, are inadequate. In contrast, by receiving adequate support and nurturance in the form of admiration, encouragement, and permission to be yourself, you develop a sufficient degree of self-acceptance, security, and confidence in living authentically. Similarly, it is when criticism is focused and specific, rather than targeting your whole person, that you become open to and accepting of your emotions, thoughts, and behaviors, as well as your desires and abilities to satisfy them.

Through such interactions you develop self-worth and trust in your creative genius as well as more realistic expectations for yourself. These experiences foster your capacity to challenge conformity, which is an essential component of the creative process. In addition, such experiences strengthen your sense of healthy narcissism, the capacity to identify, accept, believe in, and take action regarding your individual desires, needs, and goals.

Through experiences with shamed strivings, you learn to attach shame to all of the activities and processes that form the foundation of the creative venture. As a result of experiencing shamed strivings during formative years, you may refrain from seeking solitude, self-reflection and self-expression, seeking recognition, and taking any action that reflects your creative genius. In essence, shame begins to accompany any feelings of desire for autonomy in thought, emotion, or actions. Shame can also become attached to the desire for admiration and the desire to feel special.

Shame may also be communicated in more subtle ways through direct communications that imply a rejection or devaluation. The following anecdote offers a poignant example of how shame may be induced in this manner.

As a child Michael had derived great pleasure in painting. He had gained some experience in school with watercolors and by age eleven had decided to try oil painting. Michael had become sufficiently confident in his skills to attempt a scene depicting warriors of the Middle Ages engaged in combat. He drew his inspiration from scenes of battle depicted in books that described that period. After spending several weeks working on his painting in seclusion, he bravely shared it with his father. Michael's vivid description of their interaction offers a sad example of how our strivings for self-expression can be shamed.

He initially experienced great pride and excitement when he offered to show the painting to his father. Immediately upon seeing the painting, his father's facial features became tense. After a moment's hesitation, his father announced in a harsh tone of disappointment, confusion, and some denigration, "There's certainly a lot of aggression and anger there! Why did you pick this to paint?" The content and tone of his voice sent Michael into a rage. He immediately ran off into his room, ripped the painting, and did not paint again for another fifteen years.

Michael clearly showed some capacity to accept and trust his passion, as evidenced by his purchase of the oil paints and his commitment to actually complete a painting. Unfortunately, his father's comments renewed the feeling of shame that he had been fighting against in the pursuit of his passion. The seemingly disproportionate intensity of Michael's reaction was due to the fact that he had had numerous previous interactions in which he similarly felt questioned and diminished by his father. These communications further evoked in Michael the intense need to justify his feelings, thoughts, and actions. In fact, Michael had purposely painted in seclusion in an attempt to delay exposure until he had actually completed his work. His previous encounters with his father's disapproving and diminishing attitude had only heightened the perfectionism with which he approached his painting. For this reason, he was quick to experience his father's reaction as yet another shaming evaluation of not only his painting but his essential self as well. His intense hurt and shame shifted to anger. Rather than confront his father, whose approval he so strongly desired, he struck out at himself and destroyed his work. He also experienced anger toward himself for feeling inadequate.

Shame can similarly be communicated by behavior that is modeled. For example, parents who are predisposed to experience shame regarding specific concerns may communicate and instill similar shame in their children. They do this in a variety of ways that communicate absence of acceptance rather than outright criticism.

This is exemplified by how Ben and Elaine reacted when they attended a school play in which their young daughter was a participant. Following the performance, all of the children scampered off the stage and with great pride and excitement ran up the aisles to meet their parents. Most parents lavished praise on their children. Their genuine admiration and support was evidenced by their smiles, the joyful tone in their voices, and by the flood of compliments they freely gave to their young actors.

Both Ben and Elaine sheepishly admitted that they became emotionally blocked as their daughter approached them. With minimal expression, they jointly responded, "You did a good job. But we need to go home now." Both parents indicated with acute awareness and regret how paralyzed they were when it was time to share admiration and express support for their daughter. Unfortunately, both had repeatedly learned throughout their childhoods that it was not right to seek attention or to even desire it. Each had been shamed on many occasions for seeking and desiring recognition and praise. Similarly, they had internalized the message that receiving such adoration would make them both arrogant and self-centered.

Fast-forward several years and it becomes quite apparent how this form of shaming can undermine the natural desire to live authentically and embrace creative genius. It is in part the admiration and acceptance of children's attempts to live authentically, especially with regard to being creative, that instill in them the courage to continue to be creative as they grow up.

Some parents who have been shamed experience their children as extensions of themselves. As a result, they may exert tremendous influence on their children to behave in ways that help to distract them from their own shame, especially their feelings of inadequacy. These parents may be easily threatened when their children do not feel as they feel, behave as they believe they should behave, or have the same goals in life as they maintain. Such parents often uphold rigid and unrealistically high expectations for how their children should be, rewarding only those attitudes, behaviors, thoughts, and emotions that reflect and meet their expectations. They respond negatively to any contrary behavior on the part of their children by withdrawing or even verbally or physically abusing them.

Children who have been abused physically, sexually, or emotionally may be the most at risk to experience shame as adults at a level that inhibits individual movement in the creative realm. As an outcome of such abuse, instead of fully recognizing their anger and hurt and the reality that they were not responsible for the abuse they suffered, they move into adulthood carrying the burden of paralyzing shame. As noted earlier, however, many of these children do manage to become creative adults. In fact, creativity, in these cases, is frequently the vehicle by which these individuals find meaningful ways of managing their shame. It is through their creativity that they dare to live authentically and to embrace their unique identities.

Those who pursue creativity in spite of shaming experiences may do so for a variety of reasons. Some may be more driven by anger than by shame, resulting in a desire to prove that those who shamed them were wrong. Others may have had experiences with role models who helped them to overcome their feelings of shame.

Noted author and psychoanalyst Alice Miller suggests that children who are abused or neglected do best as adults when they have had a "witness" to their plight.[6] By witness, she refers to those who are available to listen to victims and give compassion while acknowledging and recognizing their pain.

This type of witnessing helps reduce the sense of isolation and shame on the part of recovering victims. In *The Untouched Key*, Miller describes in great detail how for victims of abuse and neglect creativity may be an unconscious way of "bearing witness as artists to the truths of their childhood."[7]

SHAME AS A BLOCK TO SELF-AWARENESS

Experiences of shame can be powerful deterrents to the self-reflection that is foundational for recognizing, accepting, or acting on creative desires. Powerful shame experienced early on may undermine your connection with yourself. This is often a major contributing factor when you fail to recognize your own passions. The impact of shame may lead you to deny, minimize, or repress your interests. I have worked with many individuals who required enormous amounts of reflection before they could recall what aroused their passions as children or adolescents. Many had renounced their authentic selves and in the process had lost touch with what it was like to have the openness, curiosity, and awe of childhood.

SHAME AS A BARRIER TO CREATIVE ENGAGEMENT

Even when you do recognize what is meaningful for you, shame can still inhibit the initiation or maintenance of your creative efforts. Much of what impedes creative engagement may be related to the anticipation of shame rather than the head-on experience of it. Like those individuals who avoided returning to the scenes of their automobile accidents, you may become overly sensitive and aversive to those situations that are likely to arouse the debilitating mind-body states associated with shame. One strategy to manage this fear is avoidance, never even initiating serious thoughts or actions in the pursuit of your creative dreams.

Although Joann had a strong interest in writing, she postponed actually pursuing it for years. First, she vowed that she would begin after her career as a lawyer was firmly launched. Then, she told herself that she would begin writing while at home with her first child. Several years passed and she then committed herself to begin once her child was in school full time. Throughout this period, she periodically began to write, but not for any significant amount of time. Each time she engaged in writing, she experienced tremendous tension. When reflecting on her discomfort, Joann gradually became aware that she had based much of her self-worth on achievement and earning money. Without full awareness, she had internalized shame regarding writing because it did not lead to a significant financial gain and it seemed overly self-indulgent to be pursuing something just for the pleasure of it. While she thoroughly enjoyed writing when she was younger, she had grown to view it as childish, a waste of time, and extremely costly when measured against the hourly salary she earned as an attorney.

Others may be able to sporadically engage in creative pursuits for short periods of time before the anticipation of shame inhibits progress. Still others may begin several projects and never complete any of them because attending in greater detail would bring a confrontation with shame that much closer.

FACING THE MOMENT OF CHALLENGE

Distinct "moments of challenge" to your creativity may be aroused by the shame of simply looking inward. Self-doubt and tension during those distinct moments of creative engagement are often the most challenging moments you face when embracing your creative genius. Such shame may be a reaction to feeling negatively self-centered or simply selfish when focusing on personal feelings, emotions, or longings. The act of withdrawing into your imagination may itself be associated with shame if in your past it was punished, made fun of, criticized, or was simply not supported. If you are burdened by such a background, you may experience fear, anxiety, or some degree of shame when you engage in a creative act. The fear and anxiety is experienced as your body telling you that "something is not right or something bad is going to happen." It is at these distinct moments that any past experiences related to strivings and inhibited strivings lead you to revisit the discomfort associated with past efforts that met with disapproval. Consequently, much of shame's influence is aroused as anticipation long before you actually experience it directly.

Beth readily recognized increasing tension even as she attended her first ceramics class. She had finally enrolled after spending several years considering taking the course.

Even a few minutes before I walked into the classroom, I questioned myself about attending. I felt like I needed to justify my desire to work with ceramics. I began to feel I was taking time away from my husband and my children. I thought of the many more important things I should be doing at home.

Even as a young child Beth had been encouraged to grow up too fast. While she described her parents as being loving and good providers, there was little praise and interaction regarding play. At age eight, she was told to put her dolls in the closet because she was too old to play with them. Beth also noted that she had been pushed to excel academically. She attended classes in drama and flute at the direction of her parents. Additionally, her parents were intensely focused on their careers and did not model engagement in hobbies, play, or any form of creative expression. The combination of these experiences led Beth to feel shame in regard to taking time to "play" with clay.

Mark similarly shared his experiences of self-doubt and tension as he pursued his interest in photography.

I was in the camera store totally excited about purchasing this really cool camera, but even as I paid for it, I questioned if I should be spending my money some other way. I kept asking myself if I was spending too much even though I am financially in great shape—like I didn't believe I deserved to have such a good camera. In the class and when taking pictures for the assignments, I was often thrilled about finally learning photography. At the same time, I often had doubts about the time and expense involved in my hobby and if I needed to do something more worthwhile or important.

These examples show the influence of shame reflected in self-critical thoughts sprinkled throughout each moment of creative engagement. They portray the ways tension related to shame may arise at the very moment of experiencing intense satisfaction in one's creative pursuit.

SHAME'S IMPACT ON THE FORM OF YOUR CREATIVITY

Shamed strivings can inhibit not just the degree to which you embrace being creative but the very form your creativity takes. While painting, for example, you may be influenced by shame that encourages you to withdraw, to be excessively conservative, or to choose colors that are more muted in tone and reflect on canvas your desire to hide. Such actions may stem from a mind-body set that includes thoughts such as "this is too different," "the colors are too bright or too lively," "these colors will get too much attention," "what will people think?" or "I am getting too excited with my own creativity."

I worked with Zak, a young man in his early twenties who, while experiencing a strong fear of failure, was predominantly influenced by shame. He periodically and with great pain maintained a journal of jokes, all of which focused on his perspectives on life, and all of which were extremely self-deprecating and devaluing. With encouragement, support, and strategies described in later chapters, and after much trepidation, Zak enrolled in class to learn stand-up comedy. A final project for the class involved a performance on stage with other members of the class at a Chicago nightclub.

Following Zak's performance, the instructor, classmates, and friends raved about his routine. They marveled at the quality of his material and delivery. Zak later revealed that, while he could at times believe his performance went well, he could not accept that the praise directed toward him by his peers and instructor reflected an accurate appraisal.

As Zak realized, he could only command the attention of the spotlight if he devalued himself. While this is a successful format for many comedians, it was paralyzing for him. Deeply felt shame inhibited his ability to be open to an objective evaluation of his performance. He both downplayed the quality of his work and questioned the abilities of those in his audience to offer informed assessments of his performance. This is another example of how harboring intense, negative emotions and critical devaluing self-judgments seals off your openness to positive feedback and other forms of reality checks.

Intense shame as well as more subtle shame can also contribute to the creation of fantasies that get in the way of your creative dreams. This topic is the focus of the next chapter.

NEVER BEING GOOD ENOUGH

While trying to elude shame is often the basis for perfectionism, it is also the foundation for the ongoing self-appraisal that one is "never good enough." And while the perfectionist may be able to identify in his mind's eye what "perfect" would look like, feel like, sound like, or taste like, those with this inhibiting aspect of shame experience the feeling of adequacy as an always-elusive state.

This free-floating sense of never measuring up provides another diversion from the path of creativity. It can account for difficulty in beginning to pursue creativity as well as for the many false starts in following a creative passion. Even during those brief moments when you may think positively about your work and yourself, the self-doubt of never being good enough may slowly creep in to eventually dominate your awareness.

*** FOR FURTHER EXPLORATION ***

1. What messages did you receive while growing up regarding trusting and accepting your thoughts and emotions?
2. Write a couple of sentences that describe guidelines you have internalized about the appropriateness of your pursuit of personal interests or passions.
3. What did you learn as a child regarding your desires to be independent in your opinions, feelings, or actions?
4. What guidelines are you able to identify regarding the exploration of your inner self?
5. To what extent does shame play a part in your life?
6. Can you identify key figures who supported, encouraged, or nurtured your capacity to be authentic? How did you experience their validation? Did they communicate validating messages directly or indirectly?
7. Can you recall being shamed specifically because you pursued a creative venture?
8. What messages were you provided regarding shame and creativity? More specifically, were your parents, siblings, close relatives, or others impacted by shame in their pursuit of being creative, autonomous, or different? If so, what did you learn about what it means to be autonomous or different?

REFLECTIONS

A musician must make his music; an artist must paint, a poet must write, if he is to be at peace with himself.—Abraham Maslow

Shame is a wound felt from inside, dividing us both from ourselves and one another.—George Kaufman

Shame is pride's cloak.—William Blake

We are ashamed of everything that is real about us; ashamed of ourselves, of our relatives, of our incomes, of our accents, of our opinions, of our experience, just as we are ashamed of our naked skins.—George Bernard Shaw

NOTES

1. June Price Tangney and Ronda L. Dearing, *Shame and Guilt* (New York: Guilford, 2002).

2. Ibid.

3. Michael Lewis, *Shame: The Exposed Self* (New York: Free Press, 1995).

4. Gershen Kaufman, *Shame: The Power of Caring* (Rochester, VT: Shenkman Books, 1992).

5. John Bradshaw, *Healing the Shame That Binds You* (Deerfield Beach, FL: Health Communications, 1988), p. 9.

6. Alice Miller, *The Untouched Key* (New York: Doubleday, 1990).

7. Ibid.

Chapter 8

WHEN FANTASIES GET IN THE WAY OF OUR DREAMS

Our dreams evolve from who we are and provide direction for who we wish to become. Through the powers of your imagination you are able to transcend time and space to briefly experience an altered way of being. In one flash you can picture yourself able to sketch, direct a play, compose a song, write a short story, or form a metal sculpture worthy of exhibition in the finest art gallery. In seconds, you can shift focus and envision yourself successfully mastering the demands of a new career.

Our dreams pull us into the future and goad us on to embrace the creative journey in spite of the challenges that threaten us. They lift our spirits when we have doubts or frustration and, most important, they heighten and compliment the intrinsic reward of creative engagement. And while dreams fuel our creativity, those based on fantasies thwart our creative passions and efforts.

Some dreams may at first seem to be indistinguishable from fantasy. Certainly, it is in the realm of possibility that if you persist in writing you may someday write a best-selling novel. With perseverance and determination, you may be a pianist in a symphony orchestra. It is also possible that you may become extremely skillful in creating a unique line of ceramic tiles, greeting cards, vases, or children's dolls. Statistically speaking, the probabilities of these events occurring vary, but they are within reason. However, such dreams are undermined when they are embedded in fantasy. But what one person calls a dream, ten others will label a fantasy. So how do we distinguish them?

Imagine having your book on the *New York Times* bestseller list. It is possible to achieve this if you write well, write often, improve your craft, have a great story to tell, have the right opportunities to expose your work, obtain favorable exposure and reviews, and can manage the stress these challenges create. This is a fine dream, but if you omit any of these elements of skill and hard work from consideration, the scenario transforms into a fantasy. For example, you maintain the dream but do not write often; you hesitate to share your writing with others; your story just does not arouse excitement; or you fail to do the necessary research to really provide a realistic setting for the characters. To a great extent, these are examples of how fantasy can get in the way of fulfilling your dreams. Realistic dreams become fantasies when you imagine successful outcomes while at the same time believing that you can somehow skip essential steps in the creative process.

SKIPPING ESSENTIAL STEPS

Our culture increasingly encourages us to believe we can do anything. Sometimes, with the best of intentions, our parents have echoed this same sentiment. To a certain degree, this is a good thing. Such sentiments offer hope and support the ability to think about and identify the many possibilities of being. They reflect the general tone and tradition of our culture's "can do" spirit. These are the very guidelines we need to successfully internalize if we are to be resilient in our creative quests.

At the same time, however, we are also inundated with messages that encourage us to expect instant gratification. Similarly, we are often encouraged to believe that fulfilling our dreams should require little time or energy and that reward and satisfaction should come easily. From making purchases, to learning how to paint, to learning to play a musical instrument, to instant messages, to controlling video games with our thoughts, we have become obsessed with gratification of our desires with the least expenditure of energy and within the least amount of time. Unfortunately, an impaired tolerance for frustration is the side effect of maintaining such expectations.

All creativity requires time, effort, commitment, and patience. And yet, our dreams of being creative are too often shattered by holding on to the fantasy that achieving the products of creativity should not necessitate huge investments of personal time and energy. It is unrealistic to believe you can learn to take truly great pictures in a three-hour photo class. In reality, you will likely learn only the basics by enrolling in such a course. Certainly, attending a free seminar on faux-painting at your local home-improvement store will offer you the basic guidelines for helping you to create the appearance of texture on your walls. And going to a presentation at your local bookstore on shifting your career will offer you some ideas to motivate you in certain directions. But each of these creative endeavors, as with all sustained creativity, requires time, effort, commitment, and patience in order to be even modestly competent.

Too often, we are like the adolescent mentioned earlier, who strongly desired to play the guitar but resented the time, calluses, and the extent of practice required to develop competency. We fail to recognize or acknowledge that creativity requires deep and prolonged immersion in a given subject. Certainly, making a design for a ceramic tile, offering an idea at the office regarding a minor challenge, or being creative in your selection of Christmas presents may not require a great amount of time, but even these activities require some degree of planning and research.

I worked with Lance, a client in his late twenties, who declared that he wanted to be a photographer. He expressed this dream in spite of the fact that he had never seriously practiced taking pictures. His dream of becoming a photographer emerged while he was traveling in Australia. Upon returning home, he immediately decided that he wanted to become a photographer for *National Geographic*. At the same time, he was adamant in his reluctance to attend school to learn his craft. Furthermore, he refused to interview for a job in which he would be trained as a photographer's apprentice. By his own admission, he could not imagine himself photographing children, pets, or weddings. Instead, he rigidly focused on his dream of taking a prize-winning shot of exotic animals in their natural habitats. While few areas of interest appealed to him as much as photography, he was unable to make the plunge and immerse himself in the serious effort it takes to become a skilled photographer.

I do not mean to suggest that there is only one path to fulfilling your creative dreams. Certainly, there are many individuals who have excelled in creative arenas without following some of the more traditional routes. However, even these individuals had to commit themselves for many hours, days, months, and years to perfect their skills. Even the histories of the most innovative creators of our time reflect the importance of this commitment. These indicate that, in general, the greatest artists, scientists, inventors, and others, seem to follow the "ten-year" rule.[1] This rule emphasizes that their first truly noteworthy creative achievements occurred, on average, after ten years of study in their respective fields. While all creativity does not rise to this level of achievement (and, thankfully, it does not have to), all sustained creativity requires completing meaningful steps in the process.

THE FANTASY OF PERFECTION

Dreams that inspire creative passion can rapidly turn to fantasy when you maintain rigid expectations of perfection. Striving to be perfect pushes you to achieve your best work but, at the same time, the compulsion for perfection can undermine all creative effort and satisfaction.

When you are fully open to and accepting of your creative genius, you can easily engage in dreams that push you to the limits of your perceived capacities. Such dreams may be as simple as painting a wall or installing a tile backsplash against a sink; or they could be as complex as writing historical fiction or composing a symphony. In each of these endeavors, it is your ability to be realistic in anticipating the form and quality of your achievement that allows you to embrace creative passion. In contrast, it is the fantasy derived from rigid expectations of perfection that paralyzes your efforts in moving forward with the steps necessary to achieve your dreams.

Over the years, I have had the opportunity to work with writers who ranged from those who were extremely successful to some who had obsessed for years about their pursuit without bringing any projects to completion. Those who were most successful had fully embraced, in mind and body, the conviction that they needed to be realistic in how they approached their work. More specifically, they recognized the need to be realistic in terms of the quality of their writing, the time it would take, their goals, and their ability to reach them.

In contrast, those who ruminated about writing but rarely engaged or only periodically engaged in doing so had maintained highly unrealistic fantasies that challenged their mind-body states the moment they sat down to write. Such fantasies distracted them from accessing, trusting, and being open to their vast reservoir of creativity. In general, such fantasies only hasten and guarantee the arrival of inhibiting mind-body sets that push you to abandon your creative efforts.

One of these fantasies can best be described as the "Pulitzer Prize scenario." The inhibiting theme in this situation is expressed as something equivalent to "I have to achieve the Pulitzer Prize or I should not spend time writing." Though the Pulitzer Prize scenario may not be expressed in such specific terms, similar fantasies often reflect the very high standards of excellence we set for ourselves at the moment we sit down in front of a computer and keyboard, a blank sketch tablet, or an unsculpted block of marble.

Maintaining such unrealistic and rigid expectations leaves you highly vulnerable to paralyzing tension because, instead of remaining open to the flow of your thoughts, you become inhibited by judgment and by comparing your work to some idealized version of what it should be. When preoccupied with this goal, you stifle your creativity as you experience in full force the disparity between your actual performance and the level of quality you have fantasized achieving. When you are captive to this inhibiting theme, each hour of work may be marked by seven-eighths of the time spent in critical self-evaluation and one-eighth engaged in actually creating. Clearly, the more ideal scenario would reflect a reverse balance of time, dominated by creative pursuit and with much less time spent in self-evaluation.

This discrepancy between actual achievement and the ideal of perfection fosters a sense of inadequacy associated with mind-body tension that quickly dampens your resolve to move forward. At such moments, you may hastily retreat in an effort to avoid the greater pain of shame. While you may embrace perfectionism in an effort to avoid experiencing it, rigid and unrealistically high expectations only increase the likelihood that you will feel shame.

Perfectionism distracts you from being fully present in the "here and now." It moves you out of a state of creative flow to the next stage, that of assessment. Surely, you cannot consistently remain focused on the present when you are fixated on being perfect or on anticipated future rewards. At such distinct moments, you disconnect from both the creative process and from your passion. You may myopically conclude that your goal is not attainable and throw up your hands, saying, "Why bother?" Turning your attention to the television, fetching a cup of coffee, or reading the paper, you try to distract yourself from your sense of defeat and related feelings of inadequacy.

Unrealistic expectations regarding creativity may pertain to the quality of the finished product or to the level of skill you hope to achieve. Additionally, it can refer to expectations you maintain about the creative process itself.

EVERY ASPECT OF CREATIVITY SHOULD BE EQUALLY REWARDING

One fantasy that interrupts the flight of creativity is the expectation that every aspect of the creative process should be equally rewarding. Unfortunately, the reality of the creative process is that all aspects of the creative process are not equally rewarding.

I am exhilarated when engaging in the flow of words that best reflect the ideas I want to express. I delight in identifying a metaphor that best conveys the meaning of my premise. I thrill in my assessment that I am sharing a perspective of understanding that I believe sheds light in a unique way regarding a concept I am presenting. Certainly, these moments are significantly more gratifying than those that involve editing for grammar or entering footnote notation. And yet, all creativity involves tasks that are only minimally gratifying.

All to often, however, we cease to embrace creativity when we are confronted with the aspects of the process that we label as "tedious," "boring," "uninteresting," or "wearisome." Like a child avoiding the task of taking out the garbage, our child logic responds by petulantly asking, "Do I really have to do this?" Other times we make promises such as, "I'll do it later!"

For some of us, later never comes; or it arrives so late that both creative engagement and passion are diluted. Too often we adhere to the expectation that the creative process will be an uninterrupted series of distinct moments of intense emotional pleasure. However, we would be better off to acknowledge at the outset that every creative venture involves tasks that are minimally challenging or pleasurable.

Painters often struggle to maintain a clean and organized workspace. Some musicians describe much of their work as being tedious compared to those moments when they are actually composing music or lyrics. For some, cutting material and sewing the pieces of fabric together does not yield the same degree of satisfaction as designing the dress. And the gratification of obtaining a degree and being able to start a new career is the prize for having endured classes, taking tests, doing homework, and writing papers. Whether glassblowing, writing poetry, performing dance, putting together a Web site, or refurnishing a piece of furniture, the creative process offers tremendous gratification and distinct moments of intense pleasure, but also moments that are less exciting.

While working as a teacher, Charles fantasized about developing a catering business. Each weekend, he spent hours doing research in books and purchasing ingredients, and when he had time he actually cooked. Without any hesitation, he indicated that while he enjoyed the research, he loved the cooking. And while he was able to develop an appealing menu, he realized that he was often blocked in moving forward. One challenging task was keeping his kitchen organized and clean. Another task that interfered centered on his acute trepidation regarding the business aspect of his creative endeavor.

> I have little interest in spending time figuring out finances. I know nothing about business. I feel that I should know what to do, but I don't. And that makes me feel like I am fooling myself with this dream.

He had maintained the fantasy that the entire process should be equally rewarding and that he should be equally prepared to meet all of the challenges of his creative endeavor. The reality was that he had had little exposure to the business side of catering. Besides the fantasy of each part of the creative process being equally rewarding, he maintained the fantasy that he should be skilled in a subject area in which he had no experience.

In *Authentic Happiness*, Martin Seligman differentiates pleasure and gratification, describing pleasure as that intense joy you experience while engaged in an activity.[2] At the end of active engagement, that pleasure becomes a memory. In contrast, gratification is the joy that involves a sense of having challenged yourself, coupled with the satisfaction of developing increased mastery over a subject or skill. Even when you are no longer engaged in such an activity, the skills you developed become a part of you, not just as a memory but also as part of your core being. When you paint, dance, create music, write, or work with crafts, you experience moments of intense pleasure, but it is the ongoing gratification that fuels your passion to continue the process. It is the newly acquired addition to your sense of self that is the major part of your gratification. And with each creative success, you become more resilient to meet new challenges of the creative process. However, it is often because of your determination to experience only pleasure and gratification that you face difficulties in carrying out the less rewarding aspects of the creative process.

WHEN THE DREAM YOU LIVE FOR IS NOT YOUR OWN

As described in several chapters in this section, we often become overly focused on our needs for acceptance and approval. When this is carried to the extreme, you may live a dream that is not your own. When the dream you are living is not your own, it becomes a fantasy that gets in the way of achieving your authentic dreams.

A lawyer I worked with indicated that his decision to become an attorney was more determined by the fact that his father was a lawyer than by his own desire to pursue the profession. He further reported that his mother and the rest of his extended family had all encouraged and expected him to be a lawyer as well. Even as a teen he had envisioned the excitement of presenting his oral argument to a jury regarding a high-profile case; and it was this vision that motivated him throughout his years of education. Even when imagining this scene, he recognized that the joy he experienced was very much determined by his expectation that he would be admired by others rather than on the actual experience of presenting his case. His dream focused more on being seen as a lawyer than on being a lawyer.

You may be one of many who fantasizes about writing the great American novel. The incentive for your dream may be the vision of doing book tours, the notoriety, or simply the fact that teachers praised your written work. However, without being fully connected with your own interests and the intrinsic joy of writing, focusing attention on the image of writing rather than on writing itself is a significant barrier to the creative process.

Many of the teens who seek to play guitar but quickly give it up are similarly focused on the image of being seen playing guitar rather than on the genuine pleasure of playing it. Certainly, seeking recognition and admiration may be a part of your motivation for creative engagement, but unless the creative endeavor you choose to engage in truly resonates with who you are, you cannot expect to be fully present and engaged in it. If you're not fully engaged, then it becomes just a means to reach a goal rather than the goal in itself.

CREATIVITY IS NOT ORDERLY

One of the fantasies we often maintain about creativity is that it is a process that should always be orderly. We observe a dance, hear an orchestral performance, read a short story, or observe a painting and conclude that each was conceived in an orderly manner. We observe the finished product in a brief moment. But what we observe in that moment has been preceded by hours, days, weeks, months, and maybe even years of hard work, false starts, ordering and reordering. The apparently orderly art product we encounter likely involved frustration, joy, sadness, and, most important, devotion. And as we view this "snapshot" of achievement, we all too often believe it followed a predictable path. In spite of this fantasy, much of creativity challenges order and predictability.

We view a brilliant, dramatic film set against the backdrop of three of the world's largest cities, which portrays the complexity and richness of several relationships that span almost two decadess. We experience the story as seamless and continuous. If it is extremely well done, it appears flawless, neither missing scenes nor requiring editing; we are unaware of the camera's artifice. In fact, unless we have specific interests in film production, we are usually not aware of the long and arduous production process at all. Only later, when we happen to encounter an interview with the director, do we become aware that the scenes were filmed entirely out of sequence, an order perhaps determined more by financial considerations, availability of actors and crew, and the weather during filming than any dictates of the characters' journey.

To the degree that we maintain the fantasy that creativity must follow a precise order, we become quick to evaluate our own work and ourselves negatively as failing to match up to the idealized image. In contrast, realistic thought acknowledges that creativity may not follow a specific organized sequence. Much of creativity is a process that involves doing, undoing, and redoing in a sequence that at times may seem completely out of step with our initial intentions. This was one of the most powerful lessons I learned when writing my first two books.

I learned to give myself the freedom to write four to five versions of a chapter; to revise, revise, and revise; and never to feel so overly attached to one version of a sentence that I would not consider an alternative expression. I learned to have the openness to eliminate certain portions, to rearrange their order, and even to cut and redistribute them to other chapters. Giving myself permission to write in this manner empowered me to freely explore my thoughts.

In writing *Healthy Anger: How to Help Children and Teens Manage Their Anger*, I completed close to six hundred pages to form the three-hundred-twenty-five-page book![3] Will I get better? Perhaps. It will certainly be easier to write future books if I do. But at the same time, by allowing myself the freedom not to worry about it, I find the process much more rewarding and the finished product much more to my satisfaction. Through my experiences I became more realistic and more compassionate rather than remaining driven by a child logic that demanded unreasonable adherence to rigid guidelines based on unrealistic ideas about how I should write.

This reality is similarly reflected in the confessions of movie directors who report making four or more hours of a movie before they arrive at the two-hour version that we view when it arrives in theaters. In the filming of the two-hour documentary *My Architect*, the director indicated that he had shot over a hundred hours of film before editing![4] This is truly creative freedom.

In the book *Conversations*, film editor Walter Murch offers clear examples of the creative challenges involved in the making of a movie. The first anecdote (Eleanor Coppola discussing the movie *Apocalypse Now*) addresses creative efforts that never became a part of the finished product. The second offers a glimpse of how unpredictable such efforts can be in influencing the form of the finished product.

> The hundreds of thousands of dollars spent on the set and the cast flown in from France. Now the whole thing will end up as a roll of celluloid in a vault somewhere.[5]

> A good ten days of the material was never filmed. . . . Francis and the production team just ran out of time and money to shoot the entire script. . . . His advice to me was, well let's just cut what we have together and see if we can find a way to compensate for the missing footage.[6]

The creative process does not lend itself to the exercise of full control. Much of the creative process involves alternating periods of focused control and more passive periods of responsiveness to the process.

With whatever medium you work, you need to foster openness to be global in your thoughts and imagination, alternating with moments when you exert focused attention on specific thoughts, images, sensations, movements, or sounds. Through this combination of passive alertness and active exploration, you will discover surprising connections and patterns in words, music, concepts, images, and textures.

When writing, I find myself reserving mental space for novel thoughts to come to me while at the same time providing some structure to my stream of consciousness. In contrast, I am more keenly focused when selecting the most appropriate word or phrase to provide clarity of understanding regarding a novel concept or idea that has emerged in my mental space.

When painting, artists often describe having a general sense of where they are going in their work. They describe moments of being open and more passive to the process and moments of more focused attention on the specific details of their work. Glassblowing is one form of art that calls for the rapid oscillation between letting the medium work itself and taking assertive and focused action to influence it.

A core requirement of creativity is freedom, the ability to both exert will and to be open to influence. Shaun McNiff emphasizes this key component of creativity when he states:

> Truly original expressions can never be planned in advance. Surprise rather than predictable results rule the process in which creations reveal themselves. As creators we try to stay open and receptive to what is moving through and around us.[7]

In this sense creativity is a very individual journey that does not necessarily follow a particularly orderly path.

THERE IS ONLY ONE WAY TO ACHIEVE YOUR CREATIVE GOAL

As a graduate student in psychology I wrote a book to help adolescents cope with the emotional challenges of that tumultuous period in their lives. It included individual as well as group exercises to help teens better understand and manage issues such as dependency, independence, anger, anxiety, jealousy, love, and competition. I carried writing tablets with me wherever I went. If a client at my internship canceled a session, I wrote for an hour. If I had an extra half hour following lunch, I found a quiet place to jot down some ideas. It was a piecemeal project that eventually became a comprehensive program that included a book, a workbook, and audiocassettes. That experience ran against the many images I had of writers who spent entire days at their craft. Clearly, there is more than one way to achieve your creative goal.

Years ago, when I was new to Chicago, I set up a makeshift darkroom in the extremely small bathroom of my one-bedroom apartment. A major component was a half-inch-thick board, two feet by four feet, which I had cut out to fit over the sink. In this confined area, I learned and practiced principles in film development and experienced the same pleasure I would have if I had had a full-scale darkroom.

From reports of the great writers, we hear different scenarios regarding how they practice their craft. J. K. Rowling, author of the Harry Potter series, wrote her first book in a coffee shop.[8] Maya Angelou describes doing her most creative work in a hotel room and doing the editing at home.[9] Many novelists describe going to a secluded oasis in order to protect them from any unnecessary distractions. Dostoevsky is said to have written an entire book in his mind based on notes he kept while serving a prison term in Russia.[10] We would be a world very lacking in progress and rich culture if we were forced to rely on only one setting to fully access our creative genius.

Some artists claim they need a large space to paint. This is certainly understandable in terms of needing distance to step back to observe one's art, being able to manage the chemical fumes that paints emit, and the overall feng shui essential to promote openness. At the same time, too often we maintain the fantasy that we can only create if our external surroundings are ideal—as if there is only one setting that can entice a visit from the creative muse.

One client I worked with prided herself on writing only two hours per day and went on to receive national recognition for each of the three books she wrote over an eight-year period. In contrast, I have worked with individuals who have berated themselves for only writing five hours per day.

A musician reported doing his best work in the late evening and at night. Another indicated he was most inspired in the early morning hours. As will be emphasized in chapter 15, knowing yourself, your energy levels, your moods, and your capacity for concentration will greatly determine your capacity to be fully engaged with the creative process. Clearly, tuning into your individual preferences will again highlight that there is more than one approach to use when being creative.

WHAT YOU CREATE IS YOUR BEST APPROXIMATION OF WHAT YOU HOPE TO ACHIEVE

Certain creative ventures involve the formation of concrete representations of what originally were just images, thoughts, or sounds experienced in the inner play space of your mind. They are sorted through, juxtaposed, and arranged several times over as you form a final perception. When you achieve a perfect match between what you perceive and what you create, you experience a sense of exaltation accompanied by closure. However, you may not always achieve a real sense of completion with what you create. You may make what you consider to be the last brush stroke on a painting and before the paint dries think of an additional touch you could add. You may likewise decide on a master plan to redecorate a living room and, upon revisiting a fabric store, choose to pursue an entirely different direction after noticing a pattern and material that resonates much more intensely with what you feel is "right" for the room.

One of my clients described feeling tremendous relief about giving one of his paintings to a friend. He had been working on that painting for over a year, had made ongoing revisions during that time, and never felt quite satisfied that it was fully finished. "Each time I walked past it, I felt something needed to be added or deleted. Now it is on my friend's wall and I have been able to let go of it."

I once signed a book contract in the morning and that same evening began to think of rearranging the chapters. Upon receiving the first copy from the publisher, I thought of several very relevant points I could have addressed that would have made it more complete. This continued to occur in the months following its promotion.

Your creative efforts are part of an ongoing process. They reflect only a snapshot of who you are, taken at a distinct moment in time. As such, they are markers on your path of creativity. The painting you do this month will reflect your self at this moment in time. All of what you bring to this distinct moment will then pass but will continue to influence you in the future. You sometimes need to remind yourself to let go of what you create. And only by doing so will you make room for the next project. This is an especially difficult challenge when you maintain the fantasy that you should experience an absolute sense of closure at every stage of your creative venture.

A "BIG BANG" THEORY

No, I am not referring to the theory of the creation of the universe. Rather, I refer here to the fantasy that major creative insights arise suddenly and with little effort. In part, this fantasy may be supported by certain rare stories associated with the works of the great creators. For example, it is said that Mozart awoke one morning with an entire symphony in his mind that he simply had to transpose onto music sheets.[11] Similar stories have described poets who were greeted at the break of dawn with complete poems delivered by their dreams.[12] In reality, creativity requires extensive thought and immersion in the details of the medium long before you are rewarded with the golden kernels of insight or inspiration.

Such insights are the product of the active ongoing collaboration of your unconscious and conscious minds. Consciously choosing to value and embrace novelty and to remain open and experimental keeps you receptive to all that you encounter in both your external and your internal worlds. By maintaining this perspective, you make yourself ready to notice and embrace the inspiration when it arrives. At the same time, by practicing this attitude you nurture your unconscious and give it permission and encouragement to do its magic. You exercise your unconscious mind by allowing its primal logic to make connections in ways your conscious mind alone could not fathom. Your task, then, is to use your conscious mind to order and make meaningful the daring discoveries and insights provided by your unconscious.

STAYING FOCUSED

Studies of creativity suggest that while rewards may foster your creativity, in most cases they interfere with your real capacity to be flexible and creative. More specifically, it appears that when extrinsic rewards tap into the intrinsic motivations for creating, they can foster effective creative engagement.[13] However, the drive to obtain rewards can often put into motion judgments and expectations that prematurely constrict your creative path and the capacity to think in ways that foster creative insight. Obsessing about financial rewards or public attention may provide some incentive for your creativity, but becoming overly obsessed with these interferes with the creative process.

In the movie *Swimming Upstream*, young Toni Fingleton, an Australian swimmer, struggles to win his father's approval.[14] He is driven less by his love of the sport than by his powerful desire to obtain recognition from his father. Ultimately, he made it to the Olympics, taking second place in his event. Although he achieved his goal in athletics, he did not obtain the recognition he so strongly desired. He then turned his back on his chance to go to the

Olympics for a second time and instead followed his dream to go to Harvard and escape the tension of his youth. The movie ends by showing him achieving his best time ever while swimming in a pool at Harvard. It is ironic that only after he let go of his obsession with getting his father's recognition was he really free enough to achieve his best.

There are times, however, when seeking the reward should very much influence your creative direction. In my work as chairperson on the dissertation committees for psychology students enrolled in a doctoral program, I have had firsthand experience of this. The goal of these doctoral students is to complete the program. Too often a graduate student would present a topic of research that would have demanded several years to complete. Understandably, these students yearned to make a significant contribution in the field and to pursue a subject about which they experienced great passion. It is the one role I have occupied in which I suggested strong limits on such creativity. The deadlines of the program and the reality that graduating is the priority dictated my recommendations that they delay the pursuit of their creative passions in order to graduate. I encouraged them to instead select meaningful topics that were not so overwhelming that they would ultimately interfere with their academic progress. I explained to them that they would be able to pursue their more ambitious projects once they had graduated and were free of the program's rigid deadlines.

While fantasies may at times contribute to our dreams, it is only when we let them go that we become more engaged and present in fulfilling them.

*** FOR FURTHER EXPLORATION ***

1. Based on reading this chapter, can you identify any fantasies you have regarding your creativity?
2. To what degree does your perfectionism interfere with your creativity?
3. How might your fantasies actually inhibit your openness during distinct moments of creativity?
4. What are your preconceived notions about the orderliness of your creativity? What are your notions about the physical setting for your creativity?
5. To what degree do you hold on to expectations that every aspect of creativity should be equally enjoyable and rewarding?

6. What aspects of being creative do you least enjoy? What do you do to motivate yourself to effectively manage them?

REFLECTIONS

Dreams pass into the reality of action. From the actions stems the dream again; and this interdependence produces the highest form of living.—Anais Nin

There is always the risk of ending up with something you have not intended —but isn't that the best part?—Alev Gide

Once I started working with the Polaroid, I would take a shot and if that shot was good, then I'd move the model and change the lighting or whatever . . . slowly sneaking up on what I wanted rather than having to predetermine what it was.—Chuck Close

A man is not old until regrets take the place of his dreams.—John Barrymore

It is worth mentioning, for future reference, that the creative power which bubbles so pleasantly in beginning a new book quiets down after a time, and one goes on more steadily. Doubts creep in. Then one becomes resigned. Determination not to give in, and the sense of an impending shape keeps one at it more than anything.—Virginia Woolf

NOTES

1. David Henry Feldman, "The Development of Creativity," in *Handbook of Creativity*, ed. Robert J. Sternberg (New York: Cambridge University Press, 1999).

2. Martin E. P. Seligman, *Authentic Happiness* (New York: Free Press, 2002).

3. Bernard Golden, *Healthy Anger: How to Help Children and Teens Manage Their Anger* (New York: Oxford University Press, 2003).

4. *My Architect*, DVD, directed by Nathaniel Kahn (New York: New Yorker Films, 2003).

5. Michael Ondaatje, *The Conversations: Walter Murch and the Art of Editing Film* (New York: Knopf, 2004), p. 137.

6. Ibid., p. 142.

7. Shaun McNiff, *Trust the Process: An Artist's Guide to Letting Go* (Boston: Shambhala, 1998), p. 60.

8. Connie Ann Kirk, *J. K. Rowling: A Biography (Unauthorized Edition)* (Westport, CT: Greenwood, 2003).

9. Frank Barron, Alfonso Montuori, and Anthea Barron, *Creators on Creating* (New York: Putnam's Sons, 1997).

10. Anthony Storr, *Solitude: A Return to the Self* (New York: Free Press, 1998).

11. Brewster Ghiselin, *The Creative Process* (Los Angeles: University of California Press, 1985).

12. Ibid.

13. Mary Ann Collins and Teresa M. Amabile, "Motivation and Creativity," in Sternberg, *Handbook of Creativity.*

14. *Swimming Upstream*, DVD, directed by Russell Mulcahy (Century City, CA: MGM, 2005).

Chapter 9

NO ONE IS GOING TO TELL ME WHAT TO DO— INCLUDING MYSELF

A ny creative endeavor requires discipline and an investment of time, thoughts, emotions, and money. For some, the challenge in making this commitment is hampered by conflicts regarding authority, dependency, and an intense desire for autonomy. Specifically, past difficulties with authority associated with resentment regarding imposed structure or limitations may contribute to undermine your capacity for maintaining the self-discipline essential for creativity. The core issue of this inhibiting theme revolves around child logic and conflicts regarding autonomy, dependency, and their impact on self-discipline.

AUTONOMY VERSUS DEPENDENCY

This interpersonal conflict with others can be internalized to the degree that one develops resentment and soon becomes opposed to following defined guidelines or expectations even when they are self-imposed. The ongoing sense of being controlled by these expectations becomes embedded in the form of child logic expressed as "No one is going to tell me what to do— including myself."

Under the influence of this inhibiting theme, you may even experience your choice to create as not really being your own but, rather, as a reaction to what others expect of you. Such conflict reflects a failure to genuinely "own" one's choice as being one's choice. This dilemma evolves and is most evidenced during adolescence. It is a response by some teens to balancing the desire for independence with healthy dependence, a major developmental task of adolescence.

Some children arrive at this stage of development with an identity and sense of self that is secure enough to welcome and effectively manage increased independence. They sufficiently trust themselves to become increasingly autonomous while at the same time balancing their needs for healthy nurturance, encouragement, and support in facing the challenges of their age. Consistent with this balance, they can respond positively to those limitations and structures imposed by others, whether at home, in school, or in the community. Similarly, they are able to establish goals for themselves and increasingly adhere to the self-discipline essential to attain them.

In contrast, other children reach this stage unprepared to effectively meet the demands of this task. Their difficulties are reflected in a variety of ways. Driven by insecurity and dependency, and a lack of a solid identity, some may become compliant with the demands and expectations of others. In doing so, their identities form around the satisfaction of needs, desires, and even dreams of others who are important to them. As described previously, such compliance further impedes their abilities to connect with themselves.

Some children reach this stage of development with an intense desire to be independent, though with minimal awareness of who they are. In dealing with this dilemma, many adopt a "negative identity."[1] Identified by noted psychologist Erik Erikson, this solution involves rebellion and the development of an identity that is contrary to what others desire, expect, or suggest. In the extreme, it is an identity based on identification with roles that have been presented as the most undesirable (i.e., those behaviors and attitudes that reflect the antithesis of what parents and other authority figures might desire). Although not always this severe, it is an identity based on deeply felt opposition to identify with others. It is, at the same time, an identity that is developed in order to ward off dependency needs. Through this resolution, teens can experience themselves as being independent. In reality, however, their identities are very much defined by their need to demonstrate their resistance to the influence of others.

Such a mode of self-identification is an unsuccessful attempt to deal with the difficult questions "Who am I?" and "Who do I want to be?" It is an identity driven by the perspective reflected in the internalized guideline, "I do not know what I want or who I am, but I sure don't want to be like you!" In their misguided efforts to feel independent, such teens brace themselves against the influence of others, even when a part of them finds a particular trait, thought, behavior, or attitude to be appealing.

Unfortunately, this identity-formation strategy leaves one both overly sensitive to feeling controlled and desperate to maintain control in relation to others. The intense need to feel free and be spontaneous competes with and overrides the drive to engage in a creative venture. Resentment of discipline arises, even when self-imposed, because a commitment to a sustained creative venture leads those with this inhibiting theme to reexperience the feeling of being stifled. Those who embrace this identity become blocked in the exploration and pursuit of their unique abilities and desires. As a result, they miss the opportunity to become genuinely connected with what is truly meaningful for them. At the same time, they distract themselves from the anxiety of taking a more active and assertive role in choosing who they wish to be.

Resentment associated with this inhibiting theme is often related to feelings of deprivation. You may feel deprived when you choose to be creative. Even if you haven't formed a negative identity, you may still feel a sense of deprivation when pursuing a creative goal, as when you must sacrifice spending time with friends to instead practice a musical instrument or edit a poem. You may resent the financial investment that is involved in pursuing watercolor painting or taking classes to prepare yourself to switch careers. You may also feel deprived in pursuing a single creative interest at the expense of creative interests in other areas. As a writer, for example, I have often felt restrained from pursuing photography.

For those with child logic that echoes this conflict, commitment is experienced as a rigid imposition rather than as an outgrowth of one's free choice. Strongly associated with this conflict is the internal dialogue, "I do not want to do what I do not want to do!" This dilemma is based on the distorted perspective that true freedom rests on being able to live spontaneously and on being completely independent of others. Those who suffer from this conflict often experience the same negative mind-body states whether they're trying to adhere to their own self-discipline or others are imposing discipline upon them.

THE DRIVE TO BE INDEPENDENT AND HOW IT IMPACTS CREATIVITY

To a great extent, this conflict also rests on the drive to be completely independent in spite of the fact that much of creativity depends on the input of others. In writing this book, I have had input from colleagues, friends, family, clients, writers on psychology and creativity, and artists and other creative people. I have had experiences with both mentors and students that have further contributed to my thoughts regarding the creative venture. Even fictional characters in books and movies have inspired my thinking. In addition, my publisher and agent provided feedback regarding the initial proposal that helped push me further to clarify what it was I really wanted to express. While I myself have written this book, all of these individuals have contributed to the form and content of this creative venture.

To the degree that you resent or feel threatened by recognizing and acknowledging the ideas of others, you close yourself off from the potential of your own creativity. In doing so, you constrict the boundaries of your creative vision and simultaneously become closed to the support, encouragement, and expansion that others provide.

The extreme need to experience yourself as independent often stems from a perspective that acceptance of help or feedback reflects weakness or even inadequacy. It is an attitude that derives from child logic and, when extreme, may even arouse shame.

Similarly, being obsessed with feeling independent can cause you to question the originality of your thoughts, emotions, or actions. It is the type of theme that leads you to say, "Why bother? This has been done before." When dominated by this conflict, you may believe that your creative efforts have to be absolutely unique in comparison to any work previously accomplished. Yet even the great creators were inspired and influenced by the work of others. Any creative venture, whether writing, composing or playing music, choreographing dance, taking photographs, or developing a new medicine, is nourished by work that came before.

While an intense need to be independent can negatively impact your openness to creativity, it is by emphasizing your independence of thought and action that you challenge the existing theory and practice of your particular domain of interest. Openness to creativity is like living on the edge of a pack. It is from this vantage point that you have the greatest exposure to what is novel and the broadest view of all that surrounds the pack. At the edge, you are also most vulnerable to exposure and to the potential hazards that it can bring. Such a position, as in any pack, also has the greatest potential to influence the direction that the group takes.

THE NEED FOR CONTROL AS A BLOCK TO INSPIRATION

The need for control can impede your capacity to be open to inspiration, whether it comes from outside yourself or from the depths of your unconsciousness. It leaves you closed and defensive toward novelty, ambiguity, and the acceptance of complex and multiple perspectives; the very things that allow for maximum creative inspiration. To the degree that you harbor fear and anxiety about being influenced or controlled by others, you become closed to observing, reflecting upon, and integrating the details of your world into your thought processes. By maintaining this attitude, you may become closed to the study of the history, theory, or skills that are part of the domain of your identified passion. In doing so, you invariably reduce your potential for inspiration.

The aversion to being influenced by others may similarly impede your access to your unconscious. When working in alliance, your conscious mind fosters openness and flexibility that is accepting of the novel and surprising combinations of thought patterns produced by your unconscious. As indicated earlier, the best creativity requires collaboration between your conscious and unconscious minds. In contrast, when you maintain an intense need to feel that you're in total control, you remain guarded against the thoughts and emotions you may experience both on conscious and deeper unconscious levels. You become prone to filter, question, or outright reject inspiration. In effect, your child logic stands guard at the threshold of awareness in order to keep you safe. Certainly, this is to some extent necessary, as it keeps you from being subjected in an ongoing manner to the more fluid and primal thinking of your unconscious. However, your capacity to make use of the gifts of inspiration from your unconscious rests on your capacity to be sufficiently comfortable with them.

In addition, by being closed you fail to trust your spontaneity. Some of the most productive creations have evolved from mistakes. It is in your freedom to view such events as more than distractions. You can choose to view a mistake as a new and intriguing possibility of what could be. While a perfectionist may be closed to integrating mistakes into his work because of a sense of inadequacy or fear of losing control, you can embrace your errors, consider them, and allow yourself to make use of the new directions they open.

Clients in my clinical practice often seem upset that work on their life challenges is often accompanied by an escalation in the frequency of their nightly dreams. I suggest to them that it is a sign of their progress that they dream more frequently. Such dreams tend to link the unconscious with the conscious, allowing them to become more open to look at conflicts, emotions, and thoughts that were previously too unsettling to consider.

So it is with the creative process. Fears of losing control prevent you from being receptive to inspiration both from without and from within.

A JOINT VENTURE

Much of creativity is a joint venture. Even the scientist is rarely a lone maverick working in isolation. The screenwriter works with the producer who works with the director who brings out the best from the actors while remaining surprised by the creative insights and improvised characteristics they bring to their respective roles. Each of the participants is influenced by and influences the others. And when their talents have been put on film, it is the editor who makes the major contribution of finalizing the product of this dance of creativity.

Mihaly Csikszentmihalyi emphasizes that creativity of the kind reflected by the world's greatest creators is an outgrowth of the influences of many sources and not simply the achievement of an individual. He maintains the view that such creativity is always dependent on "a culture that contains symbolic rules, a person who brings novelty into the symbolic domain, and a field of experts who recognize and validate the innovation."[2]

Thus, the culture develops the tools, theory, and guidelines for working within a particular creative domain and with a particular medium. The individual then works creatively within that domain. The individual then exposes his or her work to members of an audience who receive, review, and transmit it. In some cases, expert reviewers are the first members of the audience to consider new creative works, though, thankfully, all creativity does not have to undergo such strict review.

THE RIGHT MOOD

Many of us wait until we are in the right mood before we act on our creative desires. To some extent, this stance toward creativity reflects the similar themes of opposition previously described. It is often a challenge to do something when you are not especially in the mood to do it. However, this inhibiting theme clearly undermines creativity when it is an ingrained and frequent response to the challenges creativity presents. Our lives would be an unbelievably chaotic experience of emotions and activities if we chose to take certain actions only when we were completely in the mood to do so. "Oh, well, I'm really not in the mood to walk the dog. Oh, and that class I'm scheduled to teach today—it's just too nice outside. I'll go for a walk instead. And really, there's a great movie premiering tonight; so what if tomorrow is the deadline to submit my completed manuscript?"

Listening to and considering your mood when choosing how to spend time contributes to the excitement of life and to the creative process. In fact, many of the strategies presented in the third part of this book focus on helping foster your optimal mood for creative engagement. But rigidly prioritizing your changing moods over the discipline necessary to produce results in an attempt to feel free and spontaneous reflects a damaging subservience to your emotions. Further, it leaves you dependent on external factors that may or may not push you into the "right" mood for creative engagement, fostering an attitude of passive dependence derived from child logic that states, "I want to do only those things that I want to do when I want to do them and for only as long as I want to do them." Unfortunately, most successful creativity requires discipline rather than passive waiting for the calling of the muse. It is sad to think of all of the creativity that has remained dormant because a favorable mood never arrived.

Peter, a client I worked with, indicated an unwillingness to commit in advance to spending several hours of his weekend painting. Although he expressed great pleasure in painting, he rationalized his unwillingness to schedule painting time, saying, "How could I plan to paint ahead of time? I don't know what mood I will be in until the weekend?" When possessed by these thoughts, even the immense pleasure he experienced while painting could not alter his attitude. He could not help seeing himself as being completely at the mercy of his mood.

Your mood is your mind-body set, your predisposition at a given moment. It emanates from your genetics and personal history; from the impression of recent events in your life and in your environment; and from conditions such as the time of day, your nutrition, and how much sleep you got the night before. Decisively willing yourself to act in spite of your mood is a bold assertion of free will.

Kim offers another example of how not being in the right mood can interfere with creative commitment. She decided to rearrange her living room one weekend, a project she had been contemplating for some time. After spending a couple hours reorganizing the furniture, lamps, and other larger elements in the room, she came to an abrupt halt. She sat down for a while and experienced great satisfaction in looking over what she had accomplished. At that distinct moment, she was suddenly overcome with a feeling of "having had enough." She had rearranged the major furnishings but had failed to complete the task of arranging the many different accessories she had placed in a box several months previous. Upon recalling that moment, Kim described an overwhelming feeling of boredom. Her attention had been derailed and shifted to other concerns. She gave up on the project, promising herself that she would complete the living room within a few days.

In reflecting on the experience of that distinct moment when she suddenly lost her focus, she recalled stopping to admire her work and feeling great pleasure in the new arrangement. But she also recognized that when she anticipated putting the accessories in place she became bored and was suddenly overcome by a state of emotional and physical fatigue. She lost patience with the task and perceived it as being tedious. She recalled a lifelong expectation of her child logic that stated, "I should not have to do things that are not fun to do!"

A rebellious attitude is in fact a highly valuable asset for embracing your creative genius. Your capacity to rebel helps you to resist the temptation to see things in conventional ways instead of seeing possibilities for reordering and remaking meaning. Whether you challenge convention in art, music, dance, writing, photography, or scientific pursuit, a rebellious attitude buoys your capacity to view difference and similarity, increasing your flexibility of vision. It is only when your rebellious attitude is held hostage by rigidly maintained parameters imposed by child logic that you become constricted in your freedom to access, accept, and embrace your creative genius.

*** FOR FURTHER EXPLORATION ***

1. Are you aware of having resisted your attempts at self-discipline?
2. Do you have any sense that when you cringe at doing what you are not in the mood to do you are revisiting earlier experiences of having

been told what to do by others? Are you aware of your self-talk when experiencing this reaction?

3. How flexible are you in balancing your openness to healthy dependence and independence?

4. How open are you to the thoughts or opinions of others? Are there certain situations when you are more receptive to others' feedback? If so, what allows you to be more open?

5. To what degree do you resent being told what to do by others and by yourself?

6. Do you find yourself testing your own limits regarding self-discipline? Do you promise yourself that you'll devote time to an interest only to make apologies or excuses later on for failing to manage the tension of that commitment?

8. Have there been situations when you pursued your creative venture even though you were not in the mood? What impact did your engagement have on your mood?

9. Have you had experiences of actively working on creative projects with groups of individuals? Describe your self-talk in such contexts.

REFLECTIONS

The person who tries to live alone will not succeed as a human being. His heart withers if it does not answer another heart. His mind shrinks away if he hears only echoes of his own thoughts and finds no other inspiration.—Pearl S. Buck

Obstinacy is will asserting itself without being able to justify itself. It is persistence without a reasonable motive. It is the tenacity of self-love substituted for that of reason and conscience.—Henri Frederic Amiel

All of us, at certain moments of our lives, need to take advice and to receive help from other people.—Alexis Carrel

Freedom is not merely the opportunity to do as one pleases; neither is it merely the opportunity to choose between set alternatives. Freedom is, first of all, the chance to formulate the available choices, to argue over them— and then, the opportunity to choose.—C. Wright Mills

NOTES

1. Erik H. Erikson, "The Problem of Ego Identity," in *The Psychology of Adolescence*, ed. Aaron H. Esman (Madison, CT: International Universities Press, 1975).

2. Mihaly Csikszentmihalyi, *Creativity: Flow and the Psychology of Invention* (New York: Harper Perennial, 1997), p. 6.

Chapter 10

I DO NOT WANT TO DO IT ALONE

While some creative ventures involve active collaboration with others, much of creativity requires that you retreat in solitude. It demands that you feel physically and emotionally comfortable being alone for extended periods of time. Ultimately, it calls for the capacity to experience deep pleasure in your own company. While this is often true of short-lived creative endeavors, it is most essential for sustained creativity.

I am not suggesting that truly being creative necessitates a return to Walden Pond, but many forms of being creative require that you temporarily turn your back on your desire for social connection. The ability to think about, research, or actually engage in your creative passion requires that you overcome the anxiety of isolation. It demands that you challenge the child logic that impedes your ability to freely engage the adventure within your imagination.

While some of us are distracted from creating by our intense desires to be with others, some of the most creative individuals are prolific in their craft because they seem to have less of a need for social connection. In the film *Andy Goldsworthy's Rivers and Tides*, the artist reveals that while he dearly loves his family, many of the most deeply rewarding moments of his life are when he is at work in solitude.[1] This is clearly evident in this stunning visual recording of his thinking and of the creations he has made from the materials nature has provided, including arrangements of rock, twigs, leaves, soil, and water.

Whether planning to design a room, learning to play an instrument, developing one's skills in painting, or creating a marketing plan for a new business, the ability to comfortably be alone is essential for the creative process. For many, however, such solitude brings with it an uncomfortable mind-body set that challenges creative genius. A variety of personal, social, and cultural factors contribute to the development of this undermining inhibiting reaction.

DEPENDENCY AND CONNECTION

A major challenge to being alone, especially throughout the creative process, is a deep sense of dependency on others for support, encouragement, and specific guidance. Such dependency is reflected in self-talk such as the following:

"I need someone to assure me that I am on the right track."
"I want someone else to do it for me."
"I want someone to tell me what to do."
"I want someone to support me through every step of the process."

To a great extent, these needs are driven by a lack of confidence in one's ideas, strivings, and actions. Such self-doubt fosters a strong need for ongoing assurance and support, especially during the tension-provoking moments of challenge that occur throughout the creative process.

As emphasized throughout this book, the creative process is always accompanied by some degree of inner tension. As such, it is natural that you may periodically seek feedback when engaged in a creative venture. This inhibiting theme refers to a more powerfully distracting force that renders you overly reliant on others to help you sufficiently calm the fears and insecurities you confront throughout the creative process.

Gary was a high school freshman who was paralyzed by his insecurities when required to complete an English composition. He sheepishly admitted that, when doing this assignment, he was compelled to contact his girlfriend in order to obtain feedback after completing each paragraph of the paper. This same insecurity is a part of the child logic that can block creative movement at any age.

Elaine, a woman in her thirties, obsessed for two years about how best to decorate her living room. Piled high in a corner of that room were magazines, paint chips, carpet samples, and fabric swatches she had accumulated during her period of research. Her indecision stemmed from a lack of trust in herself and an underlying need to be reassured that she would make the right decisions. She finally gave up and contacted an interior decorator.

A writer reworks the plot to his story over and over again depending on the feedback he gets from friends, relatives, neighbors, or publishers. This is another example of the paralysis that can occur as a result of perfectionism combined with a need to have reassurance from others. Engaged in the distinct moment of creativity, it is as if you are once again an insecure child seeking your parents' approval and assurance. "Mommy, what color should I use?" "Is this good?" "What do you think I should do here?" You may not have asked these questions for decades, but even as an adult the haunting echoes of the mind-body states associated with them can still block your creative movements.

Self-doubt and the need for approval can exert their influence at any point of the creative process. They can blur your vision, preventing you from recognizing your passion. In contrast, you may be able to identify what excites you only to fall victim to self-doubt during distinct moments of decision making. Perfectionism may only buoy the lack of self-trust that heightens the need for assurance. Sometimes, such indecision stems from the fear that in making certain choices you will close doors to alternative opportunities. Any of these situations may compel you to seek direction or assurance from others.

A personal history of having relied on others to make important decisions on your behalf can contribute to this inhibiting theme. Through such interactions, you develop a sense of "learned helplessness," a deeply embedded sense of feeling inadequate to meet specific challenges.[2] The child or teen who was helped for endless hours by a parent when doing homework may become the adult who is unwittingly waiting for someone else to come along to goad him on throughout his creative journey.

THE CHALLENGE OF SOLITUDE

While the tension of self-doubt regarding decision making is one factor that thwarts creative engagement, it is often the difficulty in effectively managing the tension of solitude itself that leads many to abandon creative longings. Being alone is especially difficult if doing so forces you to revisit mind-body discomfort that taps into your deepest sense of need for internal safety and security.

According to Donald Winnicott, an expert on parent-child attachment, your capacity to be alone is very much influenced by the nature of the attachment you had with significant caretakers in your early years.[3] He contends that in order to be comfortable being alone, you need to have had a healthy attachment to caretakers who were sufficiently attentive to your needs and dependable in providing you an overall sense of security. Furthermore, the degree to which you feel comfortable being alone is very much influenced by experiences of feeling secure and comfortable playing alone in the presence of those caretakers. That is, a child who can more fully engage in play by himself has had experiences in which he had the full security of knowing that a protective caretaker was close at hand. A part of this inner tranquility rests on knowing that even when your caretaker is out of sight you can depend on her to come to your aid when needed.

Through this form of attachment you internalize a sufficient level of the comfort, security, and trust needed to both enjoy and manage solitude. An adequate history of such attachment helps you to become an adult who not only tolerates but also embraces being alone. In addition, these experiences help you to experience yourself as being stable and grounded. As suggested by psychiatrist Anthony Storr, it is in the context of this mind-body state that "the capacity to be alone thus becomes linked with self-discovery and self-realization; with becoming aware of one's deepest needs, feelings, and impulses."[4]

In contrast, solitude may become associated with anxiety when patterns of early attachment are characterized by tension related to the emotional and physical unavailability or undependability of caretakers. Such tension is related to your inability to calm yourself as well as the experience of loss, abandonment, rejection, and even emptiness triggered by solitude.

Similarly, attachment that is too intrusive, overbearing, or overly controlling may rob you of the confidence essential to trust yourself when alone. As a consequence, when you engage in solitude as an adult, you may revisit through your child logic that same sense of loss, abandonment, insecurity, rejection, or even emptiness you experienced in early childhood.

When you are not preoccupied with others and by the demands of your surroundings, you are left with a potential vacuum in your awareness. In the absence of stimulation from all that you encounter throughout the day, you may experience great challenge in dealing with the silence and stillness of solitude. It is no wonder that we bring into our homes pieces of that outside world in the form of television, radio, or music to help mute the intensity of the silence.

To a great extent, solitude is the playground for your child logic. Recognizing the absence of preoccupation, your child logic can demand attention. As if by default, any automatic reactions anchored in your past seem to surface during such solitude. Mind-body states surrounding issues of self-worth, self-trust, being alone, or feeling alone may first capture your attention at the visceral level in the form of a heightened level of tension. This may give rise to an undercurrent of self-talk that you may or may not notice. Some people may simply experience anxiety, while others recognize the experience as a deeply felt sadness. Some may experience feelings of abandonment, while others feel overwhelmed by a barrage of self-critical voices rushing in to fill the void. If you have had any significant issues that have impacted you in these areas and that have not been sufficiently addressed, times of solitude are when they demand your attention.

Over the many years I've been involved in clinical practice, I've heard clients describe the range of strategies used to deal with individual reactions to solitude. While those who live alone may be forced to confront these reactions more frequently, even those who live with others may have the same reactions when they find themselves in solitude. For example, some describe immediately turning the television on upon their return to an empty home. Others have described a realization that working long hours and socializing after work was a way to avoid this experience. I remember one client indicating that he avoided turning on the lights in the living room and headed straight for the bedroom so that he would not have to confront the intensity of solitude that that room evoked. Some who have used alcohol as a distraction to this discomfort report that the first half hour home was the major hurdle. If they became engrossed in some activity, they would be able to ward off their cravings for a drink.

Solitude also presents you with a wider variety of choices in terms of how you want to direct your attention. When in the presence of others, your attention is more easily pulled in one direction or another. In contrast, solitude reminds you of your freedom to take charge and direct your attention. It is helpful to remember that child logic is both the source of many of your negative emotions and the part of you that can help fuel your curiosity and strivings to be creative.

Self-reflection, self-discovery, and self-realization occur in the context of solitude. It is in this context that you can choose to more fully focus your attention on identifying and recognizing your deepest needs, feelings, and longings. It is in solitude that you can more clearly choose to access, recognize, and express your creative spirit. Regarding solitude, Storr further states that

> the creative person is constantly seeking to discover himself, to remodel his own identity, and to find meaning in the universe by means of what he creates. He finds this to be a valuable integrating process which, like meditation or prayer, has little to do with other people, but which has its own separate validity. His most significant moments are those in which he attains some new insight, or makes some new discovery; and these moments are chiefly, if not invariably, those in which he is alone.[5]

When embracing creativity, we explore unknown territory, we challenge convention, we surprise ourselves, and we come into full contact with our deepest fears as well as with our desires for acceptance. And as we push ourselves to expand the boundaries of our authenticity, we are challenged by the overly protective critical voices that urge us to retreat. It is often when solitude serves as a catalyst to arouse these voices that internal conflict becomes so uncomfortable that we choose to abandon creative engagement.

Clearly, our comfort or discomfort with solitude is greatly influenced by our unique personal histories. At the same time, there are also many forces in our culture that only reinforce our tendencies toward avoidance of solitude.

CHALLENGES TO SOLITUDE

Regardless of your developmental predisposition toward the management of solitude, powerful social and cultural forces challenge your efforts to fully embrace and appreciate being alone. Throughout your development, parents, teachers, preachers, peers, and the culture at large have exerted profound influences that may have functioned to thwart your capacity to turn inward. Just as you carry your child logic from the past, the wider culture directly and indirectly attempts to persuade you against choosing solitude. On one level, Western culture idealizes and glorifies the individual spirit. However, the culture simultaneously presents direct and indirect messages that threaten individuality and discourage the embrace of solitude.

Much of the media focuses on the rewards of relationships. While it addresses our needs to feel unique, marketing more frequently plays on our needs for acceptance and belonging. It emphasizes that happiness can be achieved by feeling that you are part of a relationship or a group. It further communicates that such happiness is dependent upon financial growth and the accumulation of specific possessions. Much of such marketing is geared to raise your interest and curiosity toward things rather than toward ideas or creativity.

In sum, direct and indirect messages communicate to us that seeking happiness in solitude is somehow less relevant, less meaningful, and perhaps even a reflection of eccentricity. Many seem to have accepted the notion that spending a great deal of time alone is only a reaction to fears, anxieties, and insecurities about relating to others. While these factors may contribute to some people's solitude-seeking behavior, it is not an accurate description of all people who are creative.

To a large extent our educational systems have also contributed to stifling creativity by discouraging attention to individuality in thought and in action. Educators and policymakers have increasingly focused on teaching marketable skills rather than on supporting the pursuit of individual uniqueness, genuine self-reflection, and learning for the sake of learning. In doing so, they have predominantly focused on the needs of the group rather than on those of the individual. Furthermore, such an educational model emphasizes the need to fit in with others rather than the adventure of creative exploration, whether individually or in groups.

In the conflict between the needs of society and those of the individual, educational systems seem to prioritize social needs to the degree that even creativity to meet those needs may be stifled. This is further emphasized by educational systems that predominantly focus on the need to pass standardized tests rather than including an emphasis on living authentically and creatively. Certainly, there are some systems that are progressive, but these constitute a relatively small percentage of schools.

In recent years, many corporations have similarly developed cultures that slight the creativity of individuals, focusing instead on the bottom line. Taking fewer risks, staying with the familiar, and addressing the common needs of the largest number of people become the guidelines of corporate decision making. It is as if we, as a community, have collectively adopted the inhibiting standards of our child logic.

In *Creators on Creating*, molecular biologist Kary Mullis details how one administrator gave him "free rein" to go ahead and "play" in the lab. As soon as he achieved a significant finding, other administrators stepped in with a laundry list of guidelines for how he should continue his experiments. Focusing primarily on the most immediately rewarding of his creative insights, the administrators undermined his freedom to create.[6]

While we enjoy many advantages as a result of advances in technology, some have moved us in directions that emphasize being connected with others at the expense of equally valuable solitude. Whether by using the Internet or a cell phone, we are increasingly supported and rewarded for sharing our thoughts with others with little encouragement to take time to foster connection with ourselves. Instruments like MP3s soothe us with music so as to dilute the full experience and anxiety of self-reflection and solitude.

Even psychology has predominantly focused on the capacity for healthy and meaningful relationships as evidence of sound mental health. In doing so, it has neglected to pay heed to the capacity for solitude as an equally valid measure of psychological well-being.

THE SPECIFIC CHALLENGE OF SOLITUDE AND CREATIVITY

In a culture that increasingly emphasizes conformity, being competitive, and being informed, seeking solitude requires tremendous inner strength. It is no wonder that when we are alone, many of us experience feeling lonely. We experience a level of tension that reflects a sense of isolation, if not outright rejection or abandonment.

While creativity can involve focusing on a very specific short-term goal, much of creativity involves learning the specific facts, theories, and skills regarding a given domain. In learning to sketch, for example, you have to sit with pencils and observe and record the different shades the pencils produce. You have to take each pencil and move it at different angles as you sense how it feels in your hand and how it moves across the paper. Further, you may wish to explore the theory of color and the attitudes and techniques of the masters who have preceded you. Research, education, and experimentation are all inherent aspects of sustained creativity. Each very heavily depends on your ability to sit in solitude for extended periods of time.

SOLITUDE AND THE FEAR OF THE NOVEL

The creative venture brings with it the anxiety of confronting new ideas, exploring your internal terrain, and identifying how you feel about the subject you are pursuing. Facing this challenge may lead you to feel childlike. It is the experience of first-time engagement in an area of creativity that is unfamiliar to you. This childlike feeling arises because, as you engage in your creative efforts, you may literally be revisiting the same awe and excitement that you experienced as a child.

You may feel childlike in your attempts because of your lack of experience and familiarity with the medium. As a result, you are forced to revisit in solitude a range of mind-body states that are associated with your discomfort with what is novel. The attitudes you have developed through your cumulative experiences of confronting the unfamiliar resurface during every encounter with what you perceive as novel. This tension may be associated with being alone and may force you to retreat into distraction rather than focus on the excitement of the process.

The process of learning new skills and exploring new ideas always proceeds in this direction. You may remember having had training wheels on your first bicycle and a parent who supported you as you rode it. Eventually you graduated to riding the bike without training wheels and without a parent watching over you. However, when it comes to creative pursuits, many of us still maintain child logic that depends on someone being there to prompt us in different directions and to protect us from falling. It is this same fear that underlies our discomfort in solitude and the self-reflection that usually accompanies it.

SOLITUDE IN A CROWD

Some creativity requires that you engage in solitude while in a crowd, that you maintain the ability to self-reflect on your internal experience while surrounded by others. While there is little opportunity for genuine solitude in these creative ventures, the challenge is to be freely fluid with your attention. Such situations demand the flexibility to attend to the thoughts and actions of others while being equally able to access and attend to your individual thoughts and emotions. Involvement in activities such as making a film, being part of a play, or choreographing a dance call upon your ability to shift your attention from those around you to self-reflection. And back again.

Fellini, the famous film director, described this challenge when he stated,

> I love being alone with myself, and thinking. But I can be alone only among people. I can think only if I'm pushed and shoved, surrounded by difficulties, with questions to answer, problems to solve, wild beasts to tame.[7]

By his own description, he had become so accustomed to being with others during moments of creativity that he required their presence to stimulate it. For such creators, the group is not a distraction to the creative process but rather a catalyst that helps every member of the group overcome inhibiting tension.

Whether you create individually or in collaboration with others, your capacity to be alone, both physically and in your thoughts, determines to a great extent whether you can commit yourself to the process.

*** FOR FURTHER EXPLORATION ***

1. What are your early associations with being alone? Was solitude comfortable or uncomfortable for you?
2. What emotions or themes did you associate with solitude?
3. If you experienced discomfort with solitude, what are the strategies that you used to manage such reactions?
4. What are your current associations with solitude?
5. To what degree do you feel rejection, abandonment, sadness, or low-level anxiety while being alone?
6. Currently, what are your most effective strategies for managing such reactions?
7. Growing up, what models did you have for being alone? What messages did these models convey either directly or indirectly about spending time alone?
8. Who in your life today may be threatened by your desire for solitude? How do you address this concern? How do you relate to that person or persons?

REFLECTIONS

Everyone has a talent. What is rare is the courage to nurture it in solitude and to follow the talent to the dark places where it leads.—Erica Jong

I lived in solitude in the country and noticed how the monotony of a quiet life stimulates the creative mind.—Albert Einstein

The process of creative thinking in any field of human endeavor often starts with what may be called a "rational vision," itself a result of considerable previous study, thinking, and observation.—Erich Fromm

I love people. I love my family, my children . . . but inside myself is a place where I live alone and that's where you renew your springs that never dry up.—Pearl S. Buck

NOTES

1. *Andy Goldsworthy's Rivers and Tides*, DVD, directed by Thomas Riedelshelmer (New York: New Video Group, 2001).

2. Martin E. P. Seligman, *Learned Optimism* (New York: Knopf, 1991).

3. Donald W. Winnicott, "Transitional Objects and Transitional Phenomena," *International Journal of Psycho-Analysis* 34 (1953): 89–97.

4. Anthony Storr, *Solitude* (New York: Free Press, 1988), p. 21.

5. Ibid.

6. Frank Barron, Alfonso Montuori, and Anthea Barron, *Creators on Creating* (New York: Putnam's Sons, 1997).

7. Ibid., p. 32.

Chapter 11

WILL I STILL BE ME?

I n contrast to fears of rejection by others, the fear related to this inhibiting theme is the loss of one's identity. The key struggle underlying this inhibiting theme is the concern or even a conviction that by engaging in a sustained creative endeavor you will change so significantly that you will no longer be who you currently are. Such concerns may be expressed in statements such as "If I really become successful in writing songs I'll lose some of my creative drive"; "I've been a housewife for twenty years, how could I even think of being a real estate agent"; "I know I can paint well, but I can't imagine being able to play an instrument"; or "I know I'm not creative, I've never been creative!" These same attitudes may inhibit a man from writing poetry because he views such expression as not being manly. Similarly, a sense of "closure" regarding her identity may lead a woman from a low socioeconomic background to unwittingly sabotage her financial progress.

At its core, this inhibiting theme reflects the ultimate expression of that innate conservative tendency described in chapter 3, the drive toward security and conservation of energy. This drive can lead us to maintain rigid definitions of who we are. Consequently, it undermines our openness to novelty and to the fluidity of identity that is a significant part of both authentic living and the creative journey.

THE DEVELOPMENT OF THE "SELF"

Through the course of our lives each of us develops, both consciously and unconsciously, a sense of "self," a distinct identity that defines the parameters of who we believe we are—how we think, behave, and act. Seeking and developing an identity has been described as a "self-organizing" ability. The conscious and unconscious work together to establish a self-identity that encompasses a sense of uniqueness, wholeness, and stability over time.[1] This self-identity then serves as a template against which we assess our feelings, perceptions, and behaviors. Through this process of self-definition, we gain a sense of feeling internally anchored, a sense of continuity, and a sense of cohesiveness, even though life is forever changing.

Your sense of self evolves through your interaction with family and others, as well as through the influences of your ethnicity, religion, race, social class, and nationality. It is in large part influenced by the system of rewards and punishments that you actually received or that you anticipated receiving. While as a child you may have been open to the many different ways of being, you soon internalized socially constructed guidelines to form your identity. Sometimes with full conscious choice and sometimes with no awareness at all, influenced by your needs to belong and to be loved, you adopted certain standards or guidelines for being. These may have nourished your capacity to be open and flexible in welcoming a fluid sense of self or they may have moved you to become more constrictive in establishing a rigidly defined sense of self.

If asked who you are or what you are like, you may immediately run down a list of descriptions that provide a summary of who you believe you are. You may address aspects of your personality and identify traits such as friendly, outgoing, shy, assertive, pensive, anxious, curious, or stubborn. Additionally, you may make reference to your religion, race, or nationality as another aspect of your identity. You may also list your interests, your skills, and how you spend your free time. And throughout each and every day, with and without awareness, you make reference to these parameters to guide you. When questioned about your tastes or attitudes, or when called on to behave in a certain way in a given situation, you react based upon your defined sense of self.

In part, this need to experience yourself in a consistent light serves a protective purpose. Your identified "self" provides you with a defined way of being. In a sense, you can function from within this identity as if on "automatic pilot." In this way, your self is like a shortcut that frees you from the need to evaluate at every instant how you want to feel, think, and act. As such, it helps you to avoid the anxiety and quandary of having too many possibilities of being to choose from. In every encounter you have with the world around you, with others, and with yourself, you draw on this reference point you call "self" to give meaning to events and to help you to decide how to react. In doing so, you treat your identity as if it is fixed and permanent. And although maintaining this perspective supports you in feeling cohesive and stable, you fail to recognize and acknowledge that this belief is a myth.

THE MYTH OF THE SELF

In reality, your identity is only fixed and permanent to the extent that you spend your energy steadfastly trying to adhere to the defining boundaries that you have established for it. Your identity entails only that constellation of parameters that you have established as ground rules for how you define yourself. This is the myth of the self. To the degree that you feel strongly compelled to rigidly adhere to these specific ways of being, you have erected barriers that inhibit you from more fully "being." When you do this, you fail to acknowledge and embrace a sense of self that is fluid and open to change. It means that while you may choose to "categorize" yourself in a certain way (by your skin color, nationality, or personality traits), by doing so you limit who you are and who you will be capable of becoming. A rigidly defined identity of this sort leads you to experience all new encounters through an equally rigid and predetermined lens. And yet, as described by psychiatrist and author Mark Epstein,

> being does not connote any fixed entity of self; but it does imply a stream of unimpeded awareness, ever evolving, yet with continuity, uniqueness, and integrity. It carries with it the sense of unending meeting places of interpersonal experience, convergences that are not blocked by a reactive or contracted ego.[2]

In many ways, holding on to a fixed sense of self is motivated by the same fears you experienced as a child. You learned to stay within the bounds of what was acceptable because it was safe and familiar. You wanted to belong and you wanted to avoid tension and conflict. While this conservative drive for safety and the comfort of familiarity can be protective, in the extreme it impedes your capacity to more fully become yourself. It can inhibit your embrace of an evolving "self." And when you adhere to the myth that your identity at a given moment is who you are, you fail to allow for your personal evolution.

GUARDING YOUR SENSE OF SELF

Through your watchful eye, both consciously and unconsciously, you assess and monitor yourself to determine the degree to which you are being consistent with your sense of self. Maintaining a rigid definition of who you are and who you should be may leave you little room for deviating from your perceived identity.

While this may seem energy efficient, maintaining a rigid self-identity can actually require a great deal of psychic energy. Such vigilance is an effort to defend yourself against the tension of change, ambiguity, and the doubt that accompanies "becoming." Even small steps beyond your habitual ways of feeling, thinking, or behaving can be extremely threatening to your sense of internal stability. Moments in which you step slightly outside the bounds of your habitual self may immediately push you into the realm of "not me," precipitating a great deal of anxiety in the process. At such moments you may feel a sense of disorientation. It is a reaction to fear coupled with a sense of loss, related less to your external surroundings than to a feeling of having lost your internal compass.

If I do not normally assert myself in public, I may very quickly be overwhelmed by discomfort and anxiety upon doing so. Experiencing myself as out of character, my anxiety may push me to withdraw, apologize, or experience shame and guilt. When I entertain a thought of pursuing a creative passion but have previously concluded that it does not fit with my sense of self, I once again prematurely create closure on my evolving self. Another example of such closure is when a writer, although intrigued by the idea of writing fiction, tells himself he is only a writer of nonfiction.

Such rigidity is associated with the "all or nothing" thinking I described earlier. It is a perspective that stands in sharp contrast to the fact that, as individuals, we are forever evolving, as is the world in which we live. It is encompassed in a mind-body set that fails to accept that identity is forever impacted by each new experience.

And yet, any change in your sense of self is accompanied to some degree by this sense of disorientation, a feeling of disorganization. This anxiety comes in part from the fear of the unknown as well as an unwillingness to accept that an altered self-identity may well be better. It is understandable then that you may defensively retreat from taking further action and instead exert great effort to once again adhere to the sense of self with which you feel most safe and familiar.

A SENSE OF DISORIENTATION

A sense of disorientation, that distinct moment of self-questioning and doubt, may arise at any moment during the creative journey. It is a moment when you may experience the degree of difference between your perceived sense of self and your newly evolving self as too "expansive." I experienced one such moment several years ago.

Upon the publication of my first book, a longtime friend of my co-author, Dr. Jan Fawcett, organized a cocktail party to honor the launch of our book promotion. The celebration was held in an exquisitely decorated home occupying two levels of a mid-rise building in the exclusive area of Chicago's Gold Coast. Immediately upon my arrival, I was introduced to the host and hostess and then directed to the far end of a luxurious ballroom where I was asked to sit and sign over a hundred books that were to be given to the guests. As I began, a waiter inquired about my drink preference.

I had never before published a book and yet every aspect of this setting informed me that I was now an "author." I had had visions of writing a book for many years and had even envisioned book signings, but this was no vision. Initially it felt somewhat dreamlike, extremely exciting and fulfilling, but also daunting and disorienting. I questioned why anyone would want my signature. Like a visitor to a strange culture, I even questioned the rationale of the long-standing tradition of authors signing books.

Perhaps you have had the experience of looking at a word long enough so that it no longer seems like a word but rather like a group of unrelated letters. Such was the quality of my disorientation as I signed the books. For several moments, my child logic seemed to dominate my experience. It inquired with a sense of puzzlement, "What are we doing here?" For several moments it all seemed unreal.

My mind-body reactions included intense excitement, self-doubt, pride regarding the attainment of my goal, apprehension, discomfort, and some anxiety. Brief thoughts associated with the imposter syndrome made their presence loud and clear. I questioned the significance of the event, it's impact on my career, and it's impact on my self-identity. It was not until I was well into the signing that I settled down to thoroughly enjoy the evening. My sense of self expanded to accommodate and integrate the new aspects of my identity. I was fulfilling a dream of many years.

This experience is similar to the form of mental wrestling many people have reported when they attend a photography class, begin writing, entertain fantasies of changing a career, or go through the process of decorating a newly purchased condo or home. During such distinct moments you may be flooded with thoughts, emotions, and physical states that allow all kinds of fantasies. Such moments may force you to confront the meaning and impact your creative efforts will have on your identity and, ultimately, on your life. These moments of disorientation are aroused by a sense of alienation from who you believe you are. When these moments are positive experiences, they may be marked by the familiar comment, "Pinch me so that I know it is real!" When they are not as rewarding, you may react by taking flight.

IMPACT ON PERCEPTION

When you maintain a rigid sense of self, this attitude impacts how you experience every aspect of your daily life. Your need to avoid complexity and change will lead you to put up mental and emotional barriers that insulate you from new information and the many details of new experiences. Consequently, you will be quick to define, categorize, and dismiss these new experiences.

This attitude will likely lead you to ignore most of the details of your experience through all of your senses. Jealously guarding your present sense of self makes you quick to categorize perceptions of faces, trees, colors, texture, fragrances, and even people so that you do not have to deal with novelty. In doing so, you become stuck in a pattern of seeking and finding only what is familiar and safe. To the degree that you fail to evolve and recognize the complexity and ambiguity of your own thoughts, emotions, and beliefs, you likewise mute your awareness of the complexity and ambiguity of the evolving identities of others.

In maintaining this orientation you restrict yourself to the confines of what you deem to be safe and secure.[3] However, individual growth, as with all evolution, depends on moving beyond your present limits. Emerging from a rigid sense of self threatens your sense of security, causing great anxiety. The intensity of the drive to emerge and the degree of anxiety aroused in doing so may vary at different stages of development and in different individuals. To the degree that you feel threatened in losing your sense of self, you will experience anxiety that can serve as a major inhibiting factor in your capacity for creative engagement.

CREATIVITY AND AN EXPANDING IDENTITY

Creativity is, in essence, a step into the unknown that forces you to challenge your sense of self. It is this element of living authentically that may potentially arouse anxiety as you move forward in creative engagement.

Meaningful creativity rests on your openness and ability to take this daring step as you seek out, create, and reveal novel perspectives. This involves challenging and even replacing attitudes, values, and commitments associated with your present sense of self. The capacity to see things in a "new" light; to reconfigure words, sounds, or images; and to imagine freely depend to a great extent on your comfort with emotional and mental fluidity. You must enhance your capacity to effectively manage the tension associated with ambiguity.

Even individuals who have been successful in creative endeavors may find themselves handicapped by rigid parameters that prevent them from further evolving. A painter may be hesitant to embrace an impressionistic style because all impressionistic paintings look the same to him. A musician may be quick to avoid the use of a certain rhythm because he has come to associate it with a particular song he doesn't like. A writer may believe that he is only able to write in a certain genre and never considers the possibility of trying another one; or he may become entirely focused on one style of writing within that genre. Such difficulties may similarly be reflected in the quality of work. For example, a writer may present characters that are two-dimensional, reflecting his own sense of being blocked in observing the details and complexity of his internal life. This inhibiting theme may additionally be reflected in restrained creativity or inhibition in regard to "letting go." This was reflected by an acquaintance of mine who had studied piano for eight years.

In general, he was often described as being intense or "uptight" in his demeanor, emotional expression, and behavior. His quickness to be critical of others only reflected the same high and often unrealistic standards that he had maintained for himself. This was clearly evidenced when he played piano. As he sat at the keyboard, he looked stiff. The furrows on his forehead revealed a tremendous degree of internal tension as he intently stared at the sheets of music. His body seemed bolted to the piano bench as he tilted only slightly to reach the full extension of the keyboard. His fingers seemed rigid as they moved over the keys.

He clearly knew his music. He rarely made mistakes. And yet, his rendition seemed cold and mechanical, even when playing the most emotionally moving classical pieces. He appeared overly focused on technical correctness and seemed to omit the emotion that would have given his playing life and appeal. He followed all of the rules, but was unable to bring passion to his performance.

Heightened vigilance to maintaining one's sense of self is the antithesis of what is required to experience a state of flow. This state of mind, characterized by a lack of self-consciousness, reflects a loss of self in the process and medium of the creative pursuit. As such, the experience of flow may become quite threatening for those who maintain a rigid sense of self and apprehension about violating it.

The deepest level of your psyche, sensitive to disorder and ambiguity, is the source of much of your inspiration for the creative process—the primal reservoirs you catch glimpses of in dreams, through slips of the tongue, and in the child logic. Your need to remain embedded in the rigid parameters you use to define yourself may further impair your capacity to embrace the collaboration of conscious and unconscious that is essential for the creative process.

I have met and worked with many individuals who have experienced a low-level depression characterized by overriding boredom. In many cases, these individuals fear to lose themselves in the details of creative exploration. I believe their boredom often says more about their rigidity of identity than it does about the objects for which they fail to generate an interest.

If you are able to maintain openness to change, you are liberated to attend to the details of your exploration. With free-flowing curiosity, you are receptive to multiple possibilities of being and challenged not by boredom but by the difficulty of prioritizing these possible avenues of inquiry and creativity. It is with this state of mind that you flourish in your creative journey.

FEAR OF EVOLVING A SPECIFIC IDENTITY

While you may be inhibited in creative engagement by a fear of losing your sense of self, you may instead fear that you will take on a specific identity that you might not like.

Kelly, a young woman I worked with, had exceptional skills in writing, but remained ambivalent for several years about doing anything with her skills. While she strongly desired to pursue freelance writing as a career, she instead sought training as a veterinarian technician. Although she loved working with animals, she was continually drawn to writing. When encouraged to reflect, she became increasingly aware of how her attitudes regarding her mother influenced her decision to pursue a career other than writing. For a variety of reasons, Kelly had had a conflicted relationship with her mother. Without being fully aware of it, she had vowed never to be like her mother. Her mother just happened to start out as a freelance writer before writing a full-length book.

It became apparent to Kelly that negative feelings toward her mother had contributed to her avoidance of following a similar creative path. Her enthusiasm for writing was being undermined by her sense that if she pursued writing she would be too much like her mother. Only as she began to accept and trust herself could she begin to realize that she was a separate person who could follow her unique creative path even if her path seemed to have similarities to that of her mother.

ANXIETY REGARDING GROUP IDENTITIES

While we all have a strong need for social affiliation, to feel connected with others, and to feel like we belong, some us are leery of identifying with groups. We may at times become part of a group, but prefer being involved only for brief periods of time, participating from the fringes of the group activities. We may rationalize this as desire for freedom, reluctance to limit the diversity of our interests, or as the result of disappointment with previous experiences with groups. For some, however, the aversion to group involvement stems from difficulties in setting limits and boundaries regarding frequency and quality of participation. Most relevant to our present concern, you may have an aversion to joining a particular group, even if you would like to be a member, because you have developed a negative association with it. In part, this aversion may stem from your own inability to recognize the real heterogeneity, complexity, and differences among its members because of your quickness to categorize them based upon the identity of the group as a whole. In such cases, you are only able to see the forest and remain blind to the individuality of each tree.

In reality, if you are confident in who you are and have the capacity to remain open, you can expand your identity to view yourself as a group member without feeling like your individual identity has been completely merged with the identity of the group. In contrast, if you maintain a more vague sense of who you are, connection in a relationship or a group may be experienced as threatening and result in inner turmoil.

I remember a friend who had tremendous interest in being a psychologist but decided not to major in psychology because so many students were pursuing it. His choice reflected his need to feel different and unique. Only after taking the introductory course during his second year was he hooked and only at that point was he able to listen to his inner voice rather than react to what others were doing.

Years ago, while I was working in an adolescent psychiatric unit, a mental health aide was confronting a patient named Mark concerning his behavior in a group therapy session. The aide boldly stated, "You know, if you continue doing what you're doing, you'll end up in prison by the time you're seventeen; and you know what will happen to you in there!" In response, Mark became extremely agitated. He had to be removed from the group and returned to his room.

When I spoke to him later, Mark exclaimed that he became agitated because he had truly believed that merely making that dire prediction might cause it to occur. Ideally, if Mark had felt more secure and confident in his identity, he would have been able to listen to the feedback, reflect on himself momentarily, and calmly respond that he did not share the aide's belief.

However, his sense of self was so fragile that he easily became threatened just hearing about the possibility of what could happen to him.

FEARS OF COMMITMENT

A major challenge of every loving relationship is solving the problem of how to maintain your own identity while negotiating the demands of the relationship through both assertiveness and compromise. Returning to the analogy offered earlier in this book, a commitment to sustained creativity is very much like being involved in such a relationship. Creativity can arouse many of the same fears you may have regarding commitment in a relationship. Some creators, like partners in a relationship, can totally immerse themselves in their commitment and take great pride in declaring their identity as being inextricably tied to that commitment. They do not find this threatening, rather it is their lifeblood. Some describe their creativity as a compulsion they cannot deny. They may even describe creativity as an identity that they did not fully choose—and yet they embrace it.

In contrast, fear of losing your identity serves as a major barrier for truly pursuing your creative passion. Being creative certainly makes demands. Like any relationship, it requires a commitment of time, devotion, flexibility, and work. But it is in this commitment that you become most free. It is in making the choice to embrace your evolving self that you increase the degree to which you have freedom to become who you are.

THE INDIVIDUAL JOURNEY

I have been extremely fortunate in my life to see many individuals challenge their senses of self in a wide variety of ways. In my practice, I have seen clients expand their self-concepts by learning which thoughts and emotions to trust and which ones to reject. In the process, they became more open to their humanity, including their full ranges of emotions, interests, and desires. Through their courage and hard work they move from maintaining rigid and constricting views of themselves to being more receptive to who they can become. Whether addressing relationships, careers, the use of leisure time, or attitudes about selves and others, they opened themselves up to embrace their self-unfoldings.

I have also witnessed similar courage by those who created major life changes as they switched careers—from law enforcement to social work, from social work to law enforcement, from engineering to psychology, from working in a corporation to teaching elementary school, and from teaching to nursing. These individuals made great changes in major aspects of their identities. But we do not need to change careers to be open to an evolving sense of self.

Many individuals who seek treatment for symptoms that interfere with authentic living progress when they develop an increased resilience that allows them to overcome the myth of the self. These individuals can be helped to cope with and manage the tension of emerging from a rigid sense of self toward a more fluid and evolving self-definition. They learn that they can be more true to themselves by recognizing and altering the many ways in which their rigid beliefs about the self keep them emotionally, mentally, and spiritually imprisoned.

Pursuing your creative genius can have a significant impact on your identity and the quality of your daily life. But it requires a capacity to trust and accept yourself as you live authentically. Immersing yourself in the pursuit of a creative endeavor and being open to creative inspiration enriches your life as you experience a new sense of mastery and accomplishment that is the mark of an expanding identity. It is through this process that you experience meaningful life gratification.

Yet the process of change fostered by creative engagement can at times be challenging. This is especially true when your creative passion leads in directions that can significantly alter the focus or quality of your life.

*** FOR FURTHER EXPLORATION ***

1. How open are you toward seeing your identity as evolving rather than as static?
2. What are some of your characteristics that have been constant over the years?
3. What are some of your characteristics that have changed over the years?
4. To what degree do you intensely focus on rigid attitudes that involve "all or nothing" thinking?

5. To what degree are you comfortable with the "grays" of life? Are you comfortable exploring the complexities of your experiences and attitudes?
6. To what degree do you become concerned about losing your identity as a result of pursuing your creative path? What do you believe would happen if you were to fully embrace that path?

REFLECTIONS

Creativity can be described as letting go of certainties.—Gail Sheehy

Conquering any difficulty always gives one a secret joy, for it means pushing back a boundary-line and adding to one's liberty.—Henri Frederic Amiel

To exist is to change, to change is to mature, to mature is to go on creating oneself endlessly.—Henri Bergson

A single event can awaken within us a stranger totally unknown to us. To live is to slowly be born.—Antoine de Saint-Exupery

NOTES

1. Vittorio F. Guidano, *Complexity of the Self* (New York: Guilford, 1987).
2. Mark Epstein, *Going on Being* (New York: Broadway Books, 2001), p. 31.
3. Ernest G. Schachtel, *Metamorphosis: On the Development of Affect, Perception, Attention, and Memory* (New York: Basic Books, 1959).

III

OVERCOMING
INHIBITING THEMES

The chapters in this section provide a broad range of strategies to help you unlock your creative genius. Specifically, they offer you ways to identify and reduce the impact of inhibiting themes on your creative pursuit. I begin by describing exercises you can use to foster self-reflection and increase your awareness of the inhibiting themes that may be most influential in blocking your pursuit of creative passion.

In the remaining chapters I offer a wide variety of skills to help you to enhance a positive mind-body set that can counter and overcome the tension aroused during moments of creative challenge. In effect, these are exercises and skills to assist you in developing the increased courage, trust, resilience, and commitment that are essential for sustained creative engagement.

Effectively learning these skills can be challenging and requires some degree of courage, trust, resilience, and commitment. As such, it is only natural that your attempts to learn them will force you to confront your inhibiting themes. In every step you take toward accessing who you are and expressing your creative self, you will be increasingly confronted by child logic that resists such movement.

Try not to fight or to ignore these reactions. Just acknowledge and accept them as you engage in the exercises. Most important, be realistic in your expectations. View this book as a reference, not as a list of assignments to be quickly completed and fully absorbed within a specific time frame. Like creativity, managing inhibiting themes is a process that takes time and may arouse some discomfort; it is the natural tension that accompanies growth and a newly evolving self.

Be alert to both the tension that may arise from your need to do the exercises perfectly and your fears of failure or success, guilt, shame, or any of the other inhibiting themes that may arise. And when they make their presence known, instead of being self-critical or fearful, view it as proof that your are challenging and confronting them and that you are bravely and assertively moving forward in your creative life journey.

Chapter 12

OBSERVING AND RECOGNIZING "MOMENTS OF CHALLENGE"

Access to your creative genius is impacted by your experiences in the past and by your visions for the future. But it is the nature and intensity of what you experience in the present that most strongly influences your capacity to remain engaged during a creative challenge. Thus, the essential first step in managing moments of creative challenge is to recognize and identify them, to be keenly aware of the inhibiting themes and related tensions that distract you from maintaining consistent engagement with the creative process. This chapter is devoted to helping you achieve this goal. Specifically, it offers you guidelines and skills to help observe and recognize the detailed composition of your internal experiences, those emotions, thoughts, and physical states that are aroused when you confront challenges to your creative journey.

Being aware of your internal experience at any given moment requires a variety of self-observation skills that must be learned and practiced. While each of us varies in the development of these skills and in the frequency with which we practice them, they are skills that everyone can learn.

In addition, this chapter offers you a variety of exercises in self-reflection. It begins with a discussion of mindfulness and broad and open reflection and then proceeds to exercises designed to heighten your skills in attending to various aspects of your internal experience. These exercises become increasingly structured as they offer you specific guidelines for self-exploration to better identify inhibiting themes.

MINDFULNESS

Mindfulness emphasizes (1) the creation of new categories, (2) openness to new information, and (3) awareness of multiple perspectives. Specifically, mindfulness involves being both aware and present, and attending to the uniqueness of both the moment and your experience of it.[1]

Maintaining mindfulness supports and nurtures your ability to attend to both the details and the novelty of your experience, both of which are essential elements for the creative process. Being mindful in this manner allows you to notice novel connections that may not be readily apparent. Mindfulness fosters the recognition and acceptance of mixed as well as ambivalent feelings or attitudes about an issue. When living mindfully, you become more in touch with your internal experiences, a fundamental step toward living authentically. Being mindful to your internal experience in turn entails willful attention to your awareness without being judgmental. It entails being present and attentive to your full experience (your thoughts, emotions, images, sensations, and behaviors). In *Relaxation, Meditation, and Mindfulness*, Jonathan Smith compares mindful awareness of the flow of your thoughts to "sitting beside and gazing at a quietly flowing stream. A variety of unexpected objects slowly and continuously float by. A piece of wood comes into sight and then floats away. Then a patch of leaves. And then a floating seed."[2]

For our purposes, mindfulness is an approach that will allow you to recognize and identify the inhibiting themes that challenge your creative moments. In chapter 17, "mindfulness meditation" will be discussed as a comprehensive strategy to address and reduce the impact of such inhibitions.

When mindfully identifying inhibiting themes, observations are made by seeking answers to the question "What am I experiencing?" rather than "Why am I experiencing what I am experiencing?" Asking "what" emphasizes reflection that heightens your awareness of and sensitivity to the experience. In contrast, asking "why" leads to analysis and a search for explanations. Asking questions beginning with "why" often shifts your focus to past events. On the other hand, asking "what" maximizes your engagement and presence.

Your observations may not always include information that is conveyed in full sentences or by readily identifiable emotional or physical states. They may instead be revealed in phrases or images that are anchored in the present, the past, or the future. The following exercise reflects mindful attention.

Exercise #1

Find a quiet place where you will not be disturbed. After reading these directions, spend five minutes observing your internal experiences. Specifically, note your physical states, emotions, thoughts, and images. Upon completing the exercise, list your observations on a sheet of paper with the following heading. Record your observations on the outline provided as figure 12-1 before going on to exercise #2.

Observations Log

Physical states	Emotions	Thoughts	Images

FIGURE 12-1: OBSERVATIONS LOG

Exercise #2

This time, continue to observe for five to ten minutes, but focus on the following guidelines in your reflection.

A. *Physical state*

    1. Be aware of any tension in your body. If you experience physical tension, does it feel positive like the type of excitement associated with discovery or does it entail uneasiness or vague discomfort?

    2. Where is the physical tension located? Scan your body to determine if there are other reactions.

    3. Identify any muscle tension, strain, or pain.

B. *Emotional states*

    1. Observe any positive emotions such as joy, contentment, excitement, anticipation, or hope.

    2. Note any negative emotional reaction such as anxiety, fear, low-level apprehension, or irritation.

C. *Thoughts*

    1. Are you experiencing any positive thoughts such as "this feels like a good start," "I'm good at this," or "I'm not sure where this is going, but it is interesting"?

    2. In contrast, are you experiencing negative thoughts such as "this is silly" or "this is a waste of time"?

    3. Are you experiencing distracting thoughts focused on topics other than this exercise?

D. *Images*

    1. Note images.

    2. Do they seem familiar with any past experiences you have had or are they images regarding possible future events?

Most likely you experienced additional observations when doing the second exercise. Use your log to enter any of these additional observations. By using specific guidelines for your reflection, you may have sharpened your attention to your experience, focusing it at a deeper level.

Specific guidelines for self-reflection help you to become more alert and focused in forming your observations. Describing categories such as "positive" and "negative," and offering specific examples of emotions, thoughts, physical states, and images provides markers regarding your observations. Your observations for exercise #2 involved scanning for reactions. Scanning for specifically identified experiences is different from just attending to what you experience; in a sense, it emphasizes a heightened alertness to the details of your experience.

The remaining exercises in this chapter involve structured guidelines for the use of mindfulness in better recognizing and identifying inhibiting themes.

OBSERVING MOMENTS OF CHALLENGE

The following exercise will guide your observations to help you gain increased awareness of the complexity of your thoughts, emotions, physical states, and images and, in particular, how they reflect inhibiting themes that impact your creative desires. This is the primary exercise to repeatedly practice during moments of challenge in order to help you gain increased insight regarding the forces behind them. Again, focus your observations on answering "what" you notice rather than on "why" you are having a particular experience.

Exercise #3

Identify a moment during which you feel challenged while trying to be creative. It does not have to be a moment in which you are completely paralyzed, but it should be a moment that at least causes you some discomfort. For example, perhaps you are interested in painting and have actually purchased art supplies but have not started to actually paint or you have begun several paintings but are having difficulty completing one. Maybe you think of writing but have not initiated the first page. In contrast, you may have finished a manuscript but have failed to submit it to anyone for review. The moment of challenge may be that distinct moment when you are in a committee meeting and although you form an idea for consideration regarding a shared task you hesitate and never voice it out loud. The particular moment you address may be any one that challenges you to stay engaged.

A. If possible, physically place yourself in the situation in which you are experiencing the feeling of being challenged. If your challenge is in painting, set up your easel and arrange your brushes and other supplies as you would if you were going to paint. Take a brush and dip it in one of the colors. Gradually move it closer to the easel and then . . . simply hold that position. Do not paint!

If your challenge is practicing an instrument, position it as if you are going to play it. If your challenge is experienced when trying a new recipe, take out and arrange your ingredients with the recipe on the kitchen counter. If your challenge is to sculpt, arrange your materials in front of you so that you are ready to begin shaping the clay.

Some distinct moments of challenge may not involve tangible objects or exact locations. For example, you may feel challenged to voice your personal views regarding a project at work or you may be inhibited when thinking about pursuing a specific academic goal. If this is the case, arrange your physical situation to resemble as closely as possible the conditions in which you take the initial steps to engage in these activities. Visualize or actually sit in the room at work where you may be offering your idea. Visit or imagine yourself at the school that is offering the program in which you desire to be enrolled. If you have not actually applied, sit by your desk with the school's application in front of you. You may want to select a moment that best reflects how far you have progressed in your creative endeavor.

B. Now focus your attention for a few moments on your surroundings and the objects in front of you. Actually initiate or simply visualize the first steps you would be taking as you proceed. For example, actually paint on the canvas or visualize doing so, actually write some paragraphs or picture yourself doing so, actually call the school where the course is being offered or visualize doing so. Focus your attention in this way for several minutes to help you feel as present as possible with the actual challenge of engagement in the activity. Try to immerse yourself as much as you can in attending to the details of the task. The goal at this moment is to make the situation as real as possible so as to evoke the deeper reactions that have been blocking you from full creative engagement.

Ask yourself, "What is my internal experience at this distinct moment in time?

1. Begin by focusing on your body. Do a full body scan, from the top of your head to your face and shoulders, continuing down to your toes. Again,

try to observe without judging, evaluating, or trying to change your reaction. Just observe. Notice your breathing, your muscles, your posture, and your overall physical comfort or discomfort. How comfortable or uncomfortable is your body?

Are you experiencing any form of tension? If so, where is it located? Is it in a shaking leg, in the muscles of your chest, in your gut, or in a barely noticeable change in your respiration? Is it a vague sense of overall physical tension or tension centered in a specific area of your body? Are you moving your tongue against your lips or the roof of your mouth? Perhaps you are slightly clenching your teeth together or biting your lip or tongue. Maybe you are feeling a slight strain across the muscles of your shoulders. Are you experiencing low-level fatigue that has gradually overcome your body as you have increased your engagement with the task? Might you be experiencing some tension in your eyes, as if you have been reading for hours, which causes you to feel like discontinuing the task at hand? Take time to write down your physical reactions.

In contrast, are you experiencing physical tension that is exciting? Does this tension help you to be alert and focused and to move forward and fully engage with the creative task? Make a log of your reactions. Figure 12-2 offers an example of a record you can keep. Indicate your reactions in each column. Place (+) next to each listed physical state if your reaction seems positive and (-) if it appears negative.

Observations when I (*specific activity*)

Physical states	Emotions	Thoughts
Slight overall tension (–)		
Slight tension (+)		
Slight tension in chest area (–)		
Shaking leg (–)		

FIGURE 12-2: LOGGING OF PHYSICAL STATES

2. Now shift your attention to your emotions. Again, focus on your observations rather than on analyzing them. Emotions, like thoughts, may not at first be experienced in a very clear manner. For example, you may experience images, recollections of similar experiences, or imagined scenarios triggered by your reactions. All of these may convey the emotional nature of your present experience. First, observe in a general way and identify what emotions you may be experiencing. Then, scan your emotions to determine if you are experiencing specific emotions. Are you experiencing a certain degree of joy, excited anticipation, a sense of contentment, hopefulness, a sense of empowerment, or any of a range of positive emotions that often accompany full engagement in a creative journey?

In contrast, might you be experiencing negative emotions such as fear, anxiety, guilt, shame, discouragement, hopelessness, or frustration? Being fully observant and aware of your specific emotional experience often takes several sittings. You may observe that you experience a variety of these emotions at the same time or that they alternate with each other. List the emotions that you have observed. Again, indicate whether they are positive (+) or negative (-). Your log may look like figure 12-3.

Observations when I (*specific activity*)		
Physical states	Emotions	Thoughts
Slight overall tension (–)	Slight anxiety (–)	
Slight tension (+)	Excitement (+)	
Slight tension in chest area (–)	Hope (+)	
Shaking leg (–)	Frustration (–)	
	Irritation (–)	

FIGURE 12-3: LOG OF PHYSICAL STATES AND EMOTIONS

3. Now focus on observing your thoughts. As stated previously, you may not experience complete thoughts or whole sentences but rather phrases or sentence fragments, words, or even images that reflect your thoughts. What are the thoughts you experience during the brief moment when you dip the brush in the paint and raise it to the easel, when you begin to write, or when you review the catalog regarding the course you plan to take? Do you think, "this is exciting," "this makes no sense," "how is this going to help?" "I know exactly what I want to do," "I have no idea what to do," or "this is exactly where I get stuck." Do you think, "this is difficult" or does your mind wander to thoughts such as "I wonder what Cory is up to," "I need to do the laundry, go shopping, get my haircut, and pay the bills"? Do you find your thoughts focused on your plans for the evening, your "real" work, getting a snack, or any of a variety of other concerns?

Are you aware of any self-critical judgments such as "I am not good at this," "this is a waste of time," "I really should be doing something more useful," or others such as "I will never be good at this," "I will never make money at this," "I can never compare to Jason's skill as a painter," "this isn't the way I want it to go," or "I don't know where to go from here"?

In an effort to listen at a deeper level, recall the emotions you experienced and pay close attention to any statements that shed light on them. For example, when you experienced anxiety, were you quietly and deeply thinking, "I am anxious about rejection or failure," "I am anxious about making mistakes or not being perfect," or "I am anxious about revealing myself?"

Similarly, if you felt positive emotions, try to identify thoughts associated with them. These may have included thoughts such as "this is going just as I want it to go," "it is so exciting to explore what I can do," "I really can do it," "I really am good at it," "this is fun," or "I am so hopeful—I really will complete what I am planning to do."

While the ability to identify self-talk increases with practice in self-reflection, there are times when you may not be able to recognize any internal dialogue occurring. One strategy to help identify what you may be telling yourself is to question your emotions or your physical reactions. For example, suppose you are feeling anxiety, speak to it as if it could talk to you and reveal "its" concerns. Inquire about its presence and what it may be anticipating. Similarly, if you are experiencing some form of physical tension, speak to it in the same manner, inquiring about its presence and concerns.

Your log of observations may now look like the one provided in figure 12-4. For this section of the log, "n" has been placed next to thoughts that are neutral (n) rather than positive (+) or negatie (–).

Also enter any reactions that are conveyed by or associated with images that you experience. This completed log offers you a snapshot of your mind-body set, a detailed description of the state of the mind and body reactions aroused when confronting distinct moments of creative challenge.

4. Review your observations, keeping in mind the inhibiting themes that have been outlined in part II of this book. Identify which theme(s) seem to be most reflected by your reactions. This often requires repetition of reflection over several moments of challenge. Keep in mind that several themes may influence your performance at the same time.

Observations when I (*specific activity*)		
Physical states	Emotions	Thoughts
Slight overall tension (–)	Slight anxiety (–)	"This is silly" (–)
Slight tension (+)	Excitement (+)	"I hope this works" (n)
Slight tension in chest area (–)	Hope (+)	"I've been at this point before" (n)
Shaking leg (–)	Frustration (–)	"I'm wasting my time" (–)
	Irritation (–)	"Why can't I just get into it" (–)
		"I really feel silly" (–)
		"I'm wasting time" (–)
		"I got that part right" (+)

FIGURE 13-4: A COMPLETE LOG OF REACTIONS

THE IMAGINARY VIDEOTAPE

Another approach to gain insight is to review your experience as if it were recorded on an imaginary videotape that you can review in your mind. In doing so, attend to all of the details of your experience by moving your "tape" forward or backward or by pushing the pause button to more closely attend to specific moments. For example, you may experience a vague sense of anxiety but be unable to identify any thoughts or emotions that correspond to it. Start with the experience of anxiety and slowly rewind your "tape," frame by frame, in order to better identify the fleeting thought, image, or sensation that may have contributed to your experience.

This strategy is especially helpful in determining the distinct point at which you began to experience a desire to disengage from your creative venture. You may, for example, find that you were in the middle of writing, painting, or working with your clay when you suddenly had the urge to disengage. Assuming there really was no urgent need that pulled you away from engagement, reflect and determine what specific stimulus, thought, or emotion pushed you away from engagement. This is the moment of challenge. Perhaps you experienced a moment of frustration, an image of rejection, a momentary whisper of self-criticism regarding the quality of your work, or an internal rebuke for enjoying it. Perhaps you experienced the force of inhibiting themes such as perfectionism, survivor's guilt, or fear of failure. The use of this strategy offers a very structured way to attend to your experience at a deeper level.

FINE-TUNING EMOTIONAL AWARENESS

We can only be aware of our emotions to the degree that we have learned to access them. A part of this learning includes outside recognition and validation of our emotions. Specifically, to the degree that others help us label our emotions or encourage us to reflect upon them, we learn to better recognize and access them. In contrast, when we are provided with few models for looking inward, we often will not do so.

In general, men are not encouraged to sort through and tease out what it is they are feeling. They are often socialized to renounce anxiety, self-doubt, and display of emotion in general. To the degree that this occurs, whether in men or women, emotional experience is blunted. Years ago I worked with a thirteen-year-old who could only say that he felt "good," "bad," or "so-so." He knew some words to describe emotions but was both disconnected from his experience of them and unable to differentiate between them.

As indicated previously, the capacity to distinguish, recognize, and effectively manage our emotions is a major aspect of emotional intelligence. These abilities are essential to overcoming the overriding influence of negative child logic and the pervasive power of negative emotions to dictate our thoughts and actions. This has tremendous importance when it comes to self-reflection regarding emotional states.

Some emotions may be considered more "freestanding." These emotions have few connections with other emotions and are associated with specific physical states, facial expressions, and thoughts. For example, joy and sadness may seem more clearly defined emotions than fear, anxiety, or anger. These latter three emotions are tangled in a web of relations with other emotions. We become anxious or fearful about feeling threatened, anticipating being rejected, being the target of anger, or feeling inadequate. The more keenly you can recognize your emotions, the more depth of understanding you will gain about what is both positively and negatively meaningful to you.

While a part of self-reflection involves "listening" to yourself to determine your inner experience, it can also be immensely helpful to know what to listen for. The following list of words reflects both a variety of single emotions as well as combinations of emotions. These can aid you when trying to distinguish the specific nature of your emotional experience.

depressed	cheerful	hopeful	hate-filled
alarmed	powerful	enthusiastic	frustrated
content	impatient	shamed	guilty
warm	good	angry	furious
glad	shocked	pleased	bitter
resentful	regretful	desirous	excitable
grieving	sad	cold	unhappy
agitated	thrilled	awed	loving
concerned	anguished	fulfilled	aloof
amazed	enraged	exhilarated	despairing
fond	delighted	bored	surprised
sorrowful	calm	happy	mad
terrorized	irritated	annoyed	fearful
anxious	worried	queasy	tense

OBSERVING AT A DEEPER LEVEL

Take a moment to review your observations. While you may have listed reactions you observed, go a little deeper in your observations at this time. You may have indicated anxiety or fear as well as joy, hope, or frustration. Try to observe at a deeper level what the anxiety or fear is related to. Focus your observations on what it is you may be anxious about, or fearful of. Identify your thoughts regarding these emotions. Sit with them for a moment. Again, observe rather than analyze, asking "what" rather than "why." You may recognize that you are anxious about the possibility of failure or fearful that you will be rejected in some way. You may recognize that you are anxious about feeling inadequate or that you experience shame just for trying to be creative.

One approach to identifying your reactions at a deeper level is to create a complete sentence that further elaborates on your emotional reaction. Examples of this include the following.

I am anxious that _____ .
I am fearful of _____ .
I am experiencing guilt related to _____ .
I am experiencing shame regarding _____ .

Sitting with and taking time to observe the interactions of your emotions will increase your self-awareness and capacity to both experience and understand the rich complexity of such emotions.

EXPLORING YOUR REACTIONS TO THE OUTCOME

As emphasized throughout this book, challenging moments can occur during any phase of a creative endeavor. The exercises so far described emphasize exploring how you are impacted at the beginning or middle of your creative endeavor. This next exercise is especially powerful for helping you recognize in a profound way what you anticipate experiencing when you complete your creative endeavor and share it with others. Simply anticipating a specific outcome may lead to experiencing many of the moments of challenge that impede your creative progress. Similarly, many of the barriers to creative engagement have more to do with your anticipated outcome of such engagement than the earlier or even middle phases of such engagement. Doing the following exercise will help you better determine if anticipated success in pursuing creativity plays a role in inhibiting your creative engagement. Before proceeding with exercise #4, answer the following questions to help clarify the meaning and importance of your pursuit.

1. Are you seeking to be creative just for your own pleasure?
2. To what degree do you experience concern for how others perceive your creativity?
3. Is your creative goal one that is relatively short-term, such as decorating a room, or a long-term challenge like becoming skillful in arranging music? Write a sentence that declares your goals in pursuing this path.
4. In contrast, does your creative pursuit involve seeking increased exposure to others?
5. Do you seek to eventually make your passion a part of your career so that it will actually impact how you make a living?

Exercise #4

Imagine that you have attained your goal. Picture yourself at a distinct moment in time, reflecting on the room you have decorated, the painting you have submitted for an art show, the new career you've just begun, the degree you've recently earned, or the screenplay that a studio just purchased. Reflect on this image for a while and, once again, identify how you are experiencing this moment in your mind and body.

Now imagine yourself six months to a year after you have reached your goals. Picture yourself fully engaged and present with the fruits of your passion. In what ways will your life have changed? How do you believe you will feel different about yourself? Do you perceive that the view others have of you will change? If so, how will their attitudes shift? Will your actual living environment change? Really immerse yourself in this scenario and identify the details of how your life might be impacted if you continue on your creative journey.

After reflecting for several moments on this image, once again turn your attention to how you are impacted physically, mentally, and emotionally by this imagined scenario. Identify the inhibiting themes that seem to be associated with your reactions.

RECEIVING RECOGNITION

The following exercise is especially powerful in helping you recognize the degree to which you are comfortable in receiving recognition and acknowledgment.

Exercise #5

Imagine that you are being recognized and honored for achievement in your creative endeavor. You are being acknowledged for this accomplishment in a very public way. Take time to identify what it is you have accomplished. Spend some moments revisiting all that you did to reach this point.

Now, picture yourself on a stage in a huge auditorium with several other individuals who are there only to acknowledge your achievement. Also imagine that the auditorium is filled with people who have come just for this event. Decide who is sitting in the front rows. Imagine that you will be handed a trophy, medal, or plaque as a token of such recognition.

The main speaker has just described the purpose of the gathering and the nature of your achievement. He turns toward you, looks you in the eyes, congratulates you, and hands you the object that acknowledges your achievement. He immediately begins applauding as he steps back. At that moment the audience rises, begins to applaud, and stares directly at you. Look in their eyes and the eyes of the presenter for several moments. Take time to make it as real as possible. Make a log of your reactions before proceeding to answer the following questions.

A. What did you experience in your body? Were you in touch with muscles that tingle with positive excitement? Did you experience at the physical level a sense of wholeness and empowerment that comes with the joy of recognition? In contrast, did you experience physical tension? If so, where was it located? Did you feel your body cringing, as if you were pulling back in preparation to hide or flee? Were you perhaps feeling physically nauseous?

B. What were the emotions you experienced? Did you feel overwhelmed with joy, a sense of satisfaction, and a pride in your work and achievement? Did you feel validated and assured that you were right in the directions you took? In contrast, did you experience any sense of guilt—for the recognition, for taking center stage, or for causing members of the audience to feel jealous or inadequate as a result of your accomplishment? Did you feel embarrassed, even puzzled, feeling that perhaps you had deceived them all? Were you resentful, sensing that you should have been recognized sooner for your ability? Perhaps you felt shame for even wanting to be recognized.

C. What are the fleeting thoughts that you experienced up to this point? Did you embrace thoughts like, "I am so very happy and proud and feel joy at being recognized; I have worked hard for this and I know I deserve it" or did you tell yourself, "If they only knew how much better I can be—I certainly fooled them." Or maybe you told yourself, "I know they don't mean what they are saying—I better not enjoy it or even trust it; I can't wait until this is over." Maybe you said to yourself, "This is unreal. I don't know how to react. What should I say?" Or maybe you thought, "If my father (mother, sister, brother, friend) could see me they would feel so envious; I showed them!"

This is one exercise that often brings to light inhibiting themes that have to do with shame and guilt. Imagining this scenario helps highlight the degree to which you feel comfortable with your capacity to be admired and to embrace your growing identity as you pursue your creative passion.

REVISITING THE PAST

Practicing the exercises presented in this chapter will help you to better recognize and identify specific inhibiting themes that impact your capacity to be creative. Recognizing their origins is another step in awareness that can further help you to understand how they have become a part of your child logic. Looking for their origins is not an exercise in blame. Rather, such awareness is intended to help you understand that these inhibitions make sense considering the experiences you have had in the past. Specifically, such awareness helps to highlight the fact that while you may feel threatened in the present, it is often due to a rearousal of mind-body reactions that you have experienced in the past.

Now, having identified some themes, it would be helpful to ask yourself the following questions.

1. In what ways are my current reactions similar to experiences I have had in the past?

2. What experiences have I had with parents, relatives, siblings, peers, educators, my religion, or the media that may have contributed to the development of my inhibiting themes?

As emphasized throughout this chapter, asking the question "what" rather than "why" will help you to further identify the sources of your inhibitions. Such reflection requires the same skills as those presented throughout this chapter. Take time to reflect, and be open to what comes to mind as you scan your memory to answer these questions.

IDENTIFYING YOUR INHIBITING THEMES

Through repeatedly practicing the exercises of this chapter you will develop increased awareness of the inhibiting themes that challenge your creative passion. You may find that one or more play major roles while others play comparatively minor roles in impeding creative engagement. Complete the following inventory in order to help you further refine your understanding of their impact. Indicate, by circling the appropriate number, the degree to which each of these themes contributes to feelings of tension during distinct moments of challenge.

	Not at all	Occasionally	Often	Very often
Fear of failure	1	2	3	4
Fear of success	1	2	3	4
Variations of guilt	1	2	3	4
Eluding shame	1	2	3	4
Fantasies in the way of dreams	1	2	3	4
Issues with discipline	1	2	3	4
Difficulties with solitude	1	2	3	4
Fear of losing your sense of self	1	2	3	4

Your responses will help you recognize those themes that will benefit most from using the strategies in the remaining chapters.

All creativity demands that we develop skills in observation, whether attending to the details of our immediate environments, the world around us, or to the information that we have stored in our memory banks. However, it is developing the ability to observe how we become blocked in making such observations that is a major step in accessing and embracing our creative genius. Recognizing these forces is only the first step in helping you to be more authentic in your creative journey. The remaining chapters offer a range of understanding and skills to help you effectively manage the tension of such moments and to further your courage to create.

*** FOR FURTHER EXPLORATION ***

1. If you did not complete the exercises of this chapter, what kept you from doing so? Perhaps just doing the exercises leads you to experience "moments of challenge" and a variety of emotions, thoughts, and physical states that hinder your ability to complete them. What are your reactions to thinking about doing them?

2. While we may feel challenged in one area of creativity, we may, at the same time, experience minimal discomfort engaging in another arena of creativity. For example, some individuals play piano with ease but are paralyzed in their efforts to write. Similarly, some of us may feel completely confident when offering an idea in a committee of fellow workers but avoid taking any chances in trying to surprise a spouse with vacation plans.

   Do exercise #1 and focus your observations on an activity during which you feel completely free to be creative. Be as detailed as you can in noting the range of thoughts, emotions, and physical states you experience. In doing so, you will be more aware of the factors that help pave the way for your creative engagement.

3. Focus your attention for several minutes on the idea of self-reflection, of taking time to look inward. Listen to your reactions as you attend to this concept. What emotions, thoughts, or physical reactions are aroused as you do this? In doing this exercise, you will further increase awareness of negative and positive attitudes you may have about the actual process of self-observation. Simply engaging in this process may arouse inhibiting themes.

REFLECTIONS

Knowledge of the self is the mother of all knowledge. So it is incumbent on me to know my self, to know it completely, to know its minutiae, its characteristics, its subtleties, and its very atoms.—Kahlil Gibran

Your vision will become clear only when you can look into your own heart. . . . Who looks outside, dreams; who looks inside, awakes.—Carl Jung

In the creative state, a man is taken out of himself. He lets down as if it were a bucket into his subconscious, and draws up something which is normally beyond his reach. He mixes this thing with his normal experience and out of the mixture he makes his work of art.—Erich Fromm

If I have ever made any valuable discoveries, it has been owing more to patient attention, than to any other talent.—Isacc Newton

NOTES

1. Ellen J. Langer, *Mindfulness* (Cambridge, MA: Perseus, 1989).
2. Jonathan C. Smith, *Relaxation, Meditation, and Mindfulness* (New York: Springer, 2005), p. 167.

Chapter 13

CHALLENGING INHIBITING THEMES

Challenging and replacing automatic thoughts that are associated with inhibiting themes is a primary strategy for reducing the tension aroused by them. These are the thoughts you have identified by completing the exercises described in the previous chapter. The more often you challenge these specific thoughts, the more you can reduce their negative influence.

Part of what makes inhibiting themes so powerful is that with or without your awareness you have repeatedly recited such thoughts without challenging them. These inhibiting themes may have gone unchallenged for several reasons. You may not have been fully aware of their presence. You may have tried to ignore them, withdrawing from situations that aroused them. Or you may have successfully challenged them to some degree, though they still linger. As such, the inhibiting themes have become increasingly embedded in your memory, strengthening neuronal circuitry associated with the negative emotions and physical states they arouse.

For a moment, think about how you would respond if a good friend or someone you love says things about herself that are self-critical, devaluing, pessimistic, or overly influenced by fears that do not seem justified. Most likely, if you really care about this person, you will not withdraw, tell her to be quiet, or suggest she just ignore them. Rather, you will likely respond in ways that challenge her assertions so as to further increase her confidence, optimism, and hope. You might offer comments that offer realistic feedback about her strengths, highlight the difficulties of challenges she is facing, emphasize her past successes, cite her mood as overly influencing her thoughts, or simply ask her what you could do to help. Your genuine concern to help her would keep you from being silent.

In this way you would demonstrate compassion. You would be responding from your deeply human sensitivity to her pain and suffering with the desire to alleviate it. Directing this same compassion toward yourself is a major aspect of challenging and replacing negative thoughts associated with inhibiting themes. By challenging such thoughts with positive and objective responses, you will help nurture, support, and foster more positive and realistic thinking. The only difference is that you will be challenging the thoughts that originate from a deeper part of yourself, your child logic. All of the strategies identified in this chapter offer skills to help you formulate such challenges.

IDENTIFY SELF-TALK ASSOCIATED WITH THE INHIBITING THEMES

Each chapter of part II offered examples of thoughts that reflect unrealistic expectations and conclusions that are associated with the specific inhibiting themes. While these are presented as examples, the actual phrasing of your inhibiting self-talk may be somewhat different. However, all inhibiting self-talk derives from the power of child logic, reflected as an identifiable thought and associated with certain negative emotions and physical states. In effect, self-talk is the best available approximation of the mind/body state associated with each inhibiting theme.

If you think of your mind and body as a continuum of internal experience, your physical states reflect your body's qualitative response to moving toward or away from engagement in a specific experience. These states may "percolate," stir, and give rise to sensations that reflect this visceral tendency. Your emotions then derive from these sensations and an increasingly conscious sense of desiring to engage or withdraw. Finally, your thoughts involve words that resonate with your emotional and physical experiences. When you identify and challenge your inhibiting self-talk, you are, in effect, providing a corrective interpretation that challenges the knee-jerk reaction of your body and of your child logic. By responding to your child logic in this manner, you are strengthening that part of you to better sit with the mind-body set that is aroused by inhibiting themes. The goal is to challenge and replace your reactions with these more compassionate and realistic responses so that they become a part of your automatic reaction to the tension aroused when being creative. At the physiological level, it leads to a weakening in the patterns of neuronal firings associated with negative states and the development of different and more positive patterns.

Following is a summary of self-talk associated with those inhibiting themes discussed in part II. This summary reflects unrealistic expectations and conclusions that emanate from child logic. Each of these statements is not only representative of an outcome of immature logic but also representative of the immature emotional intelligence of a young child. As such, these themes are fueled by a child's perspective that includes a weak capacity to readily identify and differentiate emotions, a minimal capacity for tolerance of frustration, and an underdeveloped ability to engage in self-soothing.

FEAR OF FAILURE

Expectations

> I know I won't do this well
> I'll never learn to do this well
> My work (idea, art, book, song, etc.) will be rejected
> I need to be perfect
> I will be laughed at
> I will be rejected
> I will be abandoned
> They will see me as being inadequate

Conclusions

> I am a failure
> I am not perfect
> I am inadequate

FEAR OF SUCCESS

Expectations

> If successful, I will be overwhelmed
> My success will hurt others
> My work will reveal me as a fraud
> If successful, I will be rejected or even abandoned

Conclusions

> I am just an imposter
> I am hurting others
> This is overwhelming
> I am successful because of luck, my looks, or personality
> I am inadequate

VARIATIONS OF GUILT

Expectations

> I do not deserve pleasure
> I do not deserve to have my needs met because of bad things I did
> I should devote my life only to the happiness of others

Conclusions

> I should feel guilty
> I should stop what I am doing

ELUDED SHAME

Expectations

> My flaws will be revealed
> I do not deserve attention, success, or pleasure

My creativity will draw too much attention to me
I do not deserve to be myself

Conclusions

I am flawed
I should hide or flee
I do not deserve attention, success, or pleasure
My creativity is drawing too much attention
I will be punished for being myself

FANTASIES IN THE WAY OF DREAMS

Expectations

I need to be perfect
I should be better at my craft by now
I should be as good as _____
I should not experience frustration in being creative
All of creativity should be equally rewarding
I need to be in the right mood to create
There is only one way to be creative
I should have complete control

Conclusions

I am not perfect—I am inadequate
I do not measure up
I am not as good as _____. I am inadequate
I am frustrated—I must be inadequate
It is frustrating that not all creativity is equally rewarding
I am not in the mood to create
I should stop right now
I can't do it the way I wanted to so I should stop

ISSUES REGARDING DISCIPLINE

Expectations

> My work should be completely original
> I should work only when I want to
> I am not "I" if I accept input from others

Conclusions

> I should not listen to anyone
> It isn't original so I should stop
> I do not want to work right now so I should stop

DIFFICULTIES WITH SOLITUDE

Expectations

> I will be helpless when alone
> I need someone else to do it for me
> I need someone to support me during every step of my project
> When I am alone, I will feel alone
> When I am alone, I will feel inadequate

Conclusions

> I am helpless
> I need support
> I am completely alone
> I am inadequate

FEAR OF LOSING SENSE OF SELF

Expectations

> I will lose my identity if I pursue my creative passion
> I will be just like _____

Conclusions

> I am losing my identity
> I have lost my identity
> I feel I am just like _____

Identify those expectations and conclusions that best capture the essence of the inhibiting theme that appears to undermine your creative engagement. As reflected in the statements above, expectations precede and influence your initiating creative thoughts and action. The examples of conclusions identify negative self-talk that results from assessing your movement forward. The more unrealistic your expectations are, the more vulnerable you are to the influence of negative self-talk while pursuing your creative passion.

Initiating creative pursuit is fraught with tension associated with the unknown. Additionally, the force of the inhibiting themes, reflected in unrealistic expectations and conclusions, is an immediate consequence of forward movement during the creative process.

Almost all unrealistic expectations and conclusions you maintain are bound by child logic. As such, they are self-centered, immature, based on the logic of dreams, and outside the rules of reality. Even when they may at times have a realistic element, they represent only a small cluster of thoughts among all of the possible thoughts that you could have about a specific concern. A major goal in overcoming their influence, then, is to recognize that you should not automatically conclude that such thoughts, emotions, or their associated physical states are reactions that reflect reality.

A challenging thought is one that offers an alternative by which you can gauge your expectations and conclusions. Challenging self-talk expands your scope of vision beyond the automatic, knee-jerk reaction of your child logic. Through repetition, challenging responses replace your child logic as the source of your automatic response. Challenging self-talk will bring to light your own errors in feeling fearful in situations where there is no threat and shame in situations where there is nothing to feel shameful about.

The challenging statement should be simple in wording and in its message. Think of how you would talk to a four-year-old and you will more readily target your message for that part of you that derives from child logic. The more concise and simple it is, the more readily it will be integrated as a part of your automatic dialogue, positively influencing your expectations and conclusions.

Challenges to your child logic can take many forms. They can be statements that educate, inform, or remind you how the world really is and how people really behave. Such statements may focus on the realistic probability that events will or will not unfold in a certain way. Such challenging thoughts will offer a reality check to your child logic, as reflected in the following examples.

Unrealistic Expectations	Challenging Thoughts
I need to be perfect or I will be rejected or abandoned.	Just because I think this does not mean it is true. I may feel this way but that does not mean it is true.
	If others really care for me, they will not reject or abandon me.
	Others will still like me even if I am not perfect. I have made mistakes before and I was not always rejected.
	If others reject or abandon me, I will feel very hurt and sad but I will still manage.
	Just because I felt rejected and imperfect as a child does not mean it is true now that I am an adult.
	I am human and humans are not perfect.

Unrealistic Conclusion	Challenging Thoughts
I need someone with me while I create.	Just because I feel that way does not mean it is true.

Just because I think that does not mean it is true.

I have been creative on my own in the past.

Unrealistic Conclusions	Challenging Thoughts
I am losing my identity by engaging in _____.	That is an example of all or nothing thinking.
	I am expanding my identity.
	Just because I think that does not mean it is true.
	Just because I feel that does not mean it is true.
	I can think of ten aspects of my identity that have not changed since I began my creative pursuit.
	As I pursue my passion I will become even more true to who I am.

Challenging statements are most effective when they also address the emotional concerns behind the unrealistic expectations and conclusions. While the specific expectation or conclusion being challenged is encapsulated in words, it derives from an inhibiting theme that is fueled by powerful negative emotions, especially fear, anxiety, shame, and guilt. Thus, the challenging statement needs to be empathic and nurturing.

Recall an incident from your childhood when you had strong feelings about an issue. Perhaps you were fearful about doing something or going somewhere. Maybe you lacked trust in yourself about trying something new. At such moments, empathy, validation, and nurturance go a long way toward helping you sit with these uncomfortable reactions.

To best formulate a challenging statement, think of what the "child" behind your child logic would need to hear or experience in order to feel comforted enough to move on. In essence, reach into that most objective, nurturing, compassionate, and parental part of yourself to help soothe the upset and anxious part.

You may be quick to respond that you do not have children or know how to respond to a child. The more you connect with your emotions, the more aware you will become of that which your child logic requires in order to be soothed. If it is difficult at first to identify a response, pretend you are acting the role of being the best possible parent. This offers another way of getting in touch with what needs to be addressed. Additionally, imagine yourself as a child who is expressing an unrealistic expectation or conclusion. Ask yourself what you need to hear to help you deal with your concern. What words would help you calm down if you were a child experiencing what your child logic is now conveying.

Challenging statements that are nurturing help the creatively inhibited part of you to mourn and grieve expectations that may not be satisfied. Such statements similarly soothe the discomfort of the unrealistic conclusions you make about yourself. You may need to mourn the expectation that you can be perfect. The following challenges reflect a nurturing tone that addresses the emotions associated with unrealistic expectations of the child logic.

Unrealistic Expectation	Challenging Thoughts
I need to be perfect or I will be rejected or abandoned.	Others will still like me even if I am not perfect.
	Unfortunately, sadly, I am human. I can strive to be perfect, but humans are not perfect.
	Even if some people do reject or abandon me, I will still be alright.
	If others reject or abandon me, I will feel very hurt and sad but I will still manage.

Unrealistic Expectation	Challenging Thoughts
All stages of creativity should be equally rewarding.	That would be nice. Sadly, creativity also involves tasks that are less rewarding. Unfortunately, when being creative we sometimes have to do things that are not very exciting.

Unrealistic Expectation	Challenging Thoughts
I should devote all my energy toward meeting the needs of others.	It is very rewarding to help others be happy—while I feel I need to devote all of my energy to doing so, I also deserve to have happiness. Those who truly care about me will also want me to be happy. I can help make others happy *and* make myself happy. I really cannot please everyone.

Unrealistic Expectation	Challenging Thoughts
I am afraid of failure.	Many of us are afraid of failure. We often feel fear whenever we try something new. We often make many mistakes while learning something new. That is okay. Failure sometimes hurts, but loved ones will help me.

Failure sometimes hurts, but I can also
learn to comfort myself.

It is like a physical injury—it feels very
uncomfortable at first but in time the discomfort goes away.

Unrealistic Expectation	Challenging Thoughts
I should be better by now.	Everyone learns at a different pace.
	Learning is sometimes frustrating.
	That would be nice, but what I am doing takes time to learn.
	It takes time and practice to develop skills in any area.

Below are examples of thoughts that challenge unrealistic conclusions
by addressing both the content and the emotion behind them.

Unrealistic Conclusion	Challenging Thought
I am not good at this, so I may as well give up.	I can see how I could feel that way even if it may not be true.
	That's just one choice among many to deal with frustration.
	Disappointment makes me think that way.
	I may not believe I am good because I have not given myself enough time to develop the necessary skills.
	It's okay, I can continue even if I feel that way.

Unrealistic Conclusion	Challenging Thoughts
My work is not at all original— I should stop right now.	Everything creative is built on the work of others.
	It feels good to feel special. My work is unique even if parts of it are based on the work of others.

FINDING EVIDENCE FOR AND AGAINST YOUR THOUGHTS

Much of unrealistic thinking is based on the distortions discussed in chapter 3. We may overgeneralize, think in rigid "all-or-nothing" terms, or focus on how we believe things should be rather than on acknowledging and accepting how they are.

An especially effective way of challenging such thoughts is to present evidence that supports the belief followed by evidence that refutes it.[1] Actually identifying and listing facts that support and refute the belief helps you to look at the reality of the situation as opposed to relying on child logic that is either too constrictive or expansive. Examples of these challenges include the following:

Unrealistic Expectations	Evidence For	Evidence Against
I need to be perfect or I will be rejected or abandoned.	I was often criticized as a child when I was not perfect.	There are many times when I have not been perfect and others did not reject or abandon me.
	Some friends have teased me for not being perfect.	I have managed being teased.

	I often got the silent treatment from my father.	No one has actually abandoned me when I was not perfect.
	Some of my friends made fun of me when I made mistakes on the piano.	I did not feel good for about a day, but I got over it.
		Actually, only two friends out of a group of eight reacted that way.
Unrealistic Expectations	Evidence For	Evidence Against
I should work only when I am in the mood.	I often feel like I do my best work when I am in the mood to do it. I have most often been creative when I was in the mood to be creative.	The more I work, regardless of my mood, the more I will progress. I have often been creative even when I did not start out in the best of moods.
		I have often improved my mood by engaging in my creative passion.
		Even when I am not fully focused I have made progress.

DIALOGUING AT A DEEPER LEVEL

While challenging thoughts can be helpful, they may not be strong enough to effectively challenge and replace a deeper belief about yourself. These beliefs, often described as "core beliefs," are not at the surface of one's awareness. Similarly, they are influenced by emotions that we are not fully aware of experiencing. Subsequently, they may require more extensive dialogue between you and that part of you that is governed by child logic. This involves exploring, probing, and reflecting on your child logic at a deeper level, while at the same time being empathic.

Dialoguing may also involve inquiry. Through inquiry you become more aware of thoughts and emotions that interact to foster the inhibiting theme. One guiding inquiry that is especially helpful is asking in an ongoing manner, "What then?" When posing this question, you probe at a deeper level to identify your core concerns. Similarly, inquiring with "tell me more" further probes the meaning attached to the strong inhibiting concerns. By repeatedly presenting these inquiries, you will eventually come to an answer that more clearly reflects the core issue.

The process of dialoguing with your child logic offers a corrective experience. By engaging with your child logic in this manner, you will be directly talking to the source of those mind-body experiences that sabotage your creative efforts. Just like a parent who offers a child skills in self-soothing, you will be helping the child-logic part of you to internalize new guidelines and standards that allow for increased openness and access to creative genius. You will be paving the way for a greater tolerance for the frustrations and anxiety that are a natural part of the creative process.

The goal of this dialogue is not to stifle, ignore, or completely distract your child logic from its hold over you. Rather, it is to change the actual makeup of your child logic. To use the analogy of repairing a software program that is corrupt, dialoguing with your child logic reflects the equivalent of replacing your software, a kind of upgrade, and one that like a new program is more suitable and relevant for how things are now.

From this vantage point, I offer a variety of responses that might help get this dialogue going. I do not mean to suggest that you completely ignore the logic that you are already using; rather, these responses emphasize the practice of going deeper and really listening to your child logic like an empathic and ideal parent. Again, listen to that part of yourself just as you would a four- or five-year-old.

Empathic responses communicate more mature logic; but equally important, they convey a recognition, validation, and acceptance of the emotions behind your inhibiting themes. These are overwhelmingly influenced by the emotions of a child and the emotional intelligence of a child. As such, the emotions dominate your child logic and may often seem impervious to attempts to reason with or calm it through the power of logic.

Such interactions involve inquiries that better identify the meaning or the implied outcome reflected by the unrealistic expectation or conclusion. The following responses reflect a variety of ways you can address the fear of failure.

Unrealistic Expectation	Challenging Thoughts
I am afraid I will fail.	Tell me more about that. What would that mean?
I will never be able to paint well. It won't look good.	And then what? What do you anticipate will happen if it doesn't look good?
I'll feel foolish. People will think I'm stupid.	And what would that mean? What if people did think that?
They'll laugh at me. They will not want to be around me. They'll reject me.	So, you believe that if your work is not perfect you'll be all alone?
They will see I am flawed.	What does that mean?
I am inadequate.	Even if I do not paint, it may mean I need more practice. It may mean I am not as skillful in painting as I am in other areas. But it does not mean that I am inadequate as a person.

Unrealistic Conclusion	Challenging Thoughts
I feel guilty to spend time pursuing my photography.	What does that mean?

I feel like it is a waste of time.	What makes it a waste of time?
I should be helping people.	What does being selfish mean?
I feel selfish.	
I feel bad. I feel like I do not deserve to be enjoying myself.	What would happen if you do?
Other people will feel hurt.	What would happen then?
They would resent me.	What would happen then?
They might leave me.	What would happen then?
I would be completely alone.	How likely is that to happen?
Unrealistic Expectation	Challenging Thoughts
I am fearful of rejection.	What comes to mind when I think of being rejected?
	What are my thoughts about rejection?
	What does it feel like to be rejected?
	What would I do if I was rejected?

In these examples, the challenges are intended not to tell your child logic how to think or how to feel. Rather, they encourage open self-reflection regarding the meaning of failure and a shared exploration of what has caused this theme to be so powerful. These questions do not begin with "why" for several reasons. As suggested earlier, asking why leads to an emphasis on explaining, finding a single reason or cause, rather than on recognition of the thinking and emotions associated with the fear.

Since the core belief is deeply embedded in emotion, it needs constant monitoring and challenge in order for you to successfully reduce the hold it may have on your automatic thoughts. It also needs empathy and compassion that addresses the intense fear, guilt, shame, or anxiety that underlies it. The core belief is the basic distortion of the child logic that fuels the cluster of unrealistic expectations and conclusions that inhibit creative engagement.

Genuine control over the decisions we make in life very much rests on our access to and recognition of our deeper experiences and how they impact our emotions, thoughts, physical states, and behaviors. To the degree that we recognize our unrealistic thoughts and underlying emotions, we are better able to choose whether to trust them or to ignore them. Through repeatedly challenging them, we are reminded that they are signs that we are feeling threatened in some way when, in fact, we may be overly exaggerating the possible threat or may not be in any real danger.

We have little control over automatic unrealistic thoughts and conclusions that enter our awareness. However, once we are aware of them, we do have a choice in deciding if we should listen to them as though they reflect reality or challenge and replace them. The more we challenge such reactions, the more adaptive we become in effectively managing those distinct moments of tension aroused during creative engagement.

MONITORING PROGRESS

One of the most important factors when making changes in your behavior is monitoring progress. Objectively noting the advances you make in shifting your thoughts, emotions, or physical states is another way of challenging the helplessness you may experience when dealing with inhibiting themes. You can use your log to make ratings of the expectations or conclusions and the challenges that form your responses to them. The following log includes ratings on a scale of 1 to 100, where 1 reflects no belief that the statement of an inhibiting theme applies to you and 100 reflects a very strong belief that the statement applies to you. This can be done over several different occasions in which you have challenged your inhibiting belief.

Inhibiting Theme	Challenging Response
I am afraid that people will dislike, reject, or abandon me if I succeed. (80)	Just because I feel that way does not mean it is true. (65)

If they truly are good friends, they will be happy for my success. (70)

Some people may dislike or abandon me but not everyone will respond that way. (80)

I do not dislike everyone who is successful. (90)

Yes, some people may be jealous. That hurts, but I'll still be alright. (60)

I have friends who would never reject me for doing well. (85)

GENERAL GUIDELINES REGARDING CHALLENGING THOUGHTS

Effectively managing the negative mind-body reactions of creative engagement entails repeatedly taking time to challenge those themes as they arise. The following guidelines offer a summary of how to address the thoughts and emotions associated with inhibiting themes.

1. Practice self-reflection exercise #2 from chapter 12 in order to gain greater general awareness of your internal experience. In contrast, exercise #3 is the key exercise to help you overcome your inhibiting tension.
2. Do this exercise when you are beginning to experience the early stages of arousal of such tension rather than waiting for it to escalate.
3. Especially when first beginning to challenge child logic, take time to write a log, outlining your unrealistic expectations or conclusions and specific challenges to them. Taking time to formulate your thoughts in writing enhances the powerful influence such thoughts can have on your child logic.
4. Pay attention to your past capacity for creative engagement as a

measure of progress. For example, if you were able to sit with a painting for thirty minutes, focus on gradually developing increased comfort. Specifically, set a goal of forty minutes, rather than immediately trying to work on a painting for several hours. If you have completely avoided reviewing a catalog of a school program, see if you can manage ten to fifteen minutes of sustained engagement.

5. The first attempts at increasing focused engagement in your creative pursuit may end up more focused on identifying and recognizing inhibiting themes rather than on making any concrete progress in your project. This is to be expected as you develop increased comfort with your pursuit. Making progress in creative engagement is very much like starting any new habit. All too often, we experience frustration because we maintain unrealistic expectations regarding such progress. To counter this tendency, remain sensitive to your internal experiences and the dosage of creative engagement you can effectively manage.

6. Repetition, repetition, repetition. Continue to practice these exercises each and every time you experience discomfort.

7. We are all creatures of habit. An important consideration in assessing your progress is to remember that even when you make progress you will still occasionally experience the same inhibiting themes that have accompanied moments of challenge in the past. In no way does the renewed experience of inhibiting themes mean that you have not made progress. Rather, such experiences emphasize the tenacity of deeply embedded past experiences. Additionally, they reflect the fact that stress inherent in your next phase of creativity may once again arouse your inhibiting tension.

8. All of our inhibiting themes developed because, as children, we experienced feelings of being threatened. In a sense, these themes are strategies we unwittingly adopted to protect ourselves; but they are coping strategies that have gone awry. They are no longer relevant and have instead become crippling. Remembering that the child logic and emotions behind them serve the purpose of self-protection can help us to be more compassionate in both understanding and challenging them.

9. Remember that the goal of using these challenges is not to eliminate all tension. Rather, the goal is to diminish the discomfort aroused by

inhibiting themes so that you can increase the intensity and frequency with which you experience a positive mind-body set when engaged in creativity.

*** FOR FURTHER EXPLORATION ***

1. Maintain logs of beliefs and the challenges you have formulated over a six-week period.
2. After reviewing your logs, make a listing of those core beliefs you most frequently identify when encountering inhibitions regarding creative engagement. After you have repeatedly challenged these beliefs, make a list of those challenges that you experience as being most helpful in reducing the degree to which you maintain such beliefs.
3. Make flash cards with the most effective challenges written on them. Review them prior to beginning your creative pursuit.
4. Make a list of the most effective challenges and post it in the area where you do the most creative work.
5. Make your own motivational poster. Find a subject that you find inspiring, one that moves you toward optimism and hope. Print your challenges on it and post it where you do your creative work.

REFLECTIONS

Children need models more than they need critics.—Joseph Joubert

There is always one moment in childhood when the door opens and lets the future in.—Graham Greene

Such as are your habitual thoughts, such also will be the character of your mind; for the soul is dyed by the thoughts.—Marcus Aurelius

Affirmations are like prescriptions for certain aspects of yourself you want to change.—Jerry Frankhauser

NOTE

1. Dennis Greenberger and Christine A. Padesky, *Mind Over Mood* (New York: Guilford, 1995).

Chapter 14

FOSTERING
POSITIVE EMOTIONS

Much of your creative drive is rooted in and echoes the natural openness and curiosity you experienced as you first encountered your world. These attitudes were fueled as well as rewarded by positive emotions of joy, excitement, and hope. And, just as these emotions stirred you to become fully engaged in discovery and exploration in those early years, they remain an essential component for your creative engagement as an adult. Any strategy that can reawaken and confirm that earlier emotional experience will further increase the degree to which you can successfully engage in your creative pursuit. While the previous chapter emphasized directly challenging and replacing thoughts, this chapter offers strategies to generate positive emotions as a way to transcend the impact of inhibiting themes.

POSITIVE EMOTIONS ENHANCE THINKING

Only in recent years has the focus of psychology expanded to include the study of "positive psychology," the identification and understanding of our strengths.[1] Toward this end, positive psychology has studied happiness, courage, resilience, content, creativity, exuberance, hope, optimism, and other character strengths that reflect and are essential for healthy functioning. This area of study has been pursued not simply to identify the ingredients for happiness but also to understand those qualities and strengths that positively impact health, relationships, work satisfaction, sense of well-being, and overall life fulfillment.

Inquiry in this field has led to the "broaden-and-build" theory of positive emotions. According to this perspective, as stated by Barbara Fredrickson, "Positive emotions seem to broaden people's momentary thought-action repertoires and build their enduring personal resources."[2] In contrast to inhibiting themes that foster constriction in thinking or promote escape from a situation, positive emotions lead us to be receptive to a wider range of thoughts and actions. Joy is seen as prompting us to play, to push limits, and to be creative. Interest, viewed as a distinct positive emotion, furthers our desire to explore, discover, and take in information. Contentment is viewed as allowing us to be in the moment and to attend to the details of our experiences. Love is viewed as being a combination of positive emotions that "creates recurring cycles of urges to play with, explore, and savor our loved ones."[3]

To the degree that you foster positive emotions at the moment of challenge, you expand your capacity to be fully present in mind and body, receptive to your curiosity, and joyful in engagement. At the same time, as you increase your openness to positive thoughts, you become less judgmental and constrictive in your self-assessment. In contrast, to the degree that you are held captive by inhibiting emotions, you devote much of your psychic energy toward protecting your sense of self from perceived threats.

Further, as described by Martin Seligman, a past president of the American Psychological Association, you may experience "spiraling emotions."[4] Though spiraling emotions may function negatively, as with the resulting disruptions of judgment and action characteristic of mania, in the present context, this phrase describes the finding that positive emotions evoke positive emotions. In other words, positive emotions allow you to produce a greater number of thoughts that increase your receptivity to the creative process. In part, this also occurs as you become better able to initiate thoughts and follow through wherever they lead. In this way, positive emotions foster an expanded flow of thoughts that subsequently yield a greater possibility of forming new connections and patterns.

MINDFULNESS, WILL, AND SHIFTING ATTENTION

Practicing mindfulness allows you to be more fully aware of all that you are experiencing at a given moment. Through the practice of mindfulness while engaging in a creative pursuit, you will open yourself to experiencing the full range of negative reactions associated with inhibiting themes. Through this same process, however, you can develop increased awareness of the range of positive reactions that creative activity arouses. As you become aware of the broader range of your reactions, you can develop an increased capacity to choose which of two distinct and contrasting mind-body sets you wish to attend to. In effect, you can develop an increased capacity to challenge your negative thoughts so as to instead focus on the positive aspects of engagement, thus relegating the inhibiting themes to the background of your attention. By becoming progressively more aware of these positive and rewarding aspects, you increasingly experience the positive imagery, thoughts, and emotions that are associated with the creative process. Through this process, you make way for a more positive mind-body set.

The better you can focus attention on the positive emotions associated with creative engagement, the more you can remain present throughout the moment of challenge. The ability to shift your emotional focus when caught in the throes of a moment of tension involves the capacity for transcendence. Through repetition, even while you may be experiencing fear, anxiety, or even shame, you can increasingly gain the wherewithal to shift attention to the rewards of creativity. When creative effort results in inhibiting tension, purposely remind yourself of the big picture and the peak moments of satisfaction you've had on your creative journey.

For example, suppose you are in the middle of painting and experience an urge to disengage, either temporarily or by stopping completely. First, become aware of the internal states that are pushing you to withdraw. Through practicing mindfulness and challenging thoughts, you can observe these internal states without a sense of urgency to listen to or act on them. Instead, you can take a moment to recall in as much detail as possible the positive emotions that you associate with creative pursuit.

Focus your attention more on "sensing" than on thinking. For example, if you paint, heighten your attention to the details of painting, noticing the colors you are using and their play upon the canvas. Note their texture, contrast, and the mood they convey. Attend to the visceral reactions you experience in your body as you move the brush. Lose yourself in the adventure. Focusing on sensing the details of your endeavor will help you to once again connect with the more positive emotions related to the act. Equally important is the fact that focusing on sensing competes with and distracts you from attending to inhibiting self-talk.

Similarly, while writing requires heightened attention to your thoughts, you can focus on being mindful of the details and content of what you are writing as opposed to the details of your self-conscious and potentially inhibiting child logic. Focus instead on the words you are composing, their arrangement on the page, the sounds they make, and the rhythm you feel in your fingers as you enter them on the computer or on a tablet.

It is in losing yourself through your senses and investing the energy of your thoughts in the creative venture that you free yourself from negative emotions and inhibiting themes. Clearly, this can be challenging when you have a history of inhibiting mind-body reactions. However, as you begin to view tension as a reminder that you have a choice regarding which of your mind-body sets to attend to, you will become increasingly empowered to choose the more rewarding focus of attention. This sense of choice is further strengthened as you practice the techniques of challenging your self-talk described in the previous chapter. As you recognize the choice, you can again draw on that most nurturing, compassionate, and objective part of you to remind your inhibiting child logic of the real joy of creative engagement.

Again, I find it useful to refer to the optical illusion of the cube as a model to depict how we have control over what we choose to attend to. See figure 14-1.

Focus your attention on the cube so that "tension of being creative" appears to be on the upper-left side of the front face of the cube and "positive aspects of creating" appears on the upper-inside face. This is your perspective when you attend to the tension you experience during the creative process. Now, focus your attention on the cube so that "positive aspects of creating" appear on the upper-front face of the cube with "tension of being creative" on the inner-rear face. This perspective represents your reaction when you are more positively engaged.

Just as we are able to choose how to attend to the foreground and the background of the cube, with practice we can increase our ability to attend to the positive tension or the satisfaction of creating when actually engaged in creative pursuit. The following exercise will help you to achieve this.

Exercise

Either imagine yourself being creatively engaged or place yourself in a real situation of engagement. Place yourself at the computer if you are writing,

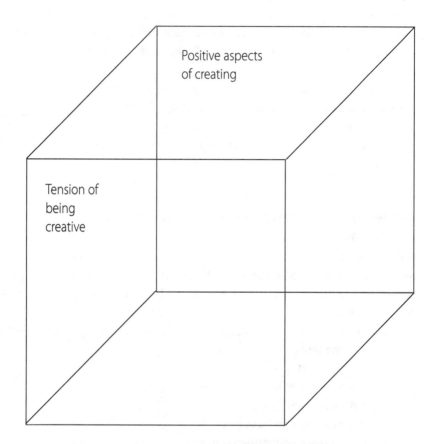

FIGURE 14-1: TENSION OF BEING CREATIVE
VS. POSITIVE ASPECTS OF CREATING

behind the camera or looking at your photos if you are a photographer, playing your musical instrument, or about to offer an idea to your fund-raising group. Take a moment to focus on the cause of heightened tension. Be mindful of that moment in an effort to better identify what you are experiencing. Recognize your reactions, including your emotions, thoughts, and physical states.

Now engage in your creative endeavor while you consciously and assertively identify and focus your attention on what is rewarding about your activity. If it is writing, do you experience the satisfaction of identifying that one word or phrase that seems to capture your idea or concept? Is it the magic of transforming and capturing your thoughts? If you are engaged in creating music, is it the physical excitement of hearing the patterns of notes and chords that so acutely resonate with the sounds in your head and the sensations of your body?

Focus attention on the tangible aspects of your creative engagement that provide the greatest pleasure. Lose yourself in the details of your engagement. Through repeated attempts to shift your focus of attention, you will increasingly experience a shift in your emotions, as well as your mind-body set in general.

"FLOW," POSITIVE EMOTIONS, AND CREATIVE ENGAGEMENT

As described previously, the state of "flow" is a mind-body set that is most reflective of committed presence and engagement in the creative process. It is a state of complete absorption in the task at hand. It is during these moments that you are most predisposed to experience a positive mind-body set.

According to Mihalyi Csikszentmihalyi, the psychologist and researcher who coined the term, flow involves:

- a task that is challenging and requires skills
- concentration
- deep, effortless involvement
- an experience of having control
- a lack of self-consciousness
- the loss of a sense of time

The experience of flow is characteristic of creative tasks that challenge you to use and expand upon your repertoire of skills.[5] At such moments, you are fully engaged in directing your energies toward something that you value and hold to be deeply and personally meaningful. Minimal energy is expended on challenging the inhibiting mind-body sets because "contrary to what happens all too often in everyday life, in moments such as these what we feel, what we wish, and what we think are in harmony."[6]

In the actual moment of creativity, you are fully engaged in observing the impact of your actions while at the same time moving forward with mindful intention to define them. When you are able to overcome the impact of inhibiting themes, you can move forward fully present and committed to your endeavor. It is in this state of mind that you can be most open to inspiration, since you are momentarily free of the need to protect yourself. For this brief duration it is as if you are once again fearless. When fully immersed in this state of mind, you experience an involvement that feels automatic and connects to the details of your engagement with your medium.

Most significant for our discussion, when fully engaged in flow, you are entirely without self-consciousness. It is this lack of self-consciousness that liberates you from fixating on negative inhibitions. Csikszentmihalyi suggests that it is only when we reflect on our work and on ourselves that we experience emotions. As such, it is when you pause to briefly assess your engagement that you experience joy, empowerment, contentment, or satisfaction.[7] In contrast, I believe that such emotions may not be fully conscious. They are instead present at a deeper level in your unconscious and in your body. They surface intermittently—after a certain word or sentence is completed, after a paint stroke is made, when a form is observed, when a string of notes are heard, or when patterns of fabric seem to resonate with an internal sense of harmony.

Flowing free of self-consciousness, it is understandable that you lose sense of time. I have certainly experienced this while writing. I similarly experienced it with an extreme intensity several years ago when I was at the Lincoln Park Zoo in Chicago, taking pictures of animals as part of an assignment for my photography class. After observing a variety of animals, I decided to photograph a group of prairie dogs. It was three in the afternoon when I returned to their cage to take pictures of them.

I watched them play with each other and noticed their facial expressions as they frolicked. I then began to frame a variety of shots before actually taking pictures. I had decided to capture images of them against the zoo landscape in such a way that the fence would disappear in the final photographs. I used an entire roll of film to complete my assignment. When I looked at my watch after taking the pictures, I saw that nearly two hours had passed. I have certainly experienced flow in many different situations, but I had never experienced time passing so quickly. I had become so unselfconscious that I was not aware of anyone around me.

Increasing your predisposition for experiencing positive emotions can be helped by fully attending to and savoring the pleasure you experience in recognizing the joy of flow. The more conscious you are of such moments, the better you will be able to recall and focus on them when you encounter the challenge of an inhibiting theme.

Engaging in flow requires intention and commitment, both of which are sabotaged by negative inhibiting themes. Developing realistic expectations, forming more realistic conclusions, challenging the excessive physical tension that arises when you dare to create; these are all ways of freeing energy for the creative process. When you are entangled by inhibiting themes, you are moved toward conserving energy. This is understandable, considering that inhibiting internalizations are so closely related to the feeling that you are threatened. It is this very situation that leads to a sense that energy is limited. Yet, when the trance of inhibition is lifted, you again experience yourself as having limitless reserves of energy.

Finding and maintaining flow takes effort. It requires mindfulness and physical effort to move beyond inertia. But once engaged in flow, it becomes more effortless. Part of the difficulty in initiating the creative process is that, while you may anticipate the joys of creativity, you are forced to get past the inhibiting tension of beginning your creative project. Such beginnings, whether sitting down to write, setting up the paints and canvas, or touching a formless pile of clay, force you to come in contact with the difficult and uneasy task of moving from inertia to engagement in flow. Again, this takes great effort and energy.

We all too often succumb to the pressure of inhibiting themes. The emotions aroused at such moments guide us in decision making and, to a great extent, move us toward safety. In contrast, positive emotions pull us forward toward a person, an object, an activity, or even a way of thinking or acting. The challenge of overcoming inhibiting themes is to recognize that they arouse negative emotions even when there is really no threat to safety. Under the influence of inhibiting themes, we are overly focused and sensitive toward aspects of the environment that are in fact safe but, through the lens of fear, guilt, shame, and anxiety, appear threatening. Like a faulty thermostat that is set to activate heat sooner than necessary, our default setting may leave us with a very low threshold for experiencing such apprehension.

To some extent, our ability to maintain creative engagement can be enhanced by a commitment to be mindful of this faulty setting. With awareness comes an increase in our capacity for a more willful focus of attention. This is the basis of the ability to shift focus to positive mind-body states as described in the following exercise.

VISUALIZATION TO ENHANCE POSITIVE EMOTIONS

Think about what is rewarding in your experiences when being creative. Fulfillment and positive reactions are not often associated with the first moments of engagement. Making those first brush strokes when painting, writing that first sentence, running your fingers over an instrument, or generating that first idea often carry with them either a level of negative tension or little emotion. While you may expect it to be different, these first steps are like a warm-up period before physical exercise. It may even feel perfunctory and highlight your ambivalence about getting started. You are moving from inertia to some form of activity in your mind and body.

A runner warms his muscles by stretching or by initially engaging in a slow run. Those who lift weights to develop strength begin their workout with weights in the lighter range so as to develop a mind-body set for greater challenges. When he was older, Picasso is said to have played piano for thirty minutes just to make his fingers more limber for his painting. And yet, all too often, when anticipating the pursuit of creative engagement, we focus attention on this initial moment. By envisioning this moment, we attend to what may be one of the most challenging experiences of the creative process—just getting started. For practice, do the following exercise.

Exercise

Take a moment to imagine yourself beginning to engage in your creative venture. Do not take your vision beyond those first initial moments of engagement. Reflect on and list your emotional reactions, your thoughts, and any physical states that arise with imagining such moments. Be aware of the specific details of the engagement that you are attending to as you have these reactions. What are the specific and distinct details of experience that foster the moments that you perceive to be especially challenging?

Now, take a moment to envision yourself at a more rewarding period of engagement. Specifically, attend to those moments of the creative process when you are experiencing peak satisfaction, those moments that reflect the pleasure and gratification of this particular form of creative engagement. Be sensitive to what you are attending to as well as to any senses that are involved in your experience. This may entail a moment that occurs an hour into the process, at the midpoint, or even toward the end of a period of engagement. Fully attend to all the details of this experience, those that make up your surroundings and, most important, your emotional reactions, thoughts, and any physical states that arise with imagining those moments.

Through doing this exercise you will create a powerfully motivating experience. It is the moment you should focus attention on whenever you think about once again resuming creative engagement. This ability to intentionally focus on and attend to what is personally meaningful and rewarding is a powerful resource in overcoming inertia and gaining creative momentum.

THE CONTAGION OF POSITIVE EMOTIONS

Internally, positive emotions help us to spiral in our thinking with regard to creative engagement. Add to this mix interactions with others who have positive emotions and we have further support and nurturance for our creative engagement. It is for this reason that I genuinely encourage that you seek involvement with others who not only have a similar creative passion but whose attitudes and actions reflect positive emotions.

All too often, in an effort to stir creative juices, we may seek support groups. Just as these can truly support and nurture positive emotions, they can also support and nurture inhibiting themes. For example, writers often seek support by attending groups of writers. However, some members may be perfectionists. Others may have spent little time writing because they are overly engaged with their inhibiting themes. For some, their underlying motivation may be to vent against inhibiting themes rather than to share feedback and support that help to enhance positive emotions.

Try to spend time with positive and creative people, those who have been fully engaged in pursuing their creative passions, rather than with those who are overwhelmed by inhibiting child logic.

RECOGNIZE, ACKNOWLEDGE, AND EMBRACE COMPETENCE

Several years ago, noted talk-show host Oprah Winfrey emphasized the use of a gratitude journal. This involved a daily recording of anything that occurred throughout the day for which one experiences appreciation. It is intended to highlight our attention to what is positive when we are more often predisposed to focus on all that is negative.

Recently, research in positive psychology has studied a variation on this approach.[8] Individuals who responded to a questionnaire on a Web site created by Martin Seligman were assessed to determine their levels of happiness and depression. They were then asked to try a number of activities over the next few weeks. Of the activities suggested, the two significant outcomes were for those who had used exercises described as "three good things" and "using your signature strengths." In the first, participants were asked to identify and record three good things that happened each day. In addition, they were asked to write down a causal explanation for each good thing.

The second exercise involved having the participants identify a "signature strength." These included twenty-four identified strengths such as curiosity, a love of learning, social intelligence, ingenuity, street smarts, bravery, and others.[9] They were then asked to use one of these strengths in a new and different way for one week. Individuals who engaged in these exercises showed a significant increase in happiness and decrease in depressive responses up to six months following their participation.

As a variation of the first exercise, I encourage you to try the following exercise.

Exercise

Note on a daily basis both your competence and your accomplishments regarding your creative pursuit. Accomplishments may include the completion of even one paragraph of a résumé, deciding on what color oil paints to purchase, reviewing a guide for comparing cameras, or writing two pages of that novel that you have thought about for years. At another point on the continuum, progress may involve finishing the first draft of a chapter for a book, completing a poem, designing a dance sequence, or signing up for a woodworking class.

The emphasis is on highlighting the progress made in spite of trepidation or inhibiting tension you may have experienced while moving forward. Write a detailed description of what you did in order to overcome any hurdles that stand in the way of achieving your goal. The following statements provide examples of highlighting competence.

"I overcame my anxiety and fears by challenging some of my negative thoughts."

"I spent time thinking about how much enjoyment I experience when I am painting."

"I asked my friend his opinion of my work."

"I continually reminded myself that it was the first draft and that I did not need to be concerned about how many drafts I develop."

"I performed breathing exercises."

"I practiced mindfulness."

"I became more compassionate with myself." (If so, how did you do this?)

"I reminded myself that my friends will still be there for me even if I do not succeed in my music."

Maintaining this journal achieves several goals. The list serves in a very concrete way as a reminder, no matter how you try to diminish it, of what you have actually accomplished during that day. The actual act of recording it in writing brings to the foreground of your attention the mastery of challenges you have faced and overcome that day.

Describing your accomplishment in detail highlights the specific steps you took to overcome your inhibiting themes. This is an extremely powerful part of the journal for several reasons. First, it highlights your ability to move forward toward increased creative engagement. Second, it further fosters your capacity to be objective, to stand back and look at your mind-body states, and to acknowledge that, in spite of some discomfort, you effectively remained engaged. A third aspect of this exercise is that it provides very specific feedback about what works. And, in doing so, it reinforces your awareness about what to do the next time inhibiting tension arises. I compare this last step to the need to receive feedback about your learning in any subject area. Suppose you were enrolled in a class for written composition. You are asked to submit a paper on Monday. After some challenge, effort, and commitment, you submit your paper but do not receive feedback in time to present your next paper on the following Monday. Without feedback you would be operating out of the same mental set, the same guidelines, the same strengths, as well as the same weaknesses in preparing your paper.

As a parallel analogy, suppose you receive your feedback orally without time to write it down. While it made sense when you heard it, after a week you may remember just a few of the details and much of the feedback will have been forgotten. This highlights the power of writing down your competencies, the specific strategies you used to move past the moments of challenge that blocked your creative endeavor.

Taken together over time, the entries of accomplishments and competencies build a powerful log that becomes increasingly difficult to ignore or minimize. It acts as a reference for strategies that you have experimented with and identified as the most effective for your unique needs. Feedback is essential to further direct your attention toward positive accomplishments and positive emotions.

LOCATION, LOCATION, LOCATION

In real estate, an expression that denotes the most highly valued property is "Location, location, location." This can also be an effective guideline when trying to enhance positive emotions. Specifically, I find that there are certain locations that have the potential to help foster positive emotions. In this case, I am not referring to those places that arouse only joy. Rather, I am focusing on those locations that energize and inspire empowerment as they instill hope and optimism. These locations may similarly arouse positive visceral reactions as they stir your emotions with excitement about "possibilities" and move you beyond a tendency to listen to your fears and anxieties.

I have found such locations in every city in which I have lived. These have often been places that seemed to create some distance from my ordinary daily life. For example, I remember as a young child growing up in the Bronx that I found the rooftop of my four-story building to be such a place. I could see the open sky, the roofs of other buildings, passengers holding straps as they moved along on the elevated train a block away from my house, even flocks of pigeons flying from their home base several blocks away. This was a very peaceful place to step back and notice myself as well as others—to stop and reflect.

When I was older, being anywhere near bodies of water had a similar impact. Whether it was an ocean, a lake, a bay, or even a river, I found that bodies of water helped me relax, evoking a sense of positive emotional energy. I am sure this is in part due to my many pleasurable memories of family adventures, making Sunday trips to Jones Beach on Long Island. Certainly, quiet corners of Central Park were another source of such inspiration. When I lived in Salt Lake City for several years following my graduate program, I often found scenic areas in the canyons or in the mountains to further arouse this very inspiring mind-set. There was an overlook point that I will never forget. It offered a panoramic view of mountains and trees that included the sliver of a lake. I often visited this place that infused me with energy and a sense of empowerment, whether in the spring or during the first hours of a snowstorm.

Such locations do not have to be outdoors. I have similarly been impacted by visits to art museums and galleries. If you cannot readily identify such a place, set out to find one.

MOVIES

Certain movies entertain us, while others challenge us to think. Some capture the essence of universal life experiences and highlight how people manage them. Many films inspire us to take action, whether political or personal in nature. Some movies simply create a pleasurable experience that leaves us with fifteen or twenty minutes of discussion regarding its high points of humor, the special effects, the acting, or the beauty of the cinematography.

On the other hand, there are certain movies that can tremendously inspire us to take chances, trust ourselves, recognize and acknowledge our strengths, or be hopeful and optimistic. Such movies are often those that depict characters who challenge convention or the forces that stifle them. These are stories of individuals who have followed their dreams, individuals who have effectively managed competing inhibiting themes that stood in the way of their expressions of the self. The joy in watching such films is that they allow us to identify with and vicariously experience the empowerment and courage that is required to overcome such challenges. We long to follow in the footsteps of the heroes of these stories.

Yes, we can easily leave the theater admiring them and then quickly conclude that our struggles are different, or focus on the many reasons why we cannot follow a similar path. In doing so, at that very instant, we are rehearsing for inertia as we revisit those persistent inhibiting themes. These movies can be powerful motivators when used in conjunction with the other strategies presented in this book. They can help us to effectively manage inhibiting themes regarding fear, anxiety, shame, and guilt.

In the last few years, as I was preparing to write this book, I became especially attracted to movies that were relevant to creativity. With regard to patience, empowerment, and positive emotions, I found *Andy Goldsworthy's Rivers and Tides* to be an especially powerful film. This movie, as previously mentioned, is about the English artist who uses natural settings and materials to create his art.[10] Some of his art is truly living (and dying), as it is impacted by currents and tides as they ebb and flow throughout the day.

More recently, I viewed *Born into Brothels*, an Oscar-winning documentary showing how one woman traveled to India, originally to interview the country's women, but instead spent her time teaching children to take pictures.[11] The movie is a gripping and powerful statement about creativity and empowerment, the resilience and openness of children, and the triumph of optimism and hope over some of the most trying living conditions.

At the same time, movies with other themes can be equally inspiring. They derive their ability to inspire not by depicting a character's triumph over a challenge but rather from the magnificent depiction of a story through images, acting, directing, or a combination of these factors. These movies offer inspiration by being magnificent examples of the creative spirit and of the products of the creative process.

CHILDREN AND PUPPIES

If we are looking for optimism, hope, and a sense of excitement about discovery, we only need to spend time observing children and puppies at play. Both carry an unlimited sense of awe and curiosity. Both seem to become exuberant about the slightest observation they make, the newest "find" of the moment. Both seem to be caught up in moments of flow, unselfconsciously engaging in exploration and truly attending to the details of their observations. Through their facial expressions and body movements, we can see the joyful embrace of what is novel. For each, every encounter appears to be unique, inviting, and captivating.

Certainly, some individuals do not experience such a positive response to either children or animals. I suggest that behind these reactions is an inhibiting theme that is being aroused regarding some aspect they exhibit. Engaging in self-reflection exercises while in the presence of children or pets may help identify these themes.

This chapter has identified a variety of strategies to help you enhance and attend to positive emotions. It is an incomplete list, since the things that move you to experience positive emotions are influenced by your own unique identity and experiences. I hope this chapter serves as a springboard of inspiration to identify additional strategies that further reflect and resonate with what can move you to the experience of positive emotions.

*** FOR FURTHER EXPLORATION ***

1. What reactions did you experience as you read this chapter? Specifically, what emotions, thoughts, or physical reactions did you experience? Did your reactions reflect your inhibiting themes?

2. If you were inspired by reading this chapter, which reactions did you experience that helped inspire you? Which strategies most appealed to you?

3. As suggested previously, merely reading a book about creativity may arouse some discomfort related to your inhibiting themes. Did you experience any negative thoughts about the strategies, about the success you would have in using them, or about their genuine usefulness? If so, what inhibiting themes may have been triggered by the suggestion that you actually take action to enhance your positive emotions?

4. What locations help foster your positive emotions?

5. What types of experiences are most helpful in enhancing your positive emotions?

6. Over the next few days, notice any articles in the news that help to enhance your positive emotions. Then identify what it is about that particular news item that leaves you feeling more positive.

7. Find a location where you believe your positive emotions are

enhanced. Sit there for a while and savor the experience. Try to identify those factors about this physical setting that help contribute to its overall impact on you. While there are factors specific to the location, you may identify specific qualities or meanings that you associate with that setting that resonate with your positive emotions.

REFLECTIONS

Each of us really understands in others only those feelings he is capable of producing in himself.—Andre Gide

Happiness is that state of consciousness which proceeds from the achievement of one's values.—Ayn Rand

Joy is but the sign that creative emotion is fulfilling its purpose.—Henri Frederic Amiel

NOTES

1. Martin E. P. Seligman and Mihaly Csikzentmihalhyi, "Positive Psychology," *American Psychologist* 55 (2000): 5–14.

2. Barbara L. Fredrickson, "The Role of Positive Emotions in Positive Psychology," *American Psychologist* 56 (2001): 218–26.

3. Barbara L. Fredrickson, "Positive Emotions," in *Handbook of Positive Psychology*, ed. C. R. Snyder and Shane J. Lopez (New York: Oxford University Press, 2002), p.123.

4. Martin E. P. Seligman, *Authentic Happinesss* (New York: Free Press, 2002).

5. Mihaly Csikszentmihalyi, *Finding Flow* (New York: Basic Books, 1997).

6. Ibid., p. 29.

7. Ibid.

8. Martin E. P. Seligman et al., "Positive Psychology Progress," *American Psychologist* 60 (2005): 410–21.

9. Seligman, *Authentic Happiness*.

10. *Andy Goldsworthy's Rivers and Tides*, DVD, directed by Thomas Riedelshelmer (2001; New York: New Video Group, 2004).

11. *Born into Brothels*, DVD, directed by Zana Briski and Russ Kaufman (2004; New York: ThinkFilm, 2005).

Chapter 15

ENHANCING PHYSICAL STATES FOR CREATIVE ENGAGEMENT

E nhancing positive physical states is another route toward maintaining a mind-body set open to the creative moment. While there may not be one clearly identifiable physical state that is most conducive to all aspects of creativity, different physical states impact your mind-body sets in ways that may help you to be more open to various aspects of creative engagement. This chapter offers a description of how these physical states can impact such openness as well as how to take advantage of them.

The experiences of pain and physical fatigue offer two notable examples of how physical states can impact your mind-body state. Both conditions impair concentration and compete with your efforts to be open, alert, and flexible in your thinking. When they are extreme, all else loses relevance. When experiencing fatigue or pain, your scope of focus narrows so that you have little attention for the details of your internal landscape or for the world around you. Clearly, both pain and fatigue drain you physically, while accompanying irritability and tension dominate your emotional experience.

The experience of fatigue or pain also leads to the development of tunnel vision with regard to time owing to a reduced capacity to focus on the past or future. These afflictions can also greatly impact your perception of your capacity to manage difficult challenges. Research suggests that people tend to assess their abilities to carry out future activities by determining how much energy they currently have, thus failing to recognize that they may have more energy in reserve when the time to carry out said activities actually arrives.[1]

239

PHYSICAL STATES AND MOOD

As I've emphasized throughout this book, our physical states strongly impact our overall mind-body sets, even when we are not fully aware of their underlying influence. The intensity of these physical states and mind-body sets in turn impacts the degree to which we can overcome moments of challenge in the creative process. These distinct moments of creative challenge involve a balance of tension and energy that either pushes us to stay engaged or moves us toward withdrawal. Psychologist Robert Thayer has studied this balance and how it impacts mood. He conceptualizes moods as encompassing four distinct patterns of reactions based on states he calls (1) calm-energy, (2) calm-tiredness, (3) tense-energy, and (4) tense-tiredness.[2]

In a state of calm-energy, you feel good. You experience yourself as alert, perhaps sociable, and confident. Physically, you may have a relatively high heart rate and metabolism in relation to what you experience during normal activities of the day. Most significantly, you are ready to take on the challenges of the day.

In a state of calm-tiredness, your cardiovascular system may be functioning at a lower level of activation. Your thoughts may tend to focus on things that require less concentration, such as reading a novel or magazine or listening to music. While you may still feel in a good mood, you are more fatigued, tired, or sleepy.

When you are in a tense-energy mood, you may experience increased tension in your muscles, breathing, and throughout your body. You may also feel animated with nervous or anxious emotional energy. Thayer suggests that when in this state you are demonstrating a "freeze response."[3] He identifies this inaction as a momentary precursor to the "fight or flight" response. It is during this fraction of a second that you decide how to manage the situation. Thayer suggests that this mood most reflects the physiological activation that is the body's response to the feeling of being threatened. Even though you feel tense, however, you may describe yourself as feeling positive; this is a reaction to feeling energized. While the tense-energy mood energizes you and increases your alertness, the accompanying anxiety tends to distract you from remaining fully focused on the types of challenges characteristic of creative pursuit.

Finally, a mood of tense-tiredness involves physical tension throughout various systems in your body accompanied by a pervasive lack of energy.

Subjectively, it is experienced as a bad mood. It encompasses fatigue as well as anxiety. Recall your state of mind at the end of a day filled with challenging demands. Your mood most likely involved an experienced sense of depletion. In addition, you were probably predisposed to make a negative assessment of your ability, exaggerate the difficulty of challenges, and feel a reduced sense of competency.

The ideal states for focused attention are when you experience calm-energy or some level of tense-energy. As such, these two states are most conducive to aspects of creativity that require focused and concentrated attention. The alert, open, and confident attitude of the calm-energy state of mind and body helps you to foster positive emotions and the open and flexible thinking that are so essential for creative engagement. However, I would suggest that even when you initiate creative engagement while experiencing calm-energy, the tension can still escalate in reaction to the arousal of your inhibiting themes. The challenge at these moments, then, is to maintain a level of calm-energy sufficient to allow you to remain engaged.

ENERGY, TENSION, AND THE RANGE OF CREATIVITY

Some forms of creativity depend on concentration for their expression. In writing, the writer focuses on finding the specific words and phrases that best convey and highlight larger concepts. The scientist or inventor needs to concentrate as much as the artist, even though the artist clearly enjoys the freedom of wider parameters for her exploration and discovery.

Throughout periods of intense concentration, we are perhaps less influenced by the negative impact of our child logic and the inhibiting themes it arouses. We are able to be fully present and open in our creative engagement.

While intense concentration is required for much of creativity, artists as well as scientists and inventors emphasize that their defining creative moments come about not only through intense concentration but frequently when they are actually less focused on "trying" to create.

In many ways, this is consistent with the underlying process of creativity. We form creative ideas when we are alert and open to the interplay of ideas, images, sounds, and so forth. If we focus too intently, we lose the greater big-picture perspective. Too much concentration and we see the "trees" at the expense of also seeing the "forest." Many moments of creativity involve an open fluidity that allows thought to move effortlessly from one focus to another.

Arrival at a key creative idea also comes about when we are able to suspend judgment and "dip into" the fertile unconscious. At such moments we are able to tap into that part of the mind that is not limited by the conventions, guidelines, and defining structures characteristic of a normal conscious awareness. We think with fewer restrictions and inhibitions, accessing the part of the child logic that is not associated with inhibiting themes. The ability to maintain these different perspectives is the defining aspect of the creative process.

I find this is true in my writing. Identifying core concepts and associated themes to explore may not always occur while I am actually writing. Rather, they may come to my awareness at any time throughout the day—while reading a newspaper or magazine article, on my way to the office, while taking a walk, when exercising at the gym, or even when doing research on an only tangentially related idea I wish to address.

During these periods I may explore some broader concept rather than the details of how to efficiently and clearly express it. For example, I have sometimes identified an analogy or metaphor that best expresses an idea I want to communicate while engaging in an activity entirely unrelated to writing. The ability to do this rests on broad thinking rather than on focused attention to detail. With more free-associative thinking, I am often better able to see novel aspects of particular comparisons than when I am overly focused on trying to identify one. Exemplary of this is the story I told in the introduction to this book about the moment late in the evening in which my reaction to rejections of my manuscript helped lead me, in part, to the conceptualization for this one.

Sometimes I have had what I consider my most productive moments because I was less structured in my focus, less intense about my need to express myself clearly, and more broad in my attentive scope. There have been times when I spent entire evenings in this mind-set, fell asleep, and woke to experience great delight in the relevance of my thoughts. I recognize that at other times I have gone too far out on a limb in my associative thinking and moved in a direction that was too tangential or provided only a minimal contribution to my work.

There are times when I let my mind linger on my writing for several moments while sleep overtakes me. In this brief transitional period from wakefulness to sleep, a window to the unconscious may sometimes open. I have thus learned to keep a writing tablet and pen by my night table so that I can catch the insights of my unconscious before they are lost to sleep.

In contrast, when I am actually writing, I become more focused on finding the specific words and phrases that will best convey and highlight the larger concepts. Certainly, this process is a part of the creative effort, but it requires a qualitatively different type of concentration and presence.

Many of our most creative moments may actually occur not during mind-body sets of calm-energy but, rather, during calm-tired moods. I believe that so long as you are free from your inhibiting themes, these states offer you closer contact with the more free-associative thinking that best fosters the creative process.

While a mood of tenseness and fatigue may also allow for some forms of creativity, it may be during this mood that you are most vulnerable to the influence of your child logic; it is in this phase that your child logic is most likely to exert its influence in the form of inhibiting themes. You are more likely to function on automatic pilot and become less able to mindfully be present and engaged in creative pursuit when feeling tense and fatigued. If I am writing late in the evening and have entered a state of fatigue and tension, I will be more likely to encounter my inhibiting themes and be less prepared in mind and body to challenge them. With increased awareness I know that it is best to not force the issue at those times. First, in doing so I know that I will at best achieve minimal productivity. Second, it creates an experience and therefore a memory of a mind-body state not conducive to feelings of productivity and competence. Trying to force creativity when in this type of vulnerable mood is risky. A serious negative outcome is the risk that such experiences will further embed and empower the inhibiting themes that we're trying so hard to control.

While most of this book is focused on how to maintain engagement, this is one context in which withdrawal serves the best interests of your ongoing creative capacity. In my own experience, I often choose to read a book to stimulate my thoughts or relax with something totally unrelated to my project when I sense that tension and fatigue have made me vulnerable. It takes practice in self-reflection to distinguish between a tense-tired mood that is fostered by inhibiting themes and an overriding mood of the day impacting your attitude regarding creativity. Inhibiting themes may be playing the dominant role in your tense-tired mood if you suddenly experience increased energy and calmness upon withdrawing from a creative activity.

Creativity stems from the wellspring of your unconscious. As such, it may arrive when you least expect it and, in fact, when you are least focused on it. And yet, through increased awareness you become more capable of living authentically through your creativity and better prepared to pick the fruits of your unconscious when they have ripened.

FINDING YOUR DAILY CYCLE OF ENERGY AND TENSION

Numerous studies suggest that the levels of our energy follow certain daily cycles. In general, our energy levels rise from a low level in the morning until they peak around noon or a little after noon. They then decrease for a bit, only to reach a second peak (though not quite as high as the first) by late afternoon. From that point on, energy levels gradually diminish.[4] More detailed studies support the idea that some of us are "morning" people while others are "night owls."[5] They report that morning persons experience 6:00–8:00 AM as being favorable for creativity and 8:00 AM–12:30 PM and 2:30–4:30 PM as being favorable for problem solving. For such individuals, 5:00–8:00 PM is best for rejuvenation while 12:30–2:30 PM and 8:00–10:00 PM are bad times for concentration.

In contrast, these studies conclude that for "night owls," the period from 10:00 AM–1:00 PM is best for creativity while 12:00–1:00 PM and 6:00–11:00 PM are good for problem solving. The periods 1:00–3:00 PM and 11:00 PM to midnight are considered bad for concentration. For these individuals, 3:00–6:00 PM is considered a good time for rejuvenation.

As with all studies, these present a pattern that reflects an average of the change in energy levels of those who participated in the study. The only way to determine your own unique pattern is by maintaining a daily record of your moods. I recommend a variation on an exercise offered by Thayer to help you address this task.[6] For one week, make a rating every hour of your mood on a scale of 1 through 5 in which 1 denotes a good mood and 5 denotes a bad mood. Also, rate the level of your tension on a scale of 1 through 100 such that 1 reflects complete calm and 100 denotes severe tension. Finally, rate your level of energy on a similar scale of 1 through 100 where 1 reflects low energy and 100 represents extremely high energy. In addition, try to identify which of those four moods you are experiencing, calm-energy, calm-tiredness, tense-energy, or tense-tiredness. By recording these observations you will gain insight into the daily time periods that may be optimal for you to pursue various aspects of your creative passion.

Simply identifying your mood cycle can help you recognize factors that inhibit or foster your creative engagement. For example, if you wish to pursue a creative activity that is distinct from your employment, you may end up targeting the late evening hours as your time to commit to such a venture. However, after completing a daily mood log you may discover that you are more likely to feel tense-tired at that time. Certainly, we may not always be able to choose ideal times for pursuing creativity. Some of us maintain careers that demand we be creative throughout the entire day. Others may only be able to clear space in their schedules for creativity at times when their moods are not optimal. But by identifying your individual cycle, you may recognize the most suitable times to address various aspects of your creative pursuit. While many are intuitively able to adjust to this cycle, those who have tried to ignore it because of unrealistic expectations may unnecessarily be adding increased stress to their moments of challenge.

While our levels of energy may follow a particular pattern, fortunately there are a variety of strategies that can be implemented to help us have greater control over them.

CREATING ENERGY THROUGH MOVEMENT

Physical movement plays a key role in increasing energy. It is for this reason that it can be an integral part of the creative process. By movement, I am not referring just to intense physical exercise or the level of energy that it provides. Regardless of what creative path you take, movement in any form can help contribute the energy you need to pursue it. Moderate movement such as a brief walk, playing with a pet, or a half hour of yoga can bolster your energy. Studies suggest that even just a few minutes of such exercises can have this effect.[7]

Research and years of clinical experience convince me that short periods of moderate physical movement can be the most powerful mood enhancer. I have found both walks and exercise to be integral to my writing. The energizing component may involve increased circulation, deeper breathing that brings in increased oxygen, exposure to daylight that boosts vitamin D, distraction from inhibiting self-talk, or the combination of these and other factors. Ultimately though, such activity contributes to a mood of calm-energy.

I suspect, in keeping with the notion of child logic, that the child within us becomes most alive through bodily movement, helping us to reconnect with sensing rather than thinking. I would suggest that when we move, our moods might be more influenced by the context of such movement than by our thoughts. The positive experience of muscle movement, increased circulation, and increased oxygen generates a positive visceral reaction that informs our emotions and subsequently our thoughts. In contrast, when we are still, our moods are more prone to a "downward" influence and a prioritizing of thought over sensation. In a sense, movement competes with thought. As such, it competes with inhibiting themes that may be activated during those most significant first moments of creative engagement. Movement stands in sharp contrast to the inertia of sitting still. Perhaps it is simply that remaining still is like being "frozen" in a state of limbo, a state of thought that involves pondering whether to move forward or retreat. In "warming up" for a creative task by first engaging in bodily movement, you preempt the uncertainty of this limbo moment. Once you begin moving, it is much easier to carry the momentum of your bodily exercise into the mental exercise of your creative endeavor, allowing you, essentially, to do an end run around your inhibiting themes.

Whether you are into painting, writing, photography, or working with crafts, exercises of some form will very much increase the likelihood of being energized. While a cup of coffee or a candy bar may increase your energy for a brief period of time, movement offers increased energy over a longer period of time.

BREATHING

Consistent with Eastern philosophy and religion, Western psychology has increasingly emphasized an attention to breathing as a way to impact one's mind-body state. This is just as relevant to moments of creative engagement as to other highly uncomfortable situations.

Tension aroused by the sense of an imminent danger is the main distraction to creative engagement. During such moments of tension, even when it is not severe, your breathing becomes more shallow and rapid, preventing air from making its way to the lower part of your lungs where oxygen is absorbed into your bloodstream to be circulated throughout your body, including to your brain. At the same time, shallow breathing allows for less discharge of carbon dioxide from your system, which leads to an increase in muscle tension.

Deep breathing is one strategy that can be effective to decrease some of this tension. The goal of this exercise is not to create a calm-tired mood but to create a calm-energized mood to help you remain present and engaged with the creative task at hand.

Exercise

At the moment you begin to recognize some level of tension that seems to push you away from remaining creatively engaged, take time to breathe in the following manner. Draw a breath deep into your lungs, noting the rise of your chest. Hold it for a second and deeply exhale from the deepest part of your lungs. Do this three times. This form of breathing is energizing, calms tension, and also competes with the physiological response to feeling threatened. It is often helpful to do this exercise as a first response to the tension of creating. Doing so can allow you to stay engaged as you reflect on your overall reactions and identify inhibiting themes that may be impacting you.

MUSCLE RELAXATION

Muscle-relaxation exercises are effective for managing both general stress and anxiety. Practicing these exercises to attain calmness in anxiety-provoking situations provides an increased capacity for self-soothing. As such, they can be especially effective in situations marked by performance anxiety. The more you rehearse these exercises, the more you remember, in mind and body, what it feels like to be calm.

I present these exercises as a strategy for managing the excessive tension aroused during creative engagement. The rationale for their use is not to achieve absolute calmness but, rather, to sufficiently reduce tension so as to remain engaged in your creative endeavor. This is in keeping with the perspective that all of creativity involves some degree of tension, even if it derives from the positive excitement of being creative. Absolute calmness may actually inhibit some of the guiding energy that accompanies you through your creative journey.

One form of this relaxation is progressive muscle relaxation. Originally outlined by Herbert Benson, it involves the alternating tensing and relaxation of muscle groups.[8] The following exercise is based on this approach.

Exercise

Find a place where you can sit comfortably and where you will not be disturbed for about fifteen minutes. Begin by tightening the muscles around your eyes (do not do this if you wear contacts). Notice the tension of the muscles around your eyes and temples and attend to how they feel when they are tense. Then let go of the tension by relaxing them while attending to how they feel when relaxed.

Now tighten your jaw muscles by clenching your teeth and attending to the muscle tension as you do so. Hold this position for a few seconds and then gradually lower your tongue and jaw as you attend to how the muscles feel when they are relaxed.

Raise and hold your shoulders as close as you can to your ears. Hold them in that position for a few seconds while you attend to the tension. Then gradually lower them as you attend to how relaxed they become.

Pushing your elbows down against the sides of your chair, tighten the muscles of your upper arms and notice their tension. Hold them in place for a few seconds and then relax them.

Place your forearms against the sides of the chair. Push down on them and notice their tension as you hold them in place for a few seconds. Relax them and notice how they feel.

Clench your fists and attend to the muscle tension in your hands and fingers. After holding them in place for a few seconds, open them and notice how the muscles of your fingers and hands feel when they are relaxed.

Pull in your abdomen as if you're trying to touch your navel to you back. Notice the tension. Then attend to how these muscles feel as you once again relax them.

Tighten the muscles of your lower torso and attend to their tension as you hold them in place for several seconds. Then relax and notice how the muscles feel.

Sitting straight, press your feet flat against the floor as you press your knees together and tighten your thighs. Hold them in that position and then notice how relaxed they feel when you let them go.

Stretch your legs straight out in front of you with your feet flat on the floor. Raise, point, and move your toes toward you as you tighten the muscles behind your lower legs. Feel the tension and then notice how relaxed they feel when you release them.

Now, stretch your legs straight out in front of you with your toes pointed away from you so you feel tension on the front muscles of your legs. Hold them in place for several seconds and then relax them.

Finally, curl your toes so you feel them become tense and then release them as you attend to how relaxed they feel.

Now take time to scan your body from head to toes and notice how relaxed your body can be.

By engaging in this exercise you will also become more sensitive to when your body is tense. Consequently, you will become even more aware of your body's response when inhibiting themes arise. The goal is to address such tension before it overwhelms and forces you to take flight.

While this exercise is effective for general relaxation, I present it here as an exercise to rehearse so you can direct your body to become calm when you are experiencing tension. Just as we train our muscles to behave a certain way when engaged in sports, we can rehearse calmness. As such, you do not have to take time out to do the entire relaxation sequence. Rather, through rehearsing, your body develops a memory for relaxing that you can quickly access.

YOGA

Yoga is an activity that can strengthen you physically, emotionally, mentally, and spiritually. While there are different approaches emphasized by various schools of yoga, all involve movement of the body accompanied by attention to breathing. These can have a tremendous impact on your overall mind-body states and the level of energy and calmness you experience. The training offered by yoga can impact concentration as well as general skills in flexibility of attention. At the same time, the practice of yoga may arouse in you the very same inhibiting themes that confront you during any creative endeavor. As such, it requires discipline, resilience, and a tolerance for frustration. The specific details of the practice are beyond the scope of this book, but understanding and practicing them can greatly impact your capacity for maintaining creative engagement.

VISUALIZING FOR ENERGY

The premise of all exercises in visualization is that our bodies react to what we picture. Therefore, while some visualization techniques can be useful to help achieve calmness, others can help achieve energy. Any aerobic exercise provides energy, even when it is engaged in briefly. In lieu of actually running, jogging, biking, or other similar exercises, simply visualizing engagement for several minutes can have a positive impact on energy.

Exercise

Find a place where you will not be disturbed. Picture an inspiring location that you have been to or would like to be, one that excites and invigorates you. Now picture yourself racing your bike or running along a road in that area. Try to imagine all of the details of the scene, including the variety of colors; the lines, curves, and textures of the different components of that scene; the air—dry or humid; sounds or silence; and any fragrance. Imagine yourself moving at a rapid pace as you observe all of the details of your scene. Picture the scenery passing you by as you continue your trek. Do this for five to ten minutes.

Unlike the previous exercise, this one could be helpful just before working on a project.

THE HEART MATH METHOD

This Heart Math Method is a combination of breathing, visualization, and mindfully arousing a memory based on the "freeze-frame technique." This approach has been researched for many years and has been proven effective in helping individuals achieve calmness.[9] It is based on research which suggests that the arousal of anxiety and tension is often associated with a difference between the cycles of electrical impulses within the heart tissue and those within certain areas of the brain. We experience increased calmness, emotionally and physically, when these cycles are synchronized.

I include it not just because of its power to relax, but because it focuses on addressing the issue of tension from a perspective of compassion. As such, it supports the overriding theme that I have been emphasizing throughout this book. Our child logic, rooted in more primal and intense emotions, is very much at the core of our inhibiting themes. As discussed throughout this book, to the degree that you can respond to these themes, in effect, to yourself, with compassion, you become less vulnerable to their potential impact. Being compassionate with yourself is especially helpful in effectively managing the shame and guilt that may make a significant contribution to inhibiting your capacity to pursue creativity. This exercise can be especially helpful at the moment you are experiencing tension when creatively engaged.

Exercise

Revisit a mood, image, or experience in which you expressed your most caring, loving, accepting, and compassionate self toward others or yourself, a person, a pet, a situation, or as part of your religion or spiritual beliefs. The compassionate mood, image, or experience may derive from an actual or an imagined experience.

While revisiting these emotions, images, accompanying thoughts, and the physical sensations associated with them, begin to notice your breathing. Imagine that as you inhale you are taking in this feeling through your heart and that it is exiting through your solar plexus. Do this repeatedly for several moments.

Now, reflect on your inhibiting themes and respond to your child logic from the compassionate mind-body set you have just established. Responding to such themes from the mind-body set of your most caring and nurturing self can be an extremely powerful approach when challenging the negative tension of inhibiting themes.

Again, as with other exercises described in this section, the application of this exercise is to manage tension and not necessarily to reduce energy. It is intended to sufficiently reduce tension so as to maintain engagement and presence in the creative process.

YOUR PHYSICAL SETTING

While I emphasized in chapter 8 that we can maintain unrealistic expectations about the necessity of an ideal environment in order to be creative, our immediate environment can very much influence the degree to which we feel secure and energized to maintain creative engagement. Certainly, some forms of creativity do require a very specific setting, as, for example, a sound studio for recording, a dance floor for choreography, and a studio equipped with a kiln for working with ceramics.

Just as it is important to identify the cycles of your energy, try to identify the setting that would be most conducive to success in sustaining engagement with a creative endeavor. Recall what has worked best for you in the past. Do you prefer a small, enclosed area or a large space? How much light do you prefer? Do you prefer that light come from a particular direction? Do you respond positively to being around plants or tropical fish?

Address all of your senses. Do you prefer music in the background? If not, might a fountain be calming and energizing for you? Are there fragrances that both energize you and calm your tension? Certain textures may further enhance the positive energy you are seeking. There may be certain furnishings that you meaningfully associate with empowerment and optimal creative functioning.

Studying feng shui may be helpful as another approach toward creating a setting conducive to your creativity. This approach holds that the arrangement of our environment influences your mind-body states, especially by affecting your overall energy. Create the ideal environment in your mind and then create one that best matches that ideal.

MUSIC

Music can provide an echo of your deepest emotions or help lead you away from experiencing them. Music has the power to soothe or to energize. Your individual experience with specific music will best determine the impact it has on you. While a certain piece may be calming to one person, that same piece may arouse sadness and discomfort in another.

For some, creativity is enhanced by instrumentals, whereas for others it is the combination of words and music that empower by conveying a message of hope. The most relevant music to favorably impact your creativity will be music that arouses in you a very positive and energizing visceral response. It is music that leaves you optimistic and eager to take chances and move against inhibiting themes. Such music physically and emotionally opens you to your potential. In doing so, it pushes you to live authentically.

Just as various aspects of the creative process require different qualities of engagement, certain forms of music may be more likely to enhance these qualities than others. For example, you may prefer hearing lyrics during certain moments of the creative process, while they would be distracting at other times. Notice in greater detail how you react to music in order to determine its optimal benefit for you.

A major task of this book has been to emphasize the important role our physical states play in influencing whether or not we embrace our creative passions. This chapter has provided a variety of strategies to highlight skills you can practice to directly and significantly impact you at a physical level to become more open to creative engagement.

*** FOR FURTHER EXPLORATION ***

1. Review the log of your moods. During which mood states do you feel most creative and most productive?
2. In what ways, if any, do you try to enhance these moods?
3. What are the signals that inform you that you are becoming too tense or too tired to continue attending to your project?
4. Inhibiting themes drain your energy for creative commitment. They similarly foster tension. Through reflection, try to distinguish the degree to which these reactions are due to such themes or to other factors of the day.
5. Physically relaxing can be uncomfortable when we have internalized negative attitudes toward it and fear the thoughts and emotions that could surface if we become relaxed. What if any inhibiting themes do you experience with regard to physical relaxation? Are you aware of specific issues that you believe will arise when you relax? Try dialoguing with that voice that tells you not to become relaxed.
6. When visiting your energizing location, reflect on your reactions, specifically the thoughts you have that foster comfort and energy.

RELECTIONS

The mind's first step to self-awareness must be through the body.—George Sheehan

Life engenders life. Energy creates energy. It is by spending oneself that one becomes rich.—Sarah Bernhardt

The body says what words cannot.—Martha Graham

NOTES

1. Robert E. Thayer, *The Origin of Everyday Moods* (New York: Oxford University Press, 1996).

2. Ibid.

3. Ibid.

4. Ibid.

5. Jeremy Kaplan, "Making the Most of Your Day . . . And Best Use of the Night," *Newsweek*, January 16, 2006.

6. Thayer, *Origin of Everyday Moods*.

7. Ibid.

8. Herbert Benson, *The Relaxations Response* (New York: Avon, 1976).

9. Doc Childre and Deborah Rozman, *Transforming Anger* (Oakland, CA: New Harbinger, 2003).

Chapter 16

PRACTICING
SELF-COMPASSION

A ll inhibiting themes share a common foundation; they are based on some form of suffering as well as the unconscious steps we take to escape experiencing that suffering. Fear of failure, fear of success, shame, guilt, and discomfort with being alone are just a few of the ways this suffering is expressed. And it is for this reason that practicing compassion toward yourself is an essential aspect of every strategy I present to help you connect with your creative genius.

SELF-COMPASSION

Compassion involves the capacity to feel the pain of others. It also rests on the ability to communicate that sensitivity and attitude and, by doing so, to acknowledge and validate another's pain. Additionally, when we practice compassion, we desire to reduce the pain of others. Through being compassionate, we serve as an ally as we support others in sitting with and moving beyond their pain.

However, genuine compassion toward others depends on the degree to which we can be compassionate with ourselves. While receiving much more attention in Eastern philosophy and religion than in the West, the concept of "self-compassion" plays a key role in helping us to access and express our creative genius. Kristen Neff, a psychologist who has studied this concept, concludes that self-compassion parallels compassion toward others.[1] It involves being sensitive and open to one's own suffering, not avoiding or eluding it; developing a desire to alleviate that suffering; and the practice of kindness toward the self.

As such, when we practice self-compassion, we practice kindness and acceptance. In doing so, we try to be understanding of our pain or failure rather than harshly self-critical. In being self-compassionate, we build on our strengths rather than tear ourselves down based on our shortcomings. Similarly, when we practice self-compassion, we identify with all of humanity. In doing so, even in our pain, we feel connected with, rather than isolated from, our humanity. Finally, when being self-compassionate, we do not overidentify with our weaknesses or failures as an inherent permanent part of who we are. In fact, Neff suggests that the measure of self-compassion is a more accurate reflection of healthy emotional well-being than simple self-esteem or self-confidence.[2]

Self-compassion is a concept that is also addressed in *How Good Do We Have to Be*, by Rabbi Harold Kushner. He examines how excessive guilt and shame stem from both a felt need for perfection and a lack of self-compassion. He observes that "it is the notion that we were supposed to be perfect, and that we could expect others to be perfect because we needed them to be, that leaves us feeling constantly guilty and perpetually disappointed."[3] Self-compassion, truly recognizing and accepting our humanity, is the antidote to this destructive and undermining notion, especially as it relates to living authentically through creative expression.

SELF-COMPASSION AND CREATIVITY

Self-compassion clearly contributes to the resilience essential to moving beyond negative mind-body states associated with creative pursuit. Being compassionate with yourself means recognizing the naturalness of needing to mourn or grieve the fact that you are not perfect. Compassion helps you to realize and accept that you create from who you are, from the ideas, attitudes, skills, and talent you bring to any given moment of the creative process. It fosters an attitude of acceptance that you can only try your best to achieve your goals based on who you are at any given moment. Practicing self-compassion allows you to recognize and accept your fears as being natural reactions to the unknown and to the disorder of creativity.

Such compassion helps you to view your shortcomings not as evidence of being flawed or inadequate but, rather, as reflective of the disappointment of not measuring up to what may be unrealistic expectations for yourself. Being compassionate means being able to be realistic in striving to do well while recognizing that you can never be perfect. Maintaining this positive attitude helps to silence the internal voice that cries out that you are not "good enough." It reminds you that not reaching a particular goal does not reflect who you are. Similarly, it helps you to nurture and support yourself even when those around you may not convey the same degree of compassion.

Being self-compassionate fosters an ongoing mind-body set that is open and accepting rather than punitive and constricting. It allows you to focus on what can be rather than on what you believe "should" be. This attitude fosters receptivity to your insights, inspiration, intuition, and to the expressions of your creative desires.

Practicing compassion toward yourself allows you to view the creative act not from the vantage point of competition but from the perspective of individual growth and evolution. It is an antidote for the form of competition that compels us to view ourselves in terms of being "better than" or "less than" others. The desire to do your best replaces the isolating attitude of measuring your self-worth by such comparisons.

Self-compassion likewise helps you to sit with and move beyond your tension. From this perspective, engagement in creativity is freed from the unrealistic expectations that constrict it. Fears of failure and success, the power of shame and guilt, and other inhibiting forces lose their hold on you when you are truly compassionate with yourself.

Such compassion helps decrease the discomfort you may experience when you're alone. Through self-compassion, you are continually viewing and experiencing what you share with humanity, fostering a strong sense of connection, whether in the middle of a crowd or when alone. Self-compassion acts in opposition to the experience of isolation fostered by fears of failure, success, or rejection as well as anxiety, guilt, and shame.

Self-compassion alleviates judgment and allows you to more easily engage in the creative process and the flow that accompanies it. It frees you to make errors, to experiment, and to translate your ideas into action without the paralyzing tension that anxiety of exposure can bring. Self-compassion allows you to take chances, to venture into new insights, and to foster new perspectives. In effect, it supports you in living authentically and helps you to sustain every aspect of creative engagement.

COMPASSION AND GUILT

To the degree that guilt serves to inhibit your ability to live authentically, it stifles your capacity for creative engagement. In doing so, it literally takes the life out of your living. Guilt is often a natural reaction to having taken certain actions. As stated earlier, some guilt is essential if we are to internalize essential guidelines for how we should treat others. In fact, guilt may be a reaction that helps us curb our impulses and become more compassionate with others and ourselves. At the same time, excessive guilt is paralyzing and toxic when it challenges and undermines the creative process.

Being self-compassionate regarding guilt does not mean denying, minimizing, or ignoring the outcome of your actions. Rather, it entails acknowledging those actions. The constructive management of guilt, however, involves identifying what can be done to effectively address and move beyond it. This may consist of undoing the action when possible. It may involve fully acknowledging that no matter what is done you will not be able to undo it. Self-compassion does not then dictate that you forever play out critical self-devaluing conversations in your mind. You are compassionate when you identify what, if anything, you can do to do the "best good" in light of your bad, past actions.

Self-compassion does not imply that you ignore or forget what you have done but, rather, supports you to take corrective action to the extent possible, forgive yourself, and move on. Actively and constructively channeling your guilt is the best remedy against it becoming pervasive and inhibiting.

So much of overcoming inhibiting themes depends on the development of awareness with regard to their impact and, as a result, the recognition that we have a choice in our thinking. It is with this in mind that I suggest the following exercise to clients as another strategy for managing guilt.

Exercise

If you have identified guilt as a contributing factor that inhibits your creative engagement, set aside a specific time to allow yourself to fully connect with that guilt. Find a place where you can sit and focus on your guilt. Challenge those thoughts associated with it. By actually structuring time to focus on guilt, you will be helped in a variety of ways. Talk to it as an expression of your child logic. Ask it the following questions.

1. What has caused this guilt?
2. What is achieved by holding on to the guilt?
3. What are you protecting or distracting me from by holding on to it?
4. What do you want me to do about this guilt?

Then dialogue with that part of you that is most compassionate, nurturing, and objective. Make peace with your guilt by identifying how you can constructively channel it.

When I have worked with clients who experienced some form of survivor's guilt, I often asked them to write a letter to the person they have survived. I asked them to express what they believe that person would want them to do with their lives. I suggested that they try to identify what it is that would be fulfilling for that person.

It is a simple task, but in most instances, this exercise leads to increased clarity and permission to move on. For example, one client recognized that her mother really would have been extremely disappointed if she did not live her dream of pursuing interior design.

Sure, occasionally individuals do this exercise and indicate that the person they have survived wished them illness or even death. The absurdity is recognized more readily when it is highlighted in this manner. So is the understanding that such ill will can only stem from the child logic of that other person, reflecting intense fear, anxiety, and pain.

Somehow, in writing such a letter, clients realize that they have developed an unhealthy obsession with pleasing the person they have survived by holding on to shame and guilt and thereby doing a sort of penance. Letting go of guilt involves a commitment to mourning, and eventually realizing that what has happened cannot be undone. Only by directly choosing what you want to do to address your guilt and by making a commitment to let it go can you help make it less toxic. Toxic guilt insulates us from our own compassion and causes us to distance ourselves from the compassion of others. It makes us resistant to accepting positive feedback from others and ourselves.

Through this exercise, you will increase your capacity to challenge survivor's guilt when it surfaces as a part of engagement in creativity.

SELF-COMPASSION AND SHAME

Self-compassion reduces the impact of toxic shame on your creative expression. Being self-compassionate involves recognizing and accepting that we are all imperfect. Being compassionate with yourself involves accepting yourself in spite of these imperfections and not highlighting them as reflections of your full essence. Some perfectionists view being self-compassionate as a reflection of weakness or denial. And yet, according to some studies, those who are highly self-compassionate actually assume more responsibility for their shortcomings. It is because they are not so destructively self-critical that they can more readily admit the part they play when they make mistakes.[4] A lack of self-compassion typically reflects the rigidity and anxiety that are an underlying part of internalized attitudes of perfectionism.

Each of us faces daily the influence our pasts have on our present thoughts, emotions, and actions. Without full awareness, we make choices based on these experiences. Guilt and shame involve beating ourselves with hindsight about the things we did not know at the time we took certain actions. Through this process, we may convince ourselves that we genuinely had options to choose from when, in fact, we may have been helpless. Guilt and shame are ways of obsessing about the "what ifs" and the "could have beens." It is often easier to accept inhibiting guilt and shame than it is to face the anxiety of moving on and exploring the unknown. This is why guilt and shame are towering barriers to creativity.

All of the strategies provided in this book reflect, in essence, how an ideal and compassionate parent could respond to her child. Maintaining the attitude of a compassionate parent chips away at shame and the unrealistic expectations and conclusions that fuel it. Such compassion fosters an attitude of "what is, is" and "what was, was," a self-view that supports the exploration of our inner landscapes, the source of both our creativity and our inhibitions. It fosters an acceptance of our longings and desires for self-expression as an inherent aspect of the human condition. All of these strategies are designed to develop the compassion needed to help our inner children give birth to themselves, a process that is an ongoing development of one's unique self.

Highly significant, these strategies provide us with skills for the tolerance of frustration, whether involved in the creative process or in meeting any of the challenges that life has to offer. It is through the practice of self-compassion that we can truly be ourselves. Self-compassion helps us to move beyond guilt or shame to an internal space that allows us to not just survive but to thrive and flourish. And when that child within us screams out declarations of belittlement for not measuring up to ideal perceptions of how we have to be or how we have to perform, these strategies teach us how to mourn and how to grieve. They offer us ways to let go of such highly unrealistic longings and, as in real mourning, grieve when we need to acknowledge that there are things over which we have little or no control. Such compassion is an inextricable part of forgiveness.

SELF-COMPASSION, FORGIVENESS, AND CREATIVITY

Just as forgiveness is a component of compassion for others, self-forgiveness is an expression of self-compassion. It is essential for helping us move beyond toxic guilt and shame so as to achieve freedom for creative engagement. To a great extent, as suggested by Robin Casarjian, forgiveness is the equivalent of love. "It is a state of being that arises from our willingness to accept, without judgment, all of who we are, our seeming shortcomings as well as our innate glory."[5]

Through practicing self-compassion, we remain alert to our suffering even when it derives from our own guilt and shame. In turn, practicing forgiveness helps us to relinquish the debilitating impact of resentment we may carry toward ourselves for actions that have provoked toxic guilt. Similarly, it helps us to mourn and, in effect, let go of unrealistic expectations and rigid and crippling internalized standards that have formed the basis of toxic shame.

While self-compassion expresses a commitment to help ourselves move beyond pain, self-forgiveness helps us to achieve this goal. Forgiveness does not mean ignoring, denying, or minimizing our emotions, thoughts, or actions. Rather, it begins with full acknowledgment and acceptance of these experiences as well as our responsibility for them. Such forgiveness is an ongoing process that involves a repeated decision to let go of the resentment we feel toward ourselves, even as we continue to periodically experience such resentment.

Self-forgiveness requires recognition that, as humans, we make mistakes, learn from them, and then strive to do better. Similarly, such forgiveness helps us to let go of unrealistic expectations and to abandon the highly self-critical and devaluing attitudes that are associated with the pain of toxic shame.

Forgiveness shares many similarities with mourning. Like mourning, forgiveness involves letting go of harmful thoughts, images, and connections. Toxic guilt involves playing over and over again what we could have done. The commitment to forgiveness therefore involves reminding ourselves that it is over, that we cannot undo what was done, and that we need to move on to make room for new learning.

Similarly, with regard to shame, forgiveness involves letting go of rigid and unrealistic expectations. In a sense, such forgiveness involves grieving for the expectation of perfection and the acknowledgment of the human inability to be perfect. It involves helping our child logic mourn his grandiosity, helping him realize he is only human.

All of the strategies provided in this book help foster self-compassion and self-forgiveness in order to enhance your access to creative genius. They free you to be open in the broadest sense to your unconscious, to your inspiration, to self-expression, and to recognizing that you deserve to live authentically through your creativity.

SELF-COMPASSION, RELATIONSHIPS, AND CREATIVITY

Throughout this book, I have compared the relationship with sustained creativity to that of a loving relationship with another person. Such engagement often requires the same commitment and love demanded by intimate relationships. Thus, the intensity of such devotion has the potential to evoke in others a variety of reactions that may be negative or positive. In turn, how they are impacted can play a decisive role in whether these relationships support or inhibit your creative passion. For this reason, I invite you to consider how your relationships impact access to your creative genius.

Honoring your creativity is not an easy task. It forces you to go against convention, to see and acknowledge perspectives that may make you uncomfortable. As you pursue your passion, it may similarly arouse anxiety in others around you, as they are confronted vicariously with challenges to their delicate senses of order. Most significantly, your creativity may challenge their abilities to stand with you as you steadfastly experiment, question, and discover yourself and the world around you. Such a quest rests on passion, but passion can be very unsettling for those who either struggle with the need for order or are competitive by temperament. Most significantly, if a relationship is to be conducive to your creativity, it must be compassionate and strong enough to support and nurture your creative desires. That can be very challenging for friends as well as for those with whom you share greater intimacy.

In an earlier chapter, I suggested that you surround yourself with others who are equally passionate, whether in the area of your specific passion or in another. Take a moment to explore the relationships you have. Are the people with whom you surround yourself available to support and encourage your pursuit? Think about it. Are your friends supportive? Are members of your family truly supportive of your creative engagement and passion? Is their support genuine? Do they express it in words as well as by their behaviors? Is it conditional? Do they offer support only when you are struggling but become less available when you are actually beginning to succeed in your endeavors? On the other hand, are they supportive only when you demonstrate some level of excellence as they define it? How do loved ones manage the time demands that your creative passion makes on your relationship? Do their own feelings of competition undermine their capacity to be genuinely supportive and nurturing of your efforts?

These are important questions to answer for a variety of reasons. Primarily, your answers may be indicative of just how much impact your inhibiting themes have on you. Even though we live a life governed by internalized inhibiting themes regarding authentic living, we may gravitate to others who can support our attempts to be authentic. In contrast, however, child logic may lead us to gravitate toward the familiar. Themes of guilt and shame about deserving to be who we are, feel what we feel, or even explore our internal landscapes may lead us to bond with others who are equally inhibited. If your early and most intimate relationships were with individuals who were threatened by your creativity or who stifled or undermined it, you may inadvertently become close with others who continue to reinforce those themes. In fact, your child logic may even lead you toward relationships that challenge you to constantly prove yourself to others. In such relationships, you may continue to be driven by the unrealistic child logic that pushes you to achieve perfection in order to get the recognition and acknowledgment that you craved but have been denied. In such relationships, you are looking to others to give you permission to be yourself and to create from that self.

I am not suggesting that you now need to turn away from such relationships. Rather, as with all behavior, the more you become aware of what leads to it, the more choice you have in the actions you take. Be alert to the fact that, with or without their full awareness, others may exert pressure on you to turn back from your pursuit. They may do so for the same underlying reasons that make us all fearful of change. Being aware of such influences may lead you to move the relationship in a more positive direction, or it may simply heighten your realization that you need to look elsewhere for that particular form of support.

Ralph Keyes, author of *The Writer's Book of Hope*, calls such individuals "encouragers." Encouragers are all of those in your life who are there to support and root you on as you pursue your craft.[6] They may be friends, mentors, a spouse, a teacher, or an agent. Find them and embrace them. They are individuals who have a passion for living authentically and who have recognized and learned to value the rewards of living creatively. They are individuals who support your audacity to create and at the same time value your uniqueness. They may often be a good source of compassion.

A child needs to be nurtured, not just in the form of blanket praise, but also in the form of genuine feedback and permission to make mistakes, comfort when she feels hurt, and the rallying support of hope and optimism. This is what encouragers do best. Their support may take many forms, from listening to your ideas and giving you feedback to helping you soothe your tension surrounding moments of challenge. Others may be resources to provide you information. Be aware of the reality that it is the rare encourager who can play all of these roles. Be alert, too, to that part of you which believes you have to do it all by yourself. Being closed to support is a severely inhibiting perspective with regard to creativity.

FURTHER FOSTERING SELF-COMPASSION

One of the best ways to further compassion for yourself is to ask the following questions when you are stifled in your creativity.

1. What do I believe I need to know before I can allow myself to further pursue my creative journey?
2. What is it I believe I need to hear before I can proceed on my creative journey?
3. What is it I believe I need to feel before I can embrace the next steps in learning to live authentically?

Once answered, respond to those answers from the perspective of the ideal parent within you. Through this process, you will gain a clear idea of what it is your child logic needs. At the same time, answering the questions will help you to identify those desires that may need to be challenged as well as when processes of mourning and forgiveness are called for. Answering them also helps to clarify the degree to which your needs are realistic or unrealistic and, in fact, whether they are even genuine needs. Some of your felt needs may be fueled by your fear, guilt, or shame. For example, the need to know the outcome, the need to "succeed," and the need for the positive response of others reflect intense desires but not genuine needs. Letting go of them is an essential step for genuine creative freedom.

MINDFULNESS MEDITATION

Mindfulness meditation is one approach that can help you to let go of your compulsive needs so that you can more assertively pursue your identified values. Through this process, you can become more self-understanding and more self-compassionate.

There are many different forms of mindfulness meditation, including those based in Buddhist religion and philosophy and those that are Western adaptations. Fully addressing these is beyond the scope of this book. However, one form, Vipassana, reflects the key aspects of this practice and is most relevant for meeting the challenges of the creative moment.

Vipassana means "insight," having "a clear awareness of exactly what is happening as it happens."[7] It is a practice that involves developing increased awareness of the many ways in which we have developed distorted lenses through which to experience reality. Meditation is not an easy approach toward self-awareness. It takes time, energy, determination, commitment, and resilience. Through its practice we gain an increased understanding of ourselves, which allows us to be more flexible, tolerant, and self-compassionate. It offers a way to gain distance from ourselves so as to see clearly our humanity, our human weaknesses, and our shared suffering. Through this process, we learn compassion for ourselves and for others.

Every creative endeavor involves attention to details. Mindful meditation is a valuable tool in helping us to become more sensitive to the details of all of our experiences, including our emotions, thoughts, images, and sensations. As such, it is an aid to creativity in that it both helps us to remove barriers to creative engagement and fosters an increased capacity to attend to details. Furthermore, in helping us be more flexible in our thinking, mindfulness meditation helps both our conscious and unconscious minds become more open to ambiguity, disorganization, and discomfort—core strengths for the creative process. As described in chapter 3, according to the Buddhist perspective, all of our inhibiting themes are the result of compulsive "attachment" or aversion to people, ideas, or things.

From this perspective, our perfectionism is an obsession that grows from an attempt to see ourselves in a certain way in order to give us a stable sense of identity. In a lifetime, we may have many "failures" and "successes." This is the natural flow of an evolving life. Our need to see ourselves as successful and our quickness to label ourselves as "failures" is viewed, from the Buddhist perspective, as a way to envision ourselves as having a fixed identity when, in fact, identity is always fluid, transient, and evolving.

Toxic shame and guilt are similarly related to unrealistic obsessions we have about control, avoidance of imperfection, and conformity to a rigid image of who we "need" to be. It is against this background that the practice of mindfulness meditation is viewed as a way to gradually strip ourselves of these false perceptions and to become more real and present with all of the details of our existence. In other words, mindfulness meditation is a process that helps us to reduce the intensity of our attachments and aversions.

Confronting the reality that all life is transient may at first appear to seem pessimistic and depressing. However, it is only when we recognize the impermanency of life that it becomes more meaningful and more valuable. The recognition and reduction of the intensity of our compulsions frees us to become more alive and in touch with life. It is from this realization that we develop choice and actually become energized, progressively freeing ourselves from compulsive cravings and aversions.

Mindfulness meditation is an approach that helps us to ignore our knee-jerk and conditioned desire for certainty and comfort. As such, it fosters the necessary resilience for managing mind-body states associated with inhibiting themes that stand in the way of creativity. It does so by helping us to be more aware of our discomfort, to sit with it, and to ignore rather than engage with it.

In several ways, this approach is significantly different from many of the approaches already discussed. Rather than encouraging you to dialogue with and challenge your thoughts and experiences, mindfulness meditation recommends viewing these as mental events, as transient and not permanent parts of the self. Thus, it is when we observe them, let them go, and assertively choose not to attend to them that we develop increased freedom to really connect with our reality.

I am offering this form of mindfulness meditation because it best conveys some of the essential elements of the practice.[8]

Mindful Meditation Exercise

Find a place where you will not be disturbed. Sit on a cushion placed over a carpeted floor or on a comfortable chair. Try to sit up straight without making yourself uncomfortable (all such meditation emphasizes the goal of being able to sit with a straight back and with your head and chest in line). If sitting on the floor, cross your legs and place your hands in your lap, one over the other, palms facing up.

The process involves focusing on your breath. Rather than focusing on picturing the breath entering and leaving or actually following your breath, focus on a point at your nostrils where you actually sense the movement of air as you inhale and exhale. Focus on your breath, but be attentive to anything that disrupts your attention. Being sensitive to thoughts, sounds, images, and physical discomfort are all a part of this practice. You might drift to thinking about your chores for the day, experience critical thoughts or impatience regarding this exercise, or have a variety of physical reactions. Gently redirect your attention to your breathing.

Ram Dass describes this process as seeing "your thoughts go by as if they were autumn leaves floating down a stream. The leaves drift by, being moved this way and that by the eddying water . . . the leaves, the thoughts, float by, but keep your attention on the water itself."[9] The emphasis is on viewing these experiences as transient and on seeing yourself as the "receiver" of experience, though not as an "I" that has to attend to, fix, or become involved in any way with it.

Through this process, we learn at the deepest level that our thoughts and feelings do not define who we are. As we watch these reactions come and go, we also learn that even suffering is transient. As emphasized by the Buddhist perspective, it is through this practice that we become liberated from craving and attachment. Similarly, this practice helps us to become more fully human and compassionate toward both ourselves and with others.

Increasingly, research is also showing how such meditation, when consistently practiced, results in neurological changes that are associated with increased levels of alertness, relaxation, and control of attention. These are clearly relevant for our emphasis on the creative moment.

When you train yourself to be receptive to your internal experiences, you are broadening your capacity to tolerate ambiguity, discomfort, and tension in general. In effect, through such meditation, you more fully open your conscious mind to awareness and sensitivity. Such openness makes you more receptive to the workings of your unconscious. Additionally, to the degree that you can be open, this attitude can transcend the "conscious-unconscious" barrier, freeing you to channel the inspiration of your unconscious more effectively into your conscious creative efforts.

The benefits of mindful meditation can be applied at the moment of challenges associated with creative engagement. Through practice, you can learn to more effectively manage distracting experiences. To the degree that you become aware of them and let them go, you can redirect your focus to the creative moment and become more fully present and engaged in it. In effect, rather than challenging or responding to the content of your thoughts during those moments of challenge, simply observe them as you would the ever-changing clouds passing overhead.

CREATING BALANCE

By balance I am referring to the need to occasionally remove ourselves from active creative pursuit. Balance implies that we spend time away from active engagement in the creative process. Nutrition, sleep, social interaction, exercise—these are all essential to our health. Even children have to disengage from play to attend to other needs. Such periodic disengagement will serve to support and energize us for resumption of the creative process.

Whether we retreat to a cottage in the woods or spend time with others, such interaction with the wider world feeds our unconscious minds. It is our observations of the details of our daily lives that provide rich sources of material to the unconscious stream of our inner lives. Through our senses—sight, sound, smell, taste, and touch—we bring to life the material and inspiration for our creative ideas. We take in the elements of experience upon which our minds work without our full awareness; day and night interacting imaginatively, free from the close scrutiny of an observing eye that demands order and meaning.

The need to take breaks from the creative process follows the same principles of an exercise program designed to strengthen muscles. When we work one muscle group, like the arms, there comes a moment when our muscles reach exhaustion and we need to move on to work another muscle group. We may move on to focus on our legs, only to pause and shift to work the muscles of our chest. Similarly, we may use different exercises to activate slightly different muscles of the same body part. Then, we require days off to allow the muscles to both integrate new growth and regain their strength.

Taking time off from creativity has the same impact. The term "incubation" is often used to describe the unconscious process our minds go through as they work to make meaning from the diverse ideas and experiences that we encounter. When we concentrate our attention on being creative, we are actively pursuing a particular focus with the full awareness of our conscious minds. Our unconscious minds are alerted to follow the same path, to be hypervigilant to the work of sorting through, reviewing, and digesting the variety of thoughts, sounds, images, and experiences that we have focused on. This activity does not simply shut down when we consciously redirect our attention. Just as the tissues of the muscles are forming new bonds, our thoughts are forming connections during incubation periods. And when we are fortunate and receptive, the fruits of its labor pass through the gates of consciousness to stir us on for the next wave of creative focus.

*** FOR FURTHER EXPLORATION ***

1. What messages about compassion did you receive when growing up?
2. What are your attitudes regarding the practice of self-compassion?
3. What behaviors do you recall experiencing as compassionate?
4. Did you learn that needing compassion reflected weakness?
5. How compassionate have you been with yourself? With regard to your emotional needs? With regard to illness? With regard to a "need" to be perfect? With regard to your creative pursuits?
6. Recall examples of being compassionate toward others. What were those experiences like? When you were compassionate, did you believe that the person toward whom you were compassionate was weak? Did you resent being compassionate toward others?

7. How readily do you acknowledge and accept the compassion of others?
8. List four ways in which you can be more self-compassionate with regard to your creativity.

REFLECTIONS

If you want others to be happy, practice compassion. If you want to be happy, practice compassion.—The Dalai Lama

The best passion is compassion.—Jamaican proverb

If your compassion does not include yourself, it is incomplete.—Siddhartha Gautama

What's gone and what's past help should be past grief.—William Shakespeare

NOTES

1. Kristen Neff, "Self-Compassion: An Alternative Way to Conceptualize and Measure Self-Attitudes," presented at the conference of the American Psychological Association, 2005.

2. Ibid.

3. Harold Kushner, *How Good Do We Have to Be?* (New York: Little, Brown, 1996), p. 8.

4. Mark Leary, Claire Adams, and Eleanor Tate, "Adaptive Self-Evaluations: Self-Compassion vs. Self-Esteem," presented at the conference of the American Psychological Association, 2005.

5. Robin Casarjian, *Forgiveness: A Bold Choice for a Peaceful Heart* (New York: Bantam, 1992), p. 135.

6. Ralph Keyes, *The Writer's Book of Hope* (New York: Henry Holt, 2003).

7. Bhante Henepola Gunaratana, *Mindfulness in Plain English* (Boston: Wisdom Publications, 2002).

8. Ram Dass, *Journey of Awakening: A Meditator's Guidebook* (New York: Bantam, 1990).

9. Ibid., p. 45.

Chapter 17

MOVING FORWARD

T his chapter offers an array of activities and exercises that can help you more effectively overcome specific challenges to the creative process. These exercises and activities are intended to further your self-awareness and provide skills to both reduce your inhibiting themes and improve your mind-body states when confronting them.

Inhibiting themes may impede creative engagement at any moment in the creative process. They can be aroused during specific phases of the creative journey; for example, when getting started, when identifying a passion, or when completing a creative endeavor. It is easy to understand how these major markers in the creative pursuit could be challenging. However, inhibiting themes may also arise in reaction to the challenge of adopting a particular attitude or frame of mind that is essential for creative pursuit. Specifically, being playful, being inquisitive, being fluid in your thinking, or attending to details may, because of your unique history, be especially challenging. As such, the degree to which inhibiting themes are activated may depend on how much a creative endeavor requires you to embrace these attitudes.

While this chapter offers exercises to address these obstacles, equally important is the emphasis on becoming more aware of how inhibiting themes may contribute to them.

OVERCOMING INERTIA

Much of the challenge of the creative process is overcoming inertia so that you can initiate the process. While any step toward creative engagement may arouse tension, it is often the first step, and every first moment of reengagement afterward, that most consistently causes tension. If you decide to pursue painting, taking the first step of researching or signing up for classes may be the trigger of inhibiting tension. After the initial involvement, you are often vulnerable to similar levels of discomfort each and every time you reengage in that commitment. The following guidelines are presented as ways to help overcome the tension of beginning.

Take Small Steps

As suggested in chapter 15, one often makes assessments of one's ability to respond to a challenge based on one's current experience of energy and tension. This point is highly relevant to our discussion of taking the first step of a creative journey. The challenge to begin is certainly exacerbated by any inhibitions you have regarding creativity. I suspect, however, that what further heightens the challenge of beginning a creative pursuit is the usually erroneous assumption that later stages in the creative process will be accompanied by the same degree of tension as the initial stage. In reality, this is rarely the case.

Ralph Keyes, in *The Courage to Write*, explains that there are times when writers will do all they can to distract themselves from getting back to writing.[1] For the writers Keyes describes, everything but writing seems to take on new importance and is quickly identified as a priority on the "to do" list. It is the tension of inhibiting themes accompanied by the natural tension of being creative that fuels these distractions.

The challenge to begin is often exacerbated by the unrealistic expectation that you need to immerse yourself in the process for hours at a time. Certainly, many forms of creativity may require significant commitments of time; however, simply overcoming the initial inertia should be considered a major success. Writing a page or even a few paragraphs is an excellent beginning for any form of writing. For painters, a few brushstrokes may represent similar success in cases where the canvas has for a long time gone untouched. It is better to walk away with some feeling of success to build upon than to withdraw with intense discomfort and a vivid memory of failure. So, using the skills you have learned to reduce discomfort, challenge yourself. But remember to start small.

I have always emphasized this mind-set, whether it involved supporting someone who was learning to play an instrument or encouraging graduate students to research dissertation topics. This approach will help you to remember that creativity is the cumulative accomplishment of specific tasks. It also emphasizes that success is not measured by the finished product alone, but also by the completion of the necessary steps in the process, each of which is a success in itself.

While some of us are able to make big changes in behavior in a relatively brief period of time, we often find ourselves quickly reverting to our old behaviors, whether dieting, starting an exercise program, or beginning a creative pursuit. We always start with great intentions but, as creatures of habit, it is easy to once again fall back into old routines. In contrast, most success stories with regard to behavior modification are based on taking small steps. This is the major premise of the Kaizen Way, an approach to personal change advocated by Dr. Robert Maurer. This name was coined by Japanese business leaders to describe the method they used to rebuild their businesses in the aftermath of the Second World War.[2] It advocates taking extremely small steps as a way of bypassing tension.

Maurer suggests that the human brain, motivated to maintain stability and security, is wired to resist change. Similarly, it reflects the fact that, as described previously, the fear center of the brain, the amygdala, can lead us to react to situations without first checking in with the cortex, the more objective administrative part. Thus, new challenges can arouse fear in the amygdala, the center of the brain that is involved in the "fight-or-flight" response. However, small steps toward change or creativity do not trigger such a response. In effect, taking small steps toward change allows you to sidestep the fight-or-flight response typical of the amygdala.

For example, if you have wanted to write a novel but keep postponing your encounter with your computer or pen, plan on writing only a paragraph. If you think you may like to paint, review a book about painting for a few minutes or purchase one small tube of paint and play with it on a small canvas. Similarly, if your interest is photography, visit a store or look at a photography magazine.

Taking small steps means you may be inspired to ask small questions. If you have no idea of what you would like to pursue as a hobby or a new career, ask yourself instead how you would like to spend an hour or two on a particular evening or weekend. Select an activity that you have never tried but have reason to believe you might enjoy. Encourage yourself to experiment.

As Maurer suggests, taking small steps "creates new connections between neurons so that the brain enthusiastically takes over the process of change and you progress rapidly toward your goal."[3] As viewed from this perspective, and as emphasized throughout this book, by taking small steps, we are less vulnerable to inhibiting themes and their accompanying tension.

Visualize the Final Moment of Creative Engagement

All too often, when intending to start a project, we picture the first few minutes of engagement. When intending to write, we may picture ourselves sitting in front of a blank page or a computer monitor. Setting up brushes, oils, and a blank canvas may be the initial images we focus on when intending to paint. When making a collage, we may first focus our attention on the task of collecting magazines and newspapers. In each instance, directing our attention to the first moments of creative engagement involves attending to a mind-body state that, as described earlier, is often dominated by tension. While moving from inertia to engagement does require extra energy, focusing on those specific moments of tension only heightens the intensity of negative mind-body states, thus forming an even greater obstacle to moving forward.

An alternate approach is to focus your attention on the moment when you have completed the anticipated task for that day. If you start small and intend to write just one page, picture yourself writing the last sentence at the bottom of the page and clicking on "save" as you close your document. If working on a sculpture, picture the end of the hour, when your mound of clay has just begun to show a rough semblance of what it will eventually be. If you intend to practice playing piano for thirty minutes, imagine yourself at the end of your practice session, that much more familiar with the composition you're learning. If you are realistic in your goals, and if you practice self-compassion, your image of the final minutes of such engagement will undoubtedly be associated with a more positive mind-body set than your image of the first minutes of such engagement.

As further ammunition to help you maintain this mind-set, recall past experiences in which once you were engaged you became increasingly calm and increasingly connected with the intrinsic pleasure of that engagement. Practice the exercises described in chapter 14 that suggest focusing on such moments as a way to shift your emotional emphasis.

IDENTIFYING AND RECOGNIZING YOUR CREATIVE PASSIONS

The origins of your specific creative passions are in your past and in your genes. As you were growing up, specific activities or subjects aroused your curiosity and compelled joyful exploration and engagement; your biology may even have played a role in your attraction to certain creative outlets. These experiences in childhood and even adolescence served as the foundation for what you have pursued as a creative adult.

For many, however, the movement into maturity was accompanied by inhibiting themes that were so intense as to mask or even deprive them of such experiences. If you find yourself challenged in this way, finding your passion will involve purposeful investigation and experimentation. Identifying your passion is a process that may take time. Be patient. After all, your lack of awareness of a particular passion suggests that inhibiting themes have been so powerfully influential in your life that they may continue to resist exposure.

With this in mind, the following activities will help you inquire into your past in an effort to uncover and reveal what it was that aroused your mind and body with moments of awe, enthusiasm, interest, curiosity, joy, and an exuberance about life. Be alert to any inhibiting themes that move to derail your efforts. Be aware that any movement toward exposing your early creative interests will challenge the inhibiting child logic that resists them out of fear, anxiety, guilt, or shame. Apply the strategies already identified if at any point during this inquiry you experience the impact of your child logic's inhibiting themes. Additionally, after completing each of these exercises, reflect on and identify the mind-body states aroused during your experiences. This reflection will further help you to identify your true passions.

1. From among the activities that you engaged in as a child and during your early teen, list your favorites.
2. Once identified, visualize yourself engaged in these activities, noting

all of the details of that engagement: the setting, whether you were alone or with friends, the time of year, the specific aspects of that activity which you enjoyed the most, and what it felt like. Write a description of the experience.

3. Review pictures of yourself as a child. If possible, find the toys or books you had as a child. Try to recall what you enjoyed most about them? What are your reactions to them now?

4. Ask those who knew you when you were younger how you spent time as a child or as a teenager. Ask them what they observed to be exciting for you and what dreams you may have expressed. Inquire if there were any subjects that you seemed especially excited about.

5. Go to a bookstore or a library and stay there for at least an hour. Let yourself gravitate toward different sections, treating it like a playground where you can explore whatever you like. What sections appeal to you? What do your interests tell you about you? If you find yourself absorbed in reading a particular book, note the mind-body reactions aroused as you are reading. If you feel paralyzed in deciding what section appeals to you, take time to reflect and gain awareness of an inhibiting theme that may be contributing to the interruption of this process.

6. What, if any, activities do you currently engage in that most resonate with that joyous, excited child part of you? What are the aspects of that activity that you find most appealing? What does this tell you about yourself?

7. Can you recall how exciting it was as a child to go on a field trip? It broke the routine of your day and addressed all of your senses. Rather than sitting in a class picturing or thinking about the subject matter, these trips gave you the opportunity to be close to it. Take a field trip to any place that piques your interest. Visit that place as if you were a child exploring it for the first time.

8. Take a one-session class on any topic that you find interesting. Keep a journal of your reactions to being in the class. Address some of the following concerns.

   a. Recognize your mind-body sets as you approached the beginning of the class, actually entered the room, and engaged with other participants and the instructor.

   b. Describe your self-talk regarding learning in general, the instructor,

the subject matter, your ability to grasp the material, your willingness to spend time on the topic, and your self-criticism.
   c. How might your reactions to this class reflect openness to your creative genius and your capacity to express your creative passion?
9. If inhibiting themes were aroused when engaging in these exercises, what strategies did you use to maintain engagement?

FLUID THINKING

The capacity for fluid thinking involves giving ourselves permission to think flexibly, to freely associate words, phrases, concepts, images, and sounds.

In the early days of psychotherapy, psychoanalysis offered an approach to flexible thinking that was known as "free association." If a patient identified a specific concern, he would be encouraged to let his thoughts freely wander, beginning with the initial focus.

Flexible thinking involves this same freedom. While giving ourselves permission to think in this manner is essential for the creative process, all too often our fears inhibit comfort in doing so. Fluid thinking requires that we give our observing and self-conscious self a rest. It requires that we be open and vulnerable to the contributions of the unconscious. This may involve the arousal of feelings and thoughts that make us uncomfortable, frighten us, or lead us to feel shame or guilt. And yet, it is only when we engage in this process that we open the gates to free creative expression.

If we are truly flexible and open in our unconscious minds, we invite ourselves to retrieve not only pleasant and positive thoughts but also those that are confusing, surprising, embarrassing, and scary. In fact, it is only when we have full access and some manageable level of comfort with whatever we retrieve that we can move on to live authentically in our creativity as well as in our lives in general.

Below are a number of exercises that encourage expanded openness to thought.

Part I

1. Write your thoughts for ten minutes, beginning with any specific idea. If you feel the urge to stop, challenge that urge with the strate-

gies you have already learned. Try not to reflect on your thoughts. Rather, let them come freely, one after the other, as if you are a child making up a song that doesn't have to have meaning. Respond to the following after completing this exercise.

    a. List the emotions, thoughts, and physical states you experienced during this exercise.

    b. Did you visit any inhibiting themes while engaged in it?

    c. Were you surprised by any of your reactions? Surprise can be experienced as negative or positive. If you were surprised, how did it feel? Did it scare or please you?

    d. Repeat this exercise, but begin your thinking with an idea that reflects your creative passion.

2. Look around and identify an object in your room. Beginning with that object, make a list of as many words as you can that come to your mind. Do this as quickly as you can for three minutes.

    a. Describe your mind and body reactions. Describe the thoughts, emotions, and physical states you experienced during this exercise.

    b. Explore your reactions, considering them as reactions you can expect to accompany your attempts to be more fluid in your thinking. Repeat these exercises and, as you do so, begin to address any negative reactions you may have experienced while trying the strategies presented in earlier chapters.

3. Select a recording of instrumental music that you do not necessarily associate with any preconceived settings or ideas. I have found that certain New Age music has been helpful for this exercise. Listen to the music for several minutes and, as you listen, imagine continually shifting images of color appearing in various patterns and textures. They may appear to morph into one another as they move, like tendrils of gasoline diffusing through a puddle of rainwater. Do not be alarmed if you are not able to do this. It can take practice, especially if you have never before tried to visualize such details. Answer the following after you do this for five to ten minutes.

    a. Describe your mind-body experience during this exercise.

    b. Was this exercise easy or challenging?

    c. In hindsight, what self-talk were you aware of as you did it? Did it become more pleasurable or did your self-consciousness increase?

Part II

1. What are your reactions to these exercises? Did you feel silly? Did you feel like you were overly focused on doing them well? Did you feel inadequate? Addressing this exercise may arouse all of the major inhibiting themes you experience with regard to any aspect of your creative endeavor.
2. Did you experience any inhibiting themes?
3. If so, try to identify them.

ATTENDING TO DETAILS

Your creativity depends on your capacity to attend to details, to those related to your inner experience as well as to those pertaining to everything around you. A child does this naturally as he uses his five senses to explore his world. Every detail to which he attends becomes a part of his history, influencing his future. Further observations both act on and are acted upon by his prevailing accumulated history. The creative endeavor involves having access to such observations as well as to the myriad ways in which the observations have been catalogued in your memory bank.

The ability to attend to details often competes with that part of us that wants order, easy recognition, and the least amount of tension. It requires much less mental effort to categorize our observations, to see them as being just another example of something with which we are already familiar. In this way, we shirk the responsibility of noticing and explaining differences from our already catalogued experiences. Unfortunately, when we perceive things leveling this way, we gradually lose the capacity to experience new sensations and perceptions with excitement. The tendency to ignore the details of our surroundings and experiences reflects the conservative drive for safety and constancy and a turning away from experiencing what is novel.

To be fully present and engaged in a creative endeavor means to be focused on the details. Attending to detail is, likewise, at the core of what it means to be mindful. In attending to details through every stage of the creative process, we become more present to the medium with which we work. We attend to details when, while painting we notice the slightest difference between two shades of yellow paints, while writing we make a decision to select one word rather than its synonym, or in conversation when we form a quip in response to something said by a friend. Full immersion in any activity, creative or otherwise, involves being absorbed by attention to details.

Doing research related to your choice of medium demands that you observe and fully notice details. And when you are inspired, maintaining creative engagement demands that you attend to details as you respond to and elaborate upon your inspiration. What is your experience of attending to the details of what you observe?

Do the following exercise in order to determine how attending to details impacts your capacity to stay engaged in a creative venture.

Exercise

Step back and view this book so that your field of vision includes the book and its surroundings. Notice the objects around you. Observe their shape, how the light falls on them, their color, the lines and curves they form, their juxtapositions, as well as their composition and texture.

Now move closer and focus your attention predominantly on the words of this page. Notice the size of the paragraphs on the page and of the sentences. Now attend to the words, their size, shape, and sound. Look for those words that have two syllables. Notice the font, the lines, curves, and feet of the letters. Notice how many times the word "notice" appears on the page. Notice how many three-syllable words there are on the page. Count how many three-letter words are in this paragraph.

1. What are your internal reactions to focusing on details? Did you experience any resistance to doing this exercise? Did you experience any tension? If so, what did you tell yourself about it?
2. By answering these questions, you can be helped to better identify the challenges you may experience in attending to details.
3. Do this same exercise for about ten minutes while attending to any aspect of your creative passion. Record observations of your mind-body states after doing this part of the exercise.

Paying attention to details provides the sustenance for creativity. Being mindful of the details of your surroundings, thoughts, emotions, and relationships at work and at home fuels every aspect of your creative inspiration.

By attending to its details, life is more intensely experienced. You see, hear, touch, taste, and smell the uniqueness of all that surrounds you. And, in the process, you become more connected with others and with yourself.

QUESTION, QUESTION, QUESTION

How do you react when you hear a child asking his parents a barrage of questions? Take a moment and think back to such an experience. Certainly, how you react depends to some extent on the context of the situation. You may be quite annoyed by such behavior in certain settings such as at a restaurant, in a theater, or at a funeral service. But what is your general attitude toward children who engage in such inquiry?

All too often parents and others want to stifle such questioning, and do so in a variety of ways. "That's enough questions for now!" "I'm busy, can't you see?" "Don't ask so many questions." These are just a few common responses parents use in an effort to bring such inquiries to a halt. However, if parents too often respond in these ways, it's almost guaranteed that they will slowly crush their children's curiosity.

Think back for a moment about your own questioning as a child and how it reflected your curiosity about the world. How did your parents, teachers, and other adults respond to it? Were your questions responded to with full attention and recognition? Were they encouraged and praised? Was the interaction they spurred interesting and exciting? In contrast, were your questioning attitudes directly stifled? Did they lead to interactions that involved tension? Were you responded to in ways that led you to believe you were being a nuisance by making your inquiries? Most important, are you aware of having responded in this manner to your own inquisitive "child," that part of you that is yearning to know how things work, why they work the way they do, or how certain changes will impact how they work? Essentially, ask yourself how much inhibiting themes have led you to inhibit and stifle your own curiosity.

Such curiosity needs to be encouraged, rewarded, and nurtured if you are to have access to and trust in your creative genius. Honoring your inner child involves making every attempt to encourage and reconnect with that part of you that embraces knowledge, skills, and new ways of thinking. It is through such questioning that you learn the theory, knowledge, and skills needed for whatever creative journey you embark upon.

Answer the following questions in order to better understand how your attitudes about questioning have impacted your openness to learning.

1. What are your attitudes toward learning? What inhibiting themes have kept your curiosity prisoner from living more authentically?
2. What are your attitudes about thinking? Whether the task involves writing a novel, painting a self-portrait, following an unfamiliar recipe, or assembling a bookcase, how comfortable are you with problem solving? Are you impatient? Do you look for shortcuts? Does it make a difference if you are thinking about something that excites you?
3. How are your attitudes toward learning different from your attitudes toward formal education?
4. How comfortable are you with thinking about thinking? Do you have any internalized messages that either support or discourage such inquiry?
5. How comfortable are you in trying new ways of thinking?
6. Do you experience any attitudes that are anti-intellectual? How has this helped you? How has it hindered you?

THE CAPACITY FOR PLAY

Creativity can be described as "structured play." While children are initially blessed with the openness to play, many of us have learned to stifle our capacity to do so. Through the pressures of growing up, some of us have heard that "play is just for children, adults work," "play is a waste of time when you could be making money," "play is unproductive and achieves nothing," "play is silly," or "you are too old to play."

When allowed to play, children freely follow their curiosity to discover, invent, and transcend their experience. Play involves a capacity to be silly and to see the fun side of life. But it is also an opportunity to imagine, to make rules, to break rules, to practice skills, and to master them. It also is a time to use various materials for self-expression. In working with them, you learn about their properties as well as your abilities, whether you are playing with pencils, crayons, clay, paints, wood, paper, cookie dough, or a varieties of liquids. Play encompasses many of the core elements of the creative process. In many ways, it can be viewed as serving as a research stage for creative considerations.

Play counterbalances your seriousness and allows you to be creative. Humor itself is a kind of play that involves seeing things from different perspectives, looking at the details of your life and the world around you from one vantage point and then forming a slightly different emphasis that allows you to step back and laugh.

Like sleep, play can also both relax and energize you. One executive I worked with years ago indicated that at 11:30 AM every day he would cancel meetings, close the door to his office for thirty minutes, and withdraw to watch cartoons. While he played golf and tennis, enjoyed going to movies, was extremely satisfied with his career choice, and could be very playful with his wife, this daily routine was one way he recharged his internal battery while at work. For that brief period each day he removed himself from the serious and demanding challenges of his job.

Much of the creative process involves giving ourselves the same freedom to be curious and playfully explore our interior and exterior realities. This attitude includes an openness to experiment, to observe, to imagine, and to manipulate things with minimal self-consciousness. Without such freedom, our creativity can become stilted, if not completely stifled.

Engage in the following exercises to further highlight your openness to being playful.

1. Draw several pictures using crayons.
2. Make several pictures using your fingers. Instead of paints, use ketchup, mustard, mayonnaise, and another condiment of your choice.
3. Find a place to run, skip, hop, and dance for several minutes.
4. Watch cartoons for at least fifteen minutes.
5. Purchase and play with a toy of your choosing (not one you had when you were a child).
6. Play a musical instrument for ten minutes. Select one that you have never before attempted to play.
7. Identify places you have visited and explored or entertainment events that you have attended. What about them created the most joy for you? What was that like?
8. Throw snowballs, make a snow angel, or ride a sled.

9. Make a collage from newspapers and magazines.
10. Find a place where you will not be disturbed. Without using words, voice sounds for five minutes as if you were a child playing by yourself.

Following the completion of each of these exercises, reflect on your mind-body reactions. Doing so will help you to more clearly identify your attitudes toward play. Were any of your inhibiting themes activated while you engaged in these exercises? If so, what did you do to reduce their impact? What can you do in the future to reduce their potential effect on your creative pursuit?

Anyone who has ever taken a family trip by car can identify the excitement of doing so. Whether intended as vacation or just taking time for exploration, the journey begins with excitement and a touch of tension regarding the unknown. However, anyone who has taken such a trip knows that incidents occur that are unplanned for: a flat tire, having to drive further because the motels in one town are completely booked, or wrong turns that lead you further away from your destination. But rarely do such incidents lead to a premature return home. In fact, such distractions are often looked upon later as amusing challenges of the trip or opportunities to explore new places. Getting lost is often part of the excitement.

As you move forward in your creative journey, I encourage you to think of it as a road trip. Accept and trust your creative genius. Know that wherever it takes you, you will forever be challenged. You may feel lost but you never really are. And when you return, your experience will have changed you. This reflects the process of your evolving identity, and it is at the core of every creative journey.

*** FOR FURTHER EXPLORATION ***

1. You can become more aware of your experienced and anticipated tension by keeping a log. For example, rate your experienced level of tension as you think about starting a creative project on a scale of 1 through 10, with 1 denoting minimal tension and 10 representing the level of tension that would ordinarily cause you to withdraw from creative engagement. Now, imagine yourself actually beginning your specific creative task and make a rating of the tension you anticipate

experiencing at that moment. Then make a rating of the tension you believe you would experience fifteen or thirty minutes into the process of working on your project. Finally, make a rating you believe would reflect your tension upon completing your creativity for the day. Making such ratings may provide you with increased awareness of the need to focus on immersion in the activity rather than on taking the first steps to initiate it.

2. Imagine that you will work on your creative project for only ten minutes. Now rate your tension in the same way you did for item 1, above. Doing this exercise may highlight a tendency to feel less threatened in making change when you take smaller steps in doing so.

3. When growing up, what direct or indirect messages did you experience with regard to engaging in play, leisure time, or hobbies? Did you have models regarding these activities?

4. What direct or indirect messages did you receive with regard to attending to the details of your environment, others, or yourself?

5. While growing up, how was your curiosity received by parents, siblings, relatives, and teachers? Can you recall feeling extremely comfortable when asking questions of any one particular individual? If so, what helped you to feel at ease doing so?

REFLECTIONS

Creativity is a type of learning process where the teacher and pupil are located in the same individual.—Arther Koestler

So you see, imagination needs moodling—long, inefficient, happy idling, dawdling and puttering.—Brenda Ueland

In the absence of clearly defined goals, we become strangely loyal to performing daily trivia until ultimately we become enslaved by it.—Robert Heinlein

During periods of relaxation after concentrated intellectual activity, the intuitive mind seems to take over and can produce the sudden clarifying insights which give so much joy and delight.—Fritjof Capra

NOTES

1. Ralph Keyes, *The Courage to Write* (New York: Henry Holt, 1995).

2. Robert Maurer, *One Small Step Can Change Your Life: The Kaizen Way* (New York: Workman, 2004).

3. Ibid., p. 28.

CONCLUSION

As I have highlighted throughout this book, I view every creative endeavor as being a significant part of authentic living. While we may not all be creative with the big "C," making highly significant contributions to the world, each of us benefits individually and as a whole from the embrace of creative genius. Embracing creative passion is a way of being that provides deep personal meaning and life fulfillment. In our creative pursuits we discover our rich and complex evolving identities. In doing so, we tap into and share our humanity as we connect with others and with ourselves. And yet, like the spiraling of positive emotions, the creativity of one person impacts and inspires others who, in turn, inspire still others.

In recent years, we have witnessed accelerating transformations of our daily lives; with changing technologies, with how companies do business, with the nature of sociopolitical and national alliances, and with the ways we conduct family life. These changes result from the shared and intersecting creative journeys of people all over the world. They are the joint outcome of our drive to explore and innovate. While some of these transformations at this time seem favorable and others appear adverse, we need to remind ourselves that we are looking at a snapshot, a brief moment in a shared evolution that is as fluid as that of any one individual. However, just as the individual experiences the conflicting pulls of the consistent and familiar and the drive to explore and seek the novel, we, as a global human community, are experiencing tremendous tension throughout our shared moments of creative challenge.

More than ever, there is an urgent need for creativity and the freedom to access and express it. Unlocking your creative genius is much more than finding a way to spend leisure time. It is a way of feeling alive and managing your life in the midst of this period of unprecedented change. The creative endeavor helps to keep you centered in your evolving identity while you contribute to the shared human journey. The creative endeavor serves as a buffer to the transformations of our era while simultaneously echoing, challenging, and helping to direct them.

If we are to feel genuinely alive, we must find and connect with creative genius. Powerful forces often make it seem easier to withdraw from the challenge, but I hope that the strategies and skills I have shared will help to foster the courage and resilience to do so. Sharing these perspectives with you has been an extremely rewarding experience. Consistent with my views about the creative journey, I feel compelled to end with the familiar and appropriate phrase—"to be continued . . ."

INDEX